NGATI DREAD

Volume Three
Revelations

ANGUS GILLIES

Rogue Monster Books

ISBN 978-0-473-19502-1

Dedicated,
to my wife Tui, my sons Cassius, Pele and
Rogie and my daughter Aroha,
and also to the future generations of Ruatoria
so that they might understand this strange thing
that happened, once upon a time, in their town

Acknowledgements
The author would like to offer his heartfelt thanks to the
Margaret King Spencer Writer's Encouragement Trust for
their timely and much-needed grant. He would also like to
thank everyone who was willing to be interviewed, all the
family and friends who supported him during this project,
particularly his wife Tui for the cover art, his father Iain for
accompanying him on some of the interviews, his brother
John and John's wife Sue, Murray Ferris and Mike Bremner
for their work at Te Rau Design and Print and the staff and
management of The Gisborne Herald newspaper,
particularly Dave Conway and Dave Thomas.

SOME OF THE CHARACTERS AND INTERVIEWEES IN VOLUME THREE

Les Atkins: Luke Donnelly's lawyer for his murder trial

Reece Bolingford: Was with Chris Campbell the day he was killed

Rangi Rick Brown: Rasta

Chris Bunyan: Policeman and former schoolmate of Chris Campbell

Barney (Pani) Campbell: Former Ruatoria policeman and Chris's brother

Chris Campbell: Rasta leader

Ike Campbell: Chris's brother

Joe Campbell: Chris's brother

Willie Campbell: Chris's father

James Carstens: Anaesthetist

Gary Condon: Former police officer

Alan Davidson: Former police officer

Luke Donnelly: Shot Chris Campbell

Russell Fairbrother: Napier lawyer

Tom Fox: Supporter of Luke Donnelly

Pop Gage (Hori Keeti): Late tohunga, who prophesied the coming of a great spiritual leader on the East Coast

Robbie Grace: Ruatoria man jailed for murder

Alan Hall: Gisborne coroner who held an inquest into Chris Campbell's death

Rex Harrison: Former Gisborne CIB detective

Cody Haua: Original Rasta

John (Hone) Heeney: Took over the Rastas when Chris died

Tom Heeney: Ruatoria deputy fire chief and John's dad

Nigel (Jimi) Hendrikse: Former police officer

Hemi Hikawai: Former CIB detective

Lyn Hillock: Former Gisborne Deputy Fire Chief

Russell Holmes: Policeman who was stationed in Ruatoria

Hughie Hughes: Electrician in Ruatoria

Dion Hutana: Rasta convicted of burning down Ngati Porou Marae

Witi Ihimaera: Novelist

Bob Kaa: Neighbourhood Support Group ("The Vigilantes")

Bill Kaihe: Was shot by Luke Donnelly

Sammy Keelan: Rasta

Iain Kelman: Surgeon

Eddie Kotuhi (Prince of Peace): Rasta

Jonathan McClutchie: Rasta

Api Mahuika: Ngati Porou Runanga chairman

Dick Maxwell: Rasta who was killed in a vicious fight

Laurie Naden: Former detective

Dave Neilson: Former detective

Sue Nikora: Early influence on the Rastas

Mike Paiti: Samoan member of the Rastas

Sir Norman Perry: Visited the Rastas in prison

Raewyn Rickard: Beau Tuhura's sister, who was also the partner of Rasta Tony Tuhou

John Robinson: Former policeman

Haile Selassie: Late Emperor of Ethiopia, considered the Second Coming by Rastafarians

Matt Sillars: Former Ruatoria sergeant

Bruce Squire: Prosecutor in Luke Donnelly's murder trial

Gordon Sutton: Childhood friend of Chris Campbell

Sarah Sykes: Secretary of Te Poho-Te-Aowera Marae

Harley Te Hau: Was with Chris Campbell the day he was killed

Te Kooti Arikirangi Te Turuki: 19th century rebel prophet, founder of Ringatu church

Roger Te Puni: Mate of Luke Donnelly

Ed Te Rauna: Former Rasta

Nehe Reuben (King Glory): Rasta

Hemi Toi Reuben: Rasta

Ron Taylor: New Zealand Herald reporter who interviewed Luke Donnelly the day Luke shot Chris Campbell

Malcolm Thomas: Gisborne police officer

Chris Thompson: Hata's brother

Hata Thompson: Original Rasta

Dr Kenneth Thompson: Did the post-mortem on Chris Campbell

Laura Thompson: Hata's mum (Aunty Ga-ga)

Tony Tuhou: Rasta

Beau Tuhura: One of the early Rasta leaders

Charlie (Cheese) Turnbull: Former Rasta

Rev. Dr Harold Turner: Late expert on world religions who visited Chris Campbell in prison

Rana Waitai: Former Gisborne Police Superintendent

Watene Wanoa: Killed Rasta Dick Maxwell in a fight

Joe Ward: Was with Chris Campbell the day he was killed
Colin Williams: Pakeha farmer, member of pioneer family
Jeremy Williams: Pakeha farmer, member of pioneer family

THE STORY SO FAR

Between 1985 and 1990, Ruatoria, a town of around eight hundred mostly Maori residents on the East Coast of New Zealand's North Island, was terrorised by a sect calling itself the Rastafarians.

The Rastas mixed the Jamaican religion with the Bible, the Ringatu faith started by the 19th century rebel prophet Te Kooti and local Maori beliefs and prophecies.

One of these prophecies was that a spiritual leader would rise in the East Coast. Many in the Rastas believed it was their top man Chris Campbell. But Campbell himself would eventually hand the leadership of the group to his right hand man John Heeney.

The Rastas had been told by their elders that 100-year leases were up on land owned by the Williams, a pioneering family descended from early Anglican missionaries who had acquired large tracts of land on the Coast. And the Rastas wanted this land returned to its original Maori owners.

They set about protesting their alienation from the land with fence-cutting sprees and hay barn arsons on the properties of Pakeha farmers. But they were soon off-side with most of the community, both Pakeha and Maori, and before long they were at war with everyone they believed represented the Establishment.

Houses, businesses, the police station-cum-courthouse, the fire station, farmhouses, woolsheds, even schools and churches were burned down. A man Rasta leader Chris Campbell converted in prison burned a marae. There were more than thirty arsons in all.

Three Rastas were jailed for "beating the devil" out of an acquaintance. One Rasta beheaded another Rasta. A horse died soon after some Rastas tried to "break it in" by dragging it behind their car. Three Rastas – Chris Campbell, Hata Thompson and Cody Haua – were found guilty of kidnapping policeman Laurie Naden. Five detectives went on trial for kidnapping and assaulting Rasta Dick Maxwell. They were found not guilty. Policemen went on trial for assaulting three other Rastas. They were all found not guilty.

We take up the story as two strong personalities are returning to Ruatoria.

Rasta leader Chris Campbell is preparing for his release from prison and his return to the brethren.

Luke Donnelly is coming home to work his mother's land and to sort out a few Rastas.

Campbell and Donnelly are on a collision course. And neither will blink, let alone change direction.

PART 8
THE COURSE IS SET

CHAPTER 1

CHRIS CAMPBELL AND LUKE DONNELLY

*It's January 2010. So far I've done two main interviews with Luke
Donnelly. The first was where he was living in Childers Road,
Gisborne, in July 2001. The second was in the car park of McDonald's
in Greenlane, Auckland, in March 2007. At this stage, he's talked to me
about everything leading up to the day he killed Chris Campbell and
everything afterwards, but not about the day itself. I can understand
that not everyone wants to talk about the day they killed someone,
especially when they've been found not guilty.*

*I was a bit nervous about meeting Luke the second time. I'd sent him
a couple of hundred pages of what I'd written so that he'd know what
people were saying about him. And quite a few weren't that
complimentary.*

*Anyway, Luke was studying at Waikato University and had some
business to attend to in Auckland that day. The plan was that we'd meet
at McDonald's between noon and 1pm. Then we'd head back to my
apartment in Mission Bay for the interview. He turned up at 11.30. I
turned up at 12.30 and found him reading the Herald in McCafe. I was
supposed to be at TV3 producing Nightline at 2pm so I said, "Shit,
Luke, let's just talk in my car."*

*"Nice office," he said as I opened the passenger door of the dark
blue Nissan Cefiro for him (the central locking didn't work). There were
some Polynesian guys kicking a soccer ball around next to us while they
waited for someone to return. I had to move a pile of CD's off the floor
so Luke had somewhere to put his feet. It's not a small car, but Luke
looked squashed in. And I always have to lean my neck forward in cars
anyway because I have a long back. Anyway, we talked until 3pm. We
talked about all sorts of incidents in which he was involved in Ruatoria.
But we didn't talk about the one thing I had told him I really wanted to*

talk about: the day he shot Chris Campbell, who later died on the operating table. (Author's note, June 2011: I couldn't get him to tell that story until much later.)

He did mention another altercation they had, though, many years before.

Second interview with Luke: This happened when we were kids growing up in Ruatoria. See, our house is here, there's a river there and they lived up here, about five or six kids and their parents in this tiny bach. And the swimming hole was just here, right between us. And we were down there. All the kids were having a swim. And Chris actually gave me a bloody whack and him and Barney (Chris's older brother, who later became a police officer stationed in Ruatoria during the Rastafarian troubles) they ganged up on me when I was a kid.

It was a sunny day. And there had been an old bridge there. But all that was left of it was an old pylon. There was a lot of silt build-up on the banks, which allowed us to climb up on the pylon. And we used to get up on it and dive off it into the river.

I can't remember exactly what happened. Either I was up there and pushed him off. Or I might have pushed him and Barney off. And they were like, "Right, we're gonna get you." And they both ganged up on me. They didn't give me a thrashing but they were sort of bullying because that's what they were. I was brought up by a widow. See, my mother's Sophie, the one I call my mother I never had no fighting skills. So these two, they bullied others. But I had enough at that young age to make a stand, not having any dukes or any ability. I think they just grabbed me and scragged me and just held me down until I submitted. I might have just gone home crying, I think, and I'd tell the old lady. And she'd say, "You go on back there and you punch them back." That's how they used to teach you. "You just go back there and whack him back."

I remember it was Chris and Barney Campbell. Joe wasn't brought up there with us. Joe was brought up in Te Araroa.

But I always remembered that. There were another couple of kids who used to push me around. But my mother would always say, "Go back there and give them a whack." This old lady, little short thing, she taught me how to fight. Every time I'd go home and say, "Aw, they gave me a hiding," she'd take me outside and give me some fighting lessons. This is how she showed me how to make a fist (with the thumb incorrectly wrapped around the index finger knuckle closest to the hand). And she said, "Now, when they come near you, you go BANG! As soon as they get beside you, you go BANG!" I always remember, that's how she taught me how to fight. "Just, on the nose, bang on the nose. That'll fix them."

It wasn't just Luke Donnelly, who had a relationship with the Campbell brothers that pre-dated the Ruatoria troubles. So did Detective Hemi Hikawai, who's now retired from the force. He went through Police College with Barney Campbell and they're still the best of friends, while Hemi's brother was a boarder at the rectory at Gisborne Boys High when Chris was at the school and they were also good mates. In fact, Chris, Barney, Hemi and his brother occasionally hung out together as they were becoming young men. And, even though they were on different sides of the Ruatoria troubles, Hemi and Chris retained their respect for each other and, it's fair to say, even their friendship. But there were definitely times when this friendship was strained.

While Chris was inside for kidnapping police officer Laurie Naden, Gisborne Police received word from staff at Paremoremo Prison, who'd been informed by other inmates, that Chris had put a bounty of forty pounds of dope on Hemi Hikawai's head. At about three grand a pound back then that's $120,000 to have Hemi knocked off.

Hemi was keen to tackle this threat head-on and received the full backing of his bosses in Gisborne. So he went to Paremoremo and confronted Chris, who was starting to put on his moko by this stage. It was no problem and Chris admitted everything and explained why. Apparently, one of Rasta John Heeney's sisters told Chris that Hemi had encouraged a witness to commit perjury during the trial for the assault of Rasta acquaintance Junior Paul. She claimed she'd overheard Hemi trying to influence Peggy Heeney as to what evidence Peggy should give against John Heeney, her son. And of course the story had grown as this one added their little bit and that one added their little bit.

Anyway, Hemi told Chris it was all bullshit and made a few threats of his own as to what would happen if anyone tried to collect the bounty.

In their own way, they sorted out their differences and were back on good terms by the time Chris came out of prison.

OTHER MEETINGS WITH CHRIS CAMPBELL IN JAIL

Rev. Dr Harold Turner, an expert in Rastafarianism who'd taught at Kingston University in Jamaica: I had a sister then, retired and living in Havelock North. I told Sir Norman Perry I was going down to visit her. (Sir Norman was a Pakeha who was born in Gisborne but lived most of his life in Opotiki and served with the Maori Battalion.) Now this must have been 1990. Norman had had a bit to do with the Rastafarians in prison and he said, "You must go to Mangaroa and meet Christopher Campbell and the superintendent," who was also a Maori.

So I went over and had a good time with the superintendent and the staff talking about the Rastafari as they met it in prison. And I arranged to go and meet Chris. I had about an hour with him and then he called some of his brothers in. Chris had Ras Tafari tattooed across his forehead and marks on his cheeks, Bible texts or something. And some of his colleagues had Bible texts on their cheeks as well. Facial moko was a new thing to me. I'd grown up with Maori in Hawke's Bay but not under these circumstances.

I knew much more about Rastafari than he did. But I was very impressed with him personally. He was articulate. He was polite. He was open. He received me very warmly. And he was on his way to a new life.

His plan was to go back to the family farm. And he wanted to think and pray and he was going to do so on Mount Zion, Hikurangi, the sacred mountain. These were his plans when he came out on parole. And I think they were quite genuine. He was looking for a new non-violent way. And of course Rastafari is essentially non-violent...

...So I met Christopher Campbell and he wanted to have some reasonings with me. That was their term for Bible study. He wanted to have some Bible reasonings. But there was a strange aspect to it. He told me about his spiritual experiences, which seemed to be a turning point for him, where he was looking for another way than the way that had got them into trouble. And one of my daughters, in middle life, she'd come back to Auckland with the rest of our family. And she was pretty much at her... she was right at the end. And she had what you might call a spiritual experience. She was in deep trouble in various respects. But she survived all these things and is doing very well now.

But this daughter, a couple of weeks after her experience, she wrote it up on four A4 pages spontaneously and gave me a copy. It's a very interesting document, very interesting indeed. I took it with me to show to my sister in Havelock North, who's actually ordained, like myself, in the Presbyterian church, even though most of my life's been spent outside the church. Acting on a hunch I put a copy of it in my pocket when I went to see Chris Campbell. And what he told me about his experience in prison chimed in so closely with my daughter's story that I said, "Well, my daughter knows about some of the things you're talking about. She's written it up. I happen to have a copy with me. I'll give it to you. I think you'll be interested in this." I can't specify what his spiritual experiences were now. It was an experience of hitting rock bottom personally, of being on his beam-ends and then something emerging to turn him around.

Soon after I met him, Chris was released on parole and then killed. So I wrote a letter to his parents after his death explaining this queer document and asking if they'd found it in his papers and if they had could they please return it. I never heard anything back from his parents…

…After I had been there and Chris was out on parole some of his buddies in prison wrote to Norman Perry wanting copies of the Ringatu printed ritual. The Ringatu ritual was entirely oral until quite late but it had been printed. They were looking for something to work on for their own services.

And a Catholic nun, who was a visitor to Mangaroa, told me later that there had been a notable difference in the behaviour of the Rastafari in the prison since we'd met. She said that the Rastafari had used to be a nuisance. They'd go to the chapel service and they'd persist in shouting out, "Jah!" Then they used to stand up and read bits of the scriptures and make a jolly nuisance of themselves. And they'd established better relations with the Black Power people in prison. Anyway, she'd heard there were some sort of changes.

I think he would have been thinking of leading the Rastafari into a more peaceful way. And I had the feeling that he was absolutely authentic in it. He'd run the full run of the other thing and it hadn't got him anywhere. And he was a man of such ability.

Many believe that Chris Campbell went through a transformation in prison. The prison experience did for him what it did for the great boxer Muhammad Ali. Like Ali, Chris was a loud and fiery young man when he went in. Slowly, he became deeper. Less of a raver, more of a thinker. Less a rebel, more a man at peace with himself and the world. At least that's the impression he gave to most people. Some wise and well-educated men recognised his potential as a leader and began to correspond with him and visit him in prison

Ngati Porou Runanga chairman Api Mahuika visited Chris and John Heeney in prison for years. For the first seven months he listened as they hurled all sorts of abuse at him. To them, Api represented their parents' generation. And they likened their parents' generation to Esau in The Bible's Old Testament. In the Book of Genesis, Esau is the eldest of Isaac's twin sons. That means he is supposed to get his father's special blessing and that he has a birthright entitling him to a position of honour in the family and to a double share in the possessions inherited from the father. But first Jacob, the youngest son, buys Esau's birthright from him for a plate of stew and then later tricks their father into giving him Esau's special blessing. (No prize for guessing which twin represents the Pakeha system.)

Chris and John were full of fire and anger at this stage. They claimed they had arms hidden away. They were gathering more soldiers in prison. They were going to raze Ruatoria to the ground. John quoted excerpts from The Bible where fire was used as a form of cleansing and purification.

Api just sat back and listened until, like tightly-sprung clocks, they eventually wound down and had nothing left to say. That's when Api started to speak. And Chris and John listened while he spoke to them for the next three years. He gave them a historical context for what they were going through. He talked to them about the Ngati Porou tribe and about their own sub-tribes and families. He talked to them about the effects their actions were having on the community. He talked to them about the future. He talked to them about all sorts of things. And he could see that many of the things he was saying stuck... they made an impact.

Sir Norman Perry was another who used to visit Chris in jail. Sir Norman was a Presbyterian who also had close associations with the Ringatu Church started by Te Kooti. Sir Norman lent Chris some books about Te Kooti and Ringatu. He stressed to Chris that Te Kooti wasn't

always a rebel, that he became a man of peace during his latter years.
He told Chris how at that time Te Kooti took great solace from Psalms
51:

> *"Have mercy on me, O God, in your goodness*
> *in the greatness of your compassion*
> *wipe out my offence.*
> *Thoroughly wash me from my guilt*
> *and of my sin cleanse me."*

When Harold Turner, a world expert in indigenous religions, met
Chris Campbell in prison, he came away convinced that Campbell had
the potential to become the next great Maori prophet.

And in the tradition of Maori prophets Chris had the self-belief,
strength and charisma that enabled him to attract followers
and believers, even in prison. Maybe Psalms 51 was being used in a
way Sir Norman Perry hadn't expected.

> *Psalms 51, IV, 15: "I will teach transgressors your ways,*
> *and sinners shall return to you.*
> *Free me from blood guilt, O God,*
> *my saving God;*
> *then my tongue shall revel in your justice."...*

Witi Ihimaera, from his novel The Dream Swimmer: Kara (Chris
Campbell) was in jail at the time Luke Donnelly arrived in Ruatoria.

Donnelly was born in Ruatoria, adopted by Sophie Haereroa, and
lived in Ruatoria in the mid-1950s. As a young man, he moved to the
Waikato where he played and coached league. He married Elizabeth and
had two children, Jason and Jessica. He owned a small clothing factory
in Hamilton. He was no angel. He had a conviction for assaulting a
rugby league referee and was known as a man who was happy to settle
scores with his fists...

...Then in February 1989 he was told Sophie Haereroa was ailing.
He returned to her 20 hectares of sheep country about 15 kilometres
south-west of Ruatoria on the main road at the junction of the road
through the Makarika Valley. His return was unusual at a time when
many people were sick of the violence and were leaving.

Sophie Haereroa died that year and was buried on the farm...

...Almost as soon as Luke Donnelly settled, the simmering feud
with the Rastafarians began. It was fuelled by the proximity of Willie
Campbell, Kara's father, who owned the adjoining property. Willie was

an uncle of the adopted father who had brought Donnelly up. They were all whanau…

…Donnelly became one of only a handful who fought back. He formed a group of four men known as the District Rangers. According to some reports, the police gave the group the quiet nod of approval but warned them not to operate outside the law.

CHAPTER 2

LUKE SIGNALS HIS ARRIVAL IN RUATORIA

So why did you go back to Ruatoria?
Luke Donnelly: Mum was terrified. She rang me. I said, "What's the matter, Mum?"

She said, "Oh, those boys keep riding their horses through. And they just keep going through the gates and letting people's stock out. I want you to come home."

I said, "Mum, I'm halfway through a law degree here. I'm at varsity."

She said, "Just come back. I feel safe when you're at home."

So I went back. That's why I went back.

From the second interview with Luke: I remember when I first arrived back in Ruatoria, these two bloody Rastas come up to the gate. And I was courteous. I said, "Oh, howzit boys."

First off, they said, "Aw you Mister Rugby League Man. Aw Mister Tough Guy Rugby League Man ay?" They'd heard that I'd been playing league and that in Waikato and whenever I used to go home and play rugby for Hikurangi they'd say, "Aw that bloody Luke Donnelly. He only knows how to play rugby league. Shouldn't be on the field. He doesn't know how to fuckin' tackle properly. And he's always fuckin' whackin' everyone around the head."

I was leaning on the gate. And I said, "You fullas know who owns these horses in here?"

They said, "They're ours."

I said, "Well, I'm moving back home now. I've taken back over the block here. So can you get you fullas' horses and put them in you fullas' paddock?"

They said, "Those horses stay where they are. We need water for those horses in the summer. They stay there." It was a ten-acre piece that was fenced off and down the bottom right through the summer there's always been water in the springs.

I said, "Well, no more. You get 'em out or I'll get 'em out."

They said words to the effect of, "You fuckin' touch those horses and you've got fuckin' trouble then."

I said, "Let me tell you guys something. On that side of this gate, you do what the fuck you want. On this side of the gate, I do what the fuck I want. You got that?"

And this guy had his fuckin' foot on the gate and he fuckin' just slammed the gate into me. He said, "Is that right, cunt?" And BANG! Fuck, he whacked me with it right in the chest.

Instinctively, I just fuckin' grabbed his foot and I fuckin' done a wishbone, you know, fuckin' hooked him straight up like this. Well, he had to get off the horse. He couldn't stay on it or I would've snapped his leg. I just about snapped his arse. He fell down between his horse and the gate And I, just in a second, whipped around the gate and fuckin' into him. Bang, bang, bang. "You wanna go? Let's do it."

And his mate was on his horse, on the other side. But his mate didn't get off. All his mate did was say, "We're gonna get you, cunt. We're gonna fuckin' get you."

Anyway, this guy's on the ground covering himself up. I said, "You get these fuckin' horses outa here. Or actually they'll be out on the road. I'll open the gate and fuckin' let them out."

So anyway, he gets up and he's bleeding around the mouth. The horse took off. Heh heh heh. The horse took off down the road. And his mate is in two minds whether to go and get the horse or to stay with his mate. That's probably why he didn't get off. But when he saw his mate back away from me, he galloped off and got the other horse and brought it back.

Meanwhile, this other idiot's standing there, saying, "We're gonna fuckin' get you mate. You wait 'til Chris gets back."

These guys were telling Chris in prison, "Aw, you know, your cousin Luke has come home and he's throwing his weight around. And he's bashing up the boys for nothing."

That was the first scrap I had when I got home. But the word spreads like wildfire. The next thing, before the end of the day I get a phone call from one of the cousins. "Aw, I heard you gave one of the Rastas a whacking. Well done."

Anyway, a few months later, after I'd got rid of most of the horses, my litle girl, one morning, she said, "Dad, Dad, Dad, that horse is biting Melrose."

Well, we had this horse called Melrose and that was in the paddock. And these horses were all meant to be gone but these buggers had stuck their stallion in with our mare. So I got up and I go out and this bloody thing is chasing her round and attacking the mare. So I thought, "Fuck, I'll fix this," went out, got my gun. I'd taught Melrose how to respond to whistle and I just whistled her up and as she was running away from this thing she just turned around, came right around and as soon as she came closer to me, I just slapped her and she kept on going. And that stallion was coming up. I loaded up just as this thing was coming up and I fuckin' whacked it. But it kept on going though. It was only a 22 I'd used. So it can't have been enough to kill it.

Anyway, it kept on going. And the next thing I hear this fuckin' yelling. "Hey, hey, ya cunt!" I look to where the voice is coming from and there's this wad of hair and bloody dreads flicking up in the air.

I'm thinking, "This bloody idiot." Well, it was Michael Paiti, the Samoan Rasta. He ran across the paddock, running up the hill towards me and he says to me, "What you fuckin' think you're doing, cunt?"

I said, "Who are you calling a cunt?"

And he's puffing. I'm thinking, "He's pretty fucked." And he was. He was puffing between every word. So I went through the gate, I walked up to him and went, "What'd you say?"

He said, "Taking a shot at the horse, what do you think you're doing? I'll put a fuckin' bullet in your head."

I said, "Is that right? Yeah? Yeah? You're gonna put a bullet in my head?" Fuck, down he went. Bang, bang, bang, bang. I got him by the bloody dreads, ay. I smashed him, whacking him in the head. He's covering himself up. I said, "Don't you fuckin' come on my place and you fuckin' tell me you'll put a bullet in my head." That annoyed me.

I could see he was so puffed that he wasn't gonna put up much of a fight. And he was all frothing at the mouth. He was so puffed he couldn't even defend himself actually. Every time I whacked him his arms would just drop down.

So I said to him, "You get that fuckin' horse outa here."

The next thing I hear his mates - two of them up on the road - but they wouldn't come down because they knew how I am with things. Michael Paiti was just walking around trying to catch the horse. I said, "You get that fuckin' thing outa here."

Anyway, they went and round about another two weeks later there was this beautiful quarter-horse Arab cross, a white one, I think it was an Appaloosa cross, that was in there. And I thought, "Oh, that's not mine."

(Author's note: Luke later told me the horse was Chris Campbell's favourite.)

Luke: I went and got my gun. But this time I didn't use a 22. I went down there with a shotgun. Walked straight up to this horse, about from here to that car. Just walked straight up to it. Proud as, this horse. I just lined her up. Bang. Fuckin' hit it right in the head. It didn't fall over to the side. It just dropped straight down. Its feet just buckled under it. It was just parked like that on its belly and its head just dropped like that. It blew off the head and the ear and that came off because I mean I used a solid shot. Fuck, did that make a mess.

It was one of the Rasta's horses.

Afterwards I went up to Gordon Shirkey's place. I said, "Gordon, give me your tractor because I haven't got anything to pull this thing across the paddock."

And he said, "Yeah-na, no worries."

So I got this tractor, pulled the fence down on the road, got the thing, dragged it up on the road and sat it down on the side of the road so they could see it. Well they had to go past to get to their house. I thought, "You'll fuckin' see your horse you bastards."

And in the hot it just fuckin' blew up. It was on its side up on the road and its bloody legs were going up like that. It was just a matter of time that it was going to just burst.

Later in the afternoon Gordon Shirkey came down and we hauled it up on to the lift at the back, put it onto there, tied it onto there. And I said, "Right, now where are you gonna take it?"

He said, "I'll take it up and just dump it in the river."

I said, "No, no. Fuck that. Dump it in their driveway."

So we went up to their place, not up to the Rasta pad, but there's another place up the river. Actually it was on the track, not on the driveway. We just took it up there and dumped it on the track...

…They had another horse in my paddock. I knew it was theirs because they'd put the mane into dreadlocks. John Taylor from the dog pound had come to register my dogs. I told him to shoot this horse with the dreadlocks. After that he and everyone around the place had free dog tucker for a while.

But horses were a prize thing for those guys. They needed their horses to get around the hills.

During a phone conversation in 2009, Luke mentioned shooting another Rasta horse back then. It was trying to attack one of the mares in his paddock. It was mounting the mare and had its teeth bared in anger as Luke sneaked quietly closer with a .22 rifle in his hand. He said he crept up right behind the horse and, while it carried on doing what stallions do to mares, Luke shot it in the balls. The horse bolted and hung around by the river for a few days. Luke saw it down there and said its "dork" hung down to the ground. It was longer than the great racehorse Sir Tristram's dork, which he had seen.

He said he heard the Rastas thought the horse had got itself caught up in a barbed wire fence because its balls were all torn up. It died after about four days when the infection spread.

Luke Donnelly: I heard an interesting story about Gordon Shirkey and his brother. Gordon was the guy who helped me move the Rasta horse that I shot. The Shirkeys were managers for Michael Cotterill. The Rastas were trying to steal their horses from down at the Mataa Bridge. And Gordon and his brother turned up from Makarika Station and they pulled a gun out on the Rastas and said, "Leave those fuckin' horses alone."

Apparently, Chris Campbell, hopped off the horse, walked straight up and grabbed the gun. Yeah, Chris grabbed the gun and says, "Aw yeah, you're gonna shoot me, ay?" And Chris pulled it up to his own head and said, "Come on, shoot."

This is early days when this happened, long before Chris's spell in prison for kidnapping.

Gordon chickened out there and they took the gun off him and Chris and them gave the brothers a bit of a whack-up. They ended up underneath their own truck that they drove down in.

The Shirkeys never got those guns back. They reported it to the police but no one ever found them.

The Shirkeys weren't the only people in those early days to have a run-in with Chris Campbell involving a gun. Former Ruatoria orchardist and electrician Roger Haugh says that Campbell pointed a rifle at him and threatened to kill him.

CHAPTER 3

HOW ROGER HAUGH'S UTOPIA COLLAPSED

Roger Haugh and his partner Val moved to Waipiro Bay in 1975. He was twenty-three and she was twenty. Roger was a keen surfer and the main attraction back then was that he had the five local point breaks and three beach breaks mostly to himself. He and Val were also keen to live self-sufficiently. In those days they saw the East Coast as a form of Utopia. And for a few years various locals let them stay on their land in unoccupied run-down houses, which they'd scrub clean and fix up. There often wasn't power. But they'd be allowed to grow vegetables.

Roger was a full-time surfer and Val did some work at Te Puia Springs Hospital. Her father was always telling her, "That's what happens when you hook up with these surfers. The women go out to work."

Eventually, they bought eleven acres off Stuart Williams (a member of the famous pioneer family) and the property had an old house on it.

Val: And when we saw the old house it was so run-down it didn't look like anyone had been living in it for years. But the strange thing was it had a calendar and it had that year on it.

The neighbours told us the story of the people who had been living in there. And it was quite a story because they were a Maori family. And the old people who had lived there originally were very tidy. The floor was so clean you could eat off it. The gardens were so beautiful that people used to drive out to the country to have a look at the gardens.

The old lady died. The old man decided to hock the property off and move away. And so when he sold the property he sold it to Stuart Williams, who farmed down the road.

The old couple's son was a fencer so Stuart Williams decided to keep him and his wife and children on in the house.

Now in the old days the farmers used to pay for the workers' power and their food and give them the house rent free and in return they'd work for the farmer. Well, apparently they stayed for a year and Stuart only got about two weeks work out of them so he had to get the police in to evict them.

But during that year, they moved out of the house because the house got so dirty. There were about three different sheds on the property. Little sheds, each with a fireplace, each with bunks in them. So they seemed to move out from the house to a shed, to another shed and then there was a chook-run with old cars in it and there were bunks in the chook run and a fireplace. They actually moved around. The kids slept in the cars. And they were pretty rough... pretty rough.

Roger: I think I took thirty truck and trailer loads of rubbish away from there. You'd go to dig your garden up and there'd be an old mattress there or stockings or tin cans or bits of steel. There was rubbish everywhere. I think they used to just open the window and throw the rubbish out actually. That's what it was like. One guy was telling me that he'd be driving past in the tractor and he'd look over and see the woman scrubbing herself in a trough and the trough was way over in the corner of the paddock well away from the house. They'd say, "Come over and have a cup of tea." And they'd be looking at the edge of the cup to try and find a clean spot to put his lips.

Anyway, I wanted to develop an orchard and it had a whole lot of pine trees on it. So I thought, "Aw, there's timber." So I could do all these things. I planted two and a half thousand stone and pip fruit trees on there. And then we milled up a whole lot of trees off the property and built a big implement shed. And we just tried to develop it into an orchard. It all worked out good but it was in the wrong place wasn't it.

Val: We discovered the house and the bottom part of the property was in an old rift. We actually had two floods through that property while we were there and one of them was Bola.

Roger was living his dream of making a living from a piece of land that he owned. By 1984 he and Val had a couple of young kids – a boy and a girl – and they still believed that the East Coast was the perfect place to bring them up; this was before the Rastas started cutting fences and burning down hay-barns. But then one night things took a sinister turn. He had a run-in with Chris Campbell, whose family land was next door.

Roger: I had a dog called Blitz. It was a cross between a bull terrier and an eye dog. A guy called Claude sold me that dog and he said, "This dog will be a good pig dog." And he was right. It was the best dog I ever had. He was really intelligent.

But anyway I couldn't keep feeding it Tux so I'd go out and shoot a hare because there were hares up and down the river bed.

Val: And they were actually ring-barking our apple trees.

Roger: I had the little green shields up but they'd come along and nibble through them. So I had to shoot them.

Val: It was a summer evening. We'd had tea and you'd decided to head on down to the river bed just before dusk because I think that's a good time to catch the hares.

Roger: So I went wandering down there. And I saw a hare on the other side of the river. So I lay down on one bank and shot across the river with my little short-barrel 22. There was no silencer so it would have been loud. It would have gone bang and ricocheted noise all round there so no matter where you were you would have known a shot went off.

I missed the flippin' thing as it worked out. I headed off across the river to get a bit closer to see what had happened and I got half-way across and then I heard Chris Campbell yell out, "You tried to kill me."

Of course, I didn't even know he was in the area at all. As I was walking across the river, he just came out of the scrub from behind me and he started yelling, "You tried to kill me!"

I was just standing there with the rifle, not pointing at him but pointing at the ground. And yeah he basically came up to me and, still telling me, "You tried to kill me," he snatched the rifle out of my hand and threw it away and kept having a go at me. I can't remember all the things he was saying but he was really angry.

He punched me one in the face. I dropped to the ground and we had a bit of a fight. He was still mad. I tried to talk him around.

Anyway, after that I went over to the creek and I was on my knees washing my face. He'd gone over and picked up the rifle and he'd come back. And he stood over me from behind. I was still on my knees washing my face. He'd put a bullet in the rifle and he said, "I'm gonna kill you." He fired the shot from behind me and it landed there, right in front of my hand, probably 50 mil in front of my hand. He fired from point blank range just past my head. I freaked and stood up.

He was pointing the gun at my chest.

So I was standing there thinking, "Where's the impact point? Where's it going to hit?"

Now just after he fired that shot, one of the Heeney girls ran out of the scrub and screamed, "What are you doing, Chris?!" Until then, I didn't even know she was there.

He said to me, "Kneel, I am going to kill you."

And I said, "I'm not kneeling." I just wouldn't kneel.

"Kneel! You gotta kneel."

But I wouldn't.

And the Heeney girl, she's screaming at Chris. So I'm hoping she had a big bearing on things because he was lining me up and I was thinking, "Aw man, I'm toast here."

And then he didn't, obviously, fire. He just decided not to shoot me. And he ejected all the bullets. And then he turned around with the rifle and he went bang on a tree branch and bent the barrel and just smashed it and threw it away. And I left it there. I didn't take it. I just walked off and he walked off.

I remember the splash of the water so I know how close that shot was to my hand… and to the back of my head.

But the worst part was when I stood up again and I was expecting him to shoot me and to feel the bullet hit me somewhere in my chest. That was so horrible. And what really makes me angry is when you talk to some of your friends and you say, "This guy threatened to kill me and this is what it was like," and they go, "Aw na, that's nothing, I could handle that." But, until you're in that situation, you never know what it's like. You're powerless, you're wasted, you're toast, you really are.

I always remember it and every time I think of it the heart rate goes up. It's not so bad now but it used to be. If I talked about it the heart would start pumping. And I always said I'd never ever get myself in a situation like that again. I'd probably use a gun in self-defence.

See, at the same time I didn't want to wrestle with the gun beween us because it could go off. I guess I was just trying to manage the situation so I could get out of it alive.

The girl may have saved my life by screaming out. Because if she hadn't been there, he could have carried on through with his threat. There would have been no witnesses.

So I went back and walked home and like woah (he shudders). I still get upset by it.

Val: I'd been putting the kids to bed, just talking to them. And I went, "Oh, Roger's here." And he was lying on the couch with his arm over his face. And he pulled his arm away and his face was just black and blue! And he said, "You better put the kids to bed quick."

So I'm freaking, wondering what the hang has happened. I stuck them back in bed and came out and he told me what had happened. We talked about it. And you decided to ring a guy down the road, John Taylor, who was the council dog controller. And John just said, "Roger, ring the cops. Tell the cops." So we did.

Roger: The policeman came out and by then it was dark and I had the feeling that they thought there was something going on. I always had this feeling that they thought it was all my fault.

Some back-story that you weren't talking about?

Roger: Exactly, but there wasn't. And Chris the whole time was telling everybody that I tried to kill him and they were all glaring at me all the time. Well I thought, "How ridiculous. If I was gonna kill him he wouldn't be here. I had a gun." He just wanted to get at me. That's all it was.

And there'd been no history before that?

Roger: No, and I can't understand why he behaved the way he did. He must have got totally freaked by the shot because it would have been loud and maybe he thought I *was* trying to kill him. But I wasn't. I didn't even know he was there. So he obviously snapped and used that as an excuse because he was wanting to have a go at me for who I was. I don't know. I don't know what was going on in his mind.

So he convinced Willie, his father, that that was true because Willie was just so… He changed after that to me, totally.

I was chairman of the local school so I'd go down there and mow the paddock. And Willie would be over at the Makarika killing shed and they'd kill animals and do all the butchering. And I'll never forget this day he just came over to the fence and just stood there and glared at me the whole time, just with a fiery look like he wanted to kill me. It was horrible because I was *really* frightened of Willie. He was a *big* man.

Yeah, I think Jeremy Williams said that Willie could whack over Chris if need be.

Roger: Aw yeah, I'd take on Chris if I had to and I'd feel comfortable about that. I was surfing all the time and I was working and I was quite tall and young and strong. But there's no way I would take Willie on. He would have been a machine. He was a big man and his whole demeanour would make you think twice about taking him on. I suppose it was tough for him, trying to make a living off the land and everything against him and this white guy comes in and I think this was how it was in the community. I was doing things. I borrowed a small amount of money and I think they probably wouldn't be able to borrow some money. So there's resentment there. It got to the stage with my neighbour Morgan Reedy that I'd knock a wall out of our old house trying to fix it up and he'd do the same. I'd do some fencing and then he'd do some fencing.

I think I affected a lot of people up there. They followed my lead. But most of them never followed through because they didn't have the dream that I had.

So were there any ramifications for you with Chris telling people you tried to kill him?

Roger: There was a public bar and a lounge bar at the Manutahi Pub. But I always drank in the public bar, never really went in the other one. Anyway, I'd had a few beers and I came out and two young boys accosted me, followed me out and then accused me of trying to kill Chris. I was always a little bit frightened because you went outside to get to the toilet and every time you went out you wondered, "Aw who's gonna follow me out here?" And occasionally things like that did happen. No one had ever accosted me but it did happen to other guys.

So these two young guys accused me of a few things and then basically jumped me and I fell to the ground with their full weight on top of me. There was a concrete curb to the footpath and I don't know how my head didn't smash on that because that could have killed me. And they were whispering in my ear, "I'm gonna kill you. I'm gonna get you."

So then my blood just started to boil. And I thought, "I just can't take this any more," and I exploded and threw the guys off and I don't know how but I just stood up. That's just how it happened. I just waved my finger at them and told them not so politely what really happened:

that I wasn't trying to kill him and it wasn't me pressing the charges against Chris, it was the police. And then they just walked off.

I didn't want to press charges against Chris. And I didn't go to court. I just gave police a written statement of what happened. I think he was charged with threatening to kill. But he thought that *I* was trying to kill *him*, too.

I didn't want to escalate it because I was frightened for my family. I came home one night and I looked at the house and it looked like it was on fire and I freaked.

But it was just lights in the house. I was starting to get really worried because he'd already threatened to burn us out lots of times.

Anyway, he got two years probation so he could do nothing wrong for two years.

But we'd tried to sort it out. Demo Johnson lived down our street and he was a good surfing mate of mine. And Demo said, "Come over cos Chris wants to meet with you."

So I went over. It was pretty freaky. You don't know if he's gonna have another go at ya. But I fully trusted Demo. He was a big strong guy and he wouldn't have let anything dodgy go down.

But Chris wanted me to drop the charges. He apologised and didn't want to go to court.

Val: I don't think he apologised did he. I remember you said, he'd been studying the Bible, he was being led by some guy who was a Rastafarian and the Rastafarian religion was foremost in his mind and he wanted to go into the religion. And part of that was to not have any dramas like what had happened with Roger and he wanted to pacify everybody and play it by the book basically.

Roger: Well, so to me it was sort of like an apology. It wasn't like, "I'm sorry," or anything like that but he was repentant.

And I said, "Well look Chris, I'm not actually pressing the charges. The police are. All I've said to them is what happened. It's out of my hands."

Roger: Two years after that shooting incident – I think it was two years to the day - I had some friends come and visit me. And this one particular friend had a rifle, a 3030 pump-action Winchester. And this particular afternoon we had a few drinks and had some shots outside my place into a whole lot of tree stumps. And that sound carried all round the valley. So Chris and the other guys would have heard that.

We didn't have gun cabinets in those days. So the rifle went into a little gap of 100 millimetres between the book cabinet and the wall in my bedroom. This was just before Chris, Cody Haua and Hata Thompson kidnapped Laurie Naden, the cop.

Val: We'd spent the day down at the beach. And Roger decided to stay down at the beach with his mates and I came home with the children. So I got home just on dark, so it must have been about 9 or 9.30. I drove into the property and I could see with the car lights that all the sheep were huddled in a group and I thought, "Aw, that's strange." So I drove the car right through the property and right *around* the property because I noticed a gate had been left open. So I closed the gate and had a look around our shed where we kept a bit of money from selling fruit. The house was locked so everything seemed okay and I went to bed. And the next morning, some time in the late morning, Roger ended up coming home and I told him things were a bit strange when I came home. And he said, "Well, just go and check that the rifle's okay."

So I went into our bedroom and the rifle was gone. And, wow, that was scary. Both the windows in the bedroom were closed but I realised the latch wasn't as I'd left it. And then I realised perhaps someone had been through the bedroom window and broken in. But they'd left it so tidy that I hadn't noticed.

Roger: Then I noticed a bucket of apples was gone too. So they took a rifle and a bucket of apples.

Val: Then they went and stole some horses from Jeremy Williams's place.

I reckon they were just leaving our property as I came home. Because as the car comes up that road you can see the lights coming. And I reckon they would have seen the lights coming and taken off. They would have only just left.

Roger: And of course the shit hit the fan after that because they'd stolen a rifle and the armed offenders squad got involved and Chris and the others went and kidnapped Laurie Naden.

The Haughs' vision of Utopia on the East Coast was finally and irrevocably smashed during and after Cyclone Bola in 1988.

Roger: I raised the alarm for Cyclone Bola for the Coast. I rang up the Catchment Board. I went outside and it was raining, raining,

raining. I thought, "This is looking like flood material." And then the water started coming through the property. And I said "Aw, our house is becoming surrounded by water."

"Is it?" So no one actually knew, nobody was actually alerted.

So my neighbour Morgan Reedy came over and helped me lift the washing machine up and out of the way and to move some of our stuff above the water. Then I was trying to shift the deer because I had deer too. I was working on the helicopters in those days. So I was chasing the deer out of the paddock to higher ground and I could see the water actually rising up my ankles. That's how quick it was rising. I could see it. And in the end I had to give up. I couldn't shift them.

So I left them and the kids were inside watching TV. And I didn't want to alarm them. And I said, "Okay, time to go now." Switched everything off and went over to Morgan Reedy's place, which was on higher ground.

Val: After Cyclone Bola Michael Cotterill came to our aid and offered us a cottage on his farm to stay in. So that was about a kilometre away from our property.

And the day of the flood we'd made an agreement with Dick Reedy to sell the property to him for half price. So that deal was done. So that meant at least we had a future.

So we'd go back to the old place each day and try and salvage what was left down there. We had a few people wandering through and pillaging, not realising that, "Hey, we might still want those."

So we decided when we had some money come through from the insurance company that we'd go and buy a section further up north. So we went away for a week to look at property and left a neighbour in charge of our dog and asked them if they would keep an eye on our pigs while we were away.

So we came back after a week and no dog. Nobody knows where Blitz the dog is. Nobody's seen him. Then we go to find the pigs. No pigs.

So we say, "What happened to the pigs?"

"Oh, oh. Yep. Saw them. They were just down the riverbed the other day. They'll be around. They'll be around."

Roger: Fed on apples, they would have been the tastiest pigs around.

Val: So anyway about a week later Demo Johnson came around and informed us that he had heard in the Manutahi Hotel that one of our neighbours had been raving about how he'd shot the dog and he'd butchered our pigs. So that was like the last straw really.

And of course this neighbour wasn't around to confront. He'd raced off to Gisborne to hide away until things had died down.

Roger: We knew Blitz didn't like him because it would bark every time he came around. It used to bark at him from one end of the property to the other as he went past on his tractor. He hated this guy. And *he* didn't like the dog either. Blitz would bark at night for some reason. I used to wonder what was up. Then we heard that someone had been sneaking through the back way to get apples for years and it was this guy.

So we decided, "We've got to get out of here." It wasn't Utopia any more. It was sad really. We had a couple of thousand trees there. We were selling fruit. We had money. We could have gone places.

Val: But we decided rather than confront the demons again, we'd just go and we were out of there within twenty-four hours. And we never went back.

Roger: I was pretty angry when I heard what had happened to the dog and the pigs. I said, "I've gotta go before I go and do something silly." Because I would have gone and I would have confronted this guy. And I would have lost the plot. I probably would have done something I'd end up in prison for. So I decided, "I gotta get out of here."

So we moved to Whangamata. Bought a section there and rented a place.

Even after the flood we couldn't even get the insurance assessor to come up because the roads were closed. So we wanted to move. But we couldn't.

Val: So Leslie Cotterill got in a plane, a private Cessna, and picked up the insurance assessor and brought him back up, which was pretty awesome.

Because we were one of about only two or three families whose homes were literally destroyed in that flood.

Roger: We couldn't even drive to our house.

These days Roger does electrical engineering, heavy industrial work for big companies. And it took him twenty years but he's finally got his eleven acres of land again, just outside Tauranga. And it's on a hill so it's not going to flood.

CHAPTER 4

LUKE GETS REACQUAINTED WITH HIS FAMILY

Ike Campbell (Chris's brother): I had run into Luke before. We'd had a couple of yarns with him over at the mailbox in the yard there. He was a hard guy to talk to. He wouldn't listen to anything you said. I was living in Ruatoria town and he came over to my place one day and punched me in the head and kicked me in the head. I sort of got to know what Luke was like just through the little dealings he was having with the old man.

One day Luke came over, and he's a bit of a boxer, apparently. And I thought he was going to hit me. But he kicked me in the head, this guy. And that's when I realised, "Gee, this guy is very dangerous."

He'd come over about some problem with the fences over here. He found some law to say that he didn't have to put up his half of the fence because it was *our* stock that was going on *his* place, that sort of carry-on.

He came back here as a bit of a Rambo. I'd heard about him. But when he was coming back here and these troubles were happening he wasn't living here. He was just coming back, stirring, and then he'd go back to Hamilton. Then he'd come back a fortnight later, stir. This is before he actually moved back. He's a stand-over character. That's all there is to it. He's a bully.

Email from former Sergeant Nigel Hendrikse: I had some interesting interactions with Luke when I was the relieving Sgt at Ruatoria... I remember once when he first met me I had to show him the actual Statute about the Dog Control Act. He just didn't want to hear it from me. However I really respected the toughness of him, that real don't fuck with me attitude.

Bob Kaa (leader of the Neighbourhood Support Group): When Luke came back the county owned that house. It used to be the road-man's house many years ago. And when he came home it was vacant. Luke had a few spare dollars in his Post account and he bought it from the county.

Of course the Campbells, they wanted that house. But they wanted it for nothing. But along comes their cousin Luke and he purchases it. And he says, "It's my fuckin' house. And you bastards keep away from it."

So why did the Campbells want the house? Well it's on family land. Despite the fact it was sold a long time ago. I don't know the history. But they were still negotiating with the county when along came Luke and he said, "Here you are. Here's fifty bucks. If you want it I'll take the house." It was a nice home.

Then of course he got into an argument with his own family. The Campbells are his own family.

The other thing he did: he also had some lease land up the Makarika Valley. As you go up Makarika Road it was up on the left, just past the marae. And, of course, who was staying there? Chris and the boys were staying there. They'd been using the house as a headquarters for the Rastafarians. So he went round there one day. He said, "Look, bros. I'll give you 'til five o'clock. You know I'm leasing here?"

"Yep."

"You know you're not supposed to be here?"

"This is *our* house."

"I'll give you fullas 'til five o'clock. All right? If you're not out I'll come back and I'll burn you out."

"Fuck off."

"I'll be back at five o'clock."

He came back at five o'clock with a can of petrol. Of course they had their Rastafarian flags flying. Luke said, "One more chance: five minutes, otherwise I'll burn you out." They told him to piss off.

Five minutes was up so he went around the house with the can splashing petrol on the weatherboards. "I'll give you one last chance." He lit the match.

"You won't do it."

He tossed the match against the petrol-soaked side of the house. BOOM! It just went up. The flags went up. The house went up. Everything went up. They came running out and of course they were gonna kill him. And of course he said, "Over my bloody dead body."

POLICE TRY TO HELP CAMPBELL

Former Sergeant John Robinson: Hemi Hikawai used to go and visit Chris Campbell in Paremoremo Prison to try and end the troubles. But in the meantime Luke Donnelly arrived on the scene.

He got that house right on the corner of Makarika Road and he was running all the land around there. The first thing he did was kick the Rastas out of their Makarika pad because it was on his land. And then he burnt it down. Of course he wasn't a popular man with the Rastas after that.

Then he started having conflicts with Willie Campbell over stock. I can remember going out there. The fences weren't good and the stock were getting mixed up - and Luke was loading the stock truck. We got called down to Makarika sale yards to help Willie Campbell go through the stock before it got loaded to see if any of his were in there with Luke's. The two of them were at loggerheads. Here was this stranger suddenly appeared on the scene throwing his weight around. And no one threatened Donnelly.

Another time one of Willie's horses jumped the fence because there was a mare on heat and broke the fence down getting through. And that didn't help matters.

Anyway they actually ended up having a fight. Willie was a tough bugger and could handle himself. But he was sixty odd by this time. He actually got knocked around a bit. And that didn't help at all either because Chris was coming out of jail and he wasn't going to let his father get hurt by Donnelly.

Detective Hemi Hikawai, January 2000: We'd started this liaison with Chris. We knew he had a release date. So we decided it was important to keep this liaison going. So after that I made several visits to the prison. What we wanted was the ability to be able to talk to him if he did get out and start down that old track again. Hopefully, we would have built up a rapport, him and I, where before anyone on either side got killed we could talk our way through it.

And the night before he was released he was brought here to Gisborne and he was released from here. And I spent about four hours in this office talking with Chris. I asked him, "What's gonna happen when you get out, Chris?"

I always remember him telling me, "I just want to be left alone." He used to call me James. "Whatever I've done, James, I've paid for it. I've paid my dues. Whatever I've done to that community the courts have imposed a sentence on me and I've paid my dues. All I wanna do is be left alone."

I said to him, "You've got Luke Donnelly up there spouting off and everything else. What's gonna happen there, Chris?"

He said, "If Luke Donnelly stays on his property, Luke will have no problems from me. But if he comes poking his fuckin' nose over my way, he'll get more fuckin' trouble than he knows how to deal with. But I'm not going back there to cause trouble, James. I'm going back to get on with my life. I've paid my dues and I just wanna be left alone."

And there were incidents involved with Rastafarians that occurred after he was released and before he was shot and Campbell was nowhere near them.

I think that spell in prison had taken the sting out of Chris Campbell. I don't have a crystal ball but I know that I spoke to Campbell the night before he was released and he told me he didn't want any trouble. He was just going back there to mind his own business and get on with his life.

Interview with Hata Thompson's mum Laura (Aunty Ga-ga) and brother Chris:

Laura: When Chris came out of prison he wasn't looking back on that situation because he was already going forward.

Chris: And he'd increased his hatred for the system while he was inside because he felt he was persecuted at the time. And when he came out he came out with like a *real* vengeance.

Laura: Yeah.

Is that right? Because Hemi Hikawai said that he believes Chris came out wanting to not go back to prison and to change his ways. Do you think that that might have just been what Chris was putting across?

Chris: No offence, I think Hemi Hikawai was just covering his own arse at the end of the day...

Laura: Yeah.

Chris: ...because Hemi was a mongrel.

Laura: Mongrel.

Ha ha ha... Hemi was over the top?

Chris: Yeah, he was extreme. He was an extremist to the point of being a modern advent of Ropata Wahawaha (the polarising Te Aowera ancestor who sided with the police against the rebel prophet Te Kooti). He was another brother doing it to a brother, he being a Maori who's got the bloody audacity at the end of the day to say I've got the suit on so I am law and order. And yet you look at him today and he's on the Gisborne District Council. How extreme art thou, Hemi? Hemi would be likened unto a potato: black on the outside but white on the inside. His true heart was of another perspective, another culture, and another kaupapa.

Rasta John Heeney reckoned Hemi Hikawai was possessed by a demon and had been for a long time. But he said that in a way he was a friend to some of the Rastas. He said Chris Campbell particularly liked Hemi and the two were good friends.

Another Rasta, Joe Nepe, said he held nothing against Hemi Hikawai. He said that Hemi was just doing his job and he was good at it. He reckoned Hemi had even given Chris Campbell a joint to smoke in the back of the car as he drove him around Gisborne when Chris got out of jail. Hemi himself didn't smoke, according to Joe.

Former Rasta Dion Hutana: Hemi Hikawai basically got the convictions for the burning of the Ngati Porou marae. This is how it happened. You can put this in the book.

When Chris Campbell arrived at the trial to be my "McKenzie friend" (a layperson who assists a defendant in court) Hemi Hikawai came and grabbed Chris from the cells and took him for a ride around Gisborne. Everyone who was in the Gisborne cop shop saw it. Hemi and Barney, Chris's brother, were good mates. And Hemi knew Barney and Chris from way back. Now I don't know what kind of discussions that they had, but *one* discussion they had was that Hemi asked Chris, "Aw, come on, Chris, get them to go guilty. You know they did it." And we did. So we (Dion and Eddie Kotuhi) decided to change our plea to guilty. And that was one of the reasons why. It was after a passenger we'd had in the car had given evidence. And Chris was in the cells with us. He said, "There's no way you can win this. You may as well just go guilty."

And I just said, "Aw, okay then." So we did. We went guilty.

So Hemi got Chris and said, "Look, you know they did it, they know they did it, we know they did it. Let's just get it over and done with. It's gonna mean a helluva lot to the community if we can get a guilty verdict here."

Aw, I don't know if that was what was said. But Chris gave me a briefing of that encounter and that was part of it. And then, oh well, when we came back Chris had a big joint on him and we smoked it.

So that had come from Hemi, too? Hahahaha.

Hahahahahahahaha.

Actually, Joe Nepe had told me this.

Ay?

*Joe Nepe had told me that Hemi had taken Chris out. I've already got a mention of it. Joe Nepe said that everyone reckoned Hemi had taken Chris out for a ride and smoked dope with him. Well, I don't know about smoked dope **with** him, but gave him some.*

Chris told me that too. When he came back to the cells, we were all in the sun room and the dining room and next thing we were smoking a joint. And, you know, we knew where it came from.

And you were in the sun room at the Gisborne cop shop?

Yeah.

And everyone was leaving yiz to yourselves?

Ay?

Everyone was leaving you to your own devices? No one was hassling you or anything?

Na.

Sheesus. That's creative policing. Hahaha.

Hahahahaha. Aw, good we can laugh about it now. Well, that happened, too. And it was that night when me and the bro woke up and we had a karakia. We did our Ringatu prayers. And we talked for a while, then, straight up, he just said, "Brethren, do you know that there's a bullet waiting for me?"

And you know how you get that gulpy thing in your throat? I swallowed hard. And then, yeah, thirty-eight days later, woah, it happened.

From the second interview with Luke: These guys were parked outside my house on the road in their light blue Falcon. And they were getting boxes of matches and lighting them and throwing them up in the air and yelling out, "We're gonna burn your fuckin' house, cunt."

This was before I'd had the scrap with Hata Thompson. And my mate Roger Te Puni happened to be with me that day. And me and Roger were getting ready to go to rugby league training because I was helping with the local team, the Raiders.

I said to Roger, "Get ready, jump in the car. We'll fuckin' bail these bastards up."

As soon as they heard the car start and I raced out of the garage, down the drive, they took off. And I chased them. Fuck, I was going for it, about a hundred and twenty k's. And they turned in and shot into Whakapaurangi Road, pulled up by the house, jumped out and then Roger yelled out, "Watch out! He's got a gun!"

Cody Haua had pulled a gun out and he had it across the bonnet of his car. But I didn't see it. So I was looking for this gun and the next thing, he pulls it and says, "Get off our fuckin' place." That's Cody.

Tony Tuhou was there and he came after me. He said, "Aw, we'll fuckin' do you."

I said, "I'll fuckin' break your neck as you stand there, ya cunt."

So he backed off because he could see that I was ready to lash out. But Cody had the gun.

Then Cody's mother – that was our aunty, Aunty Punky – she came out. She could hear the yelling going on and all the swearing. But she was a bit blind and she couldn't see long distances. So I backed off when I saw the gun but I said to Cody, "You'll fuckin' keep."

The aunty came out. She was in the house next door. I said, "Oh, hello, aunty. It's me. It's Luke."

And Cody yelled out, "Aw, Mum, it's one of those Williams," trying to say that I was one of the Pakehas, one of the Williams. "We don't want those bloody Pakehas around here."

I said, "Aunty, it's me, me, Luke."

"Oh, Luke." And then she said to Cody, "Don't you start that. This is your own family here."

And I said to her, "Cody's got a gun. He's pointing the gun at me." Well, the old lady said, "You just cut that out." So he puts the gun back down.

I said, "It's all right now, aunty. It's okay."

And she said, "Well, never mind, boy. You fullas are all family. You gotta be good to each other."

"Okay, aunty."

So me and Roger hopped back in the car and took off.

CHAPTER 5

HATA V LUKE IN THE MAIN STREET

At the time of writing, Matt Sillars is an inspector with the New Zealand police based in Auckland. But in 1990 he had a four-month stint as the sergeant in Ruatoria (including four weeks in Gisborne). Like so many before him, Sillars must have wondered what he'd walked into. The arson and other crime weren't as frenetic as they had been during the late '80s. But with Luke back in the community and Chris Campbell coming out of jail, things were heating up again and the Rastafarian troubles were slowly but surely coming to a head. Sillars says he never really felt he had great support from the community while he was there. He wasn't a local and, considering there were farmers who'd lived around Ruatoria for forty years who weren't considered locals, he was always going to struggle to be accepted. He also had only one other fulltime Ruatoria policeman to help him out. And they were shockingly outnumbered. This was never more evident than on Friday, June 22, 1990, when Sillars found himself in the middle of a fight in the main street between Rasta Hata Thompson and Luke Donnelly.

Hata Thompson: It was in the afternoon. And Luke Donnelly started giving me heaps in the street. He told me he was gonna make an example of me in front of everyone in the whole fuckin' town. Quite a lot of people had stopped what they were doing to watch. It was a fair dinkum scrap. I had bare feet and he had big steel-capped boots. He tried to put the boot into me quite hard, but he couldn't. He got the better of me by grabbing hold of my dreadlocks and pulling them as hard as he could. This cop turned up and said, "Cut it out." And I stopped fighting. And as soon as I stopped, Lukie got up and poked me in the eye. And I was blinded at that point. I couldn't see old Lukie. But he didn't beat me up.

He said, "I've got you now; you can't see."

I said, "No you haven't."

We kept rolling around and wrestling on the ground. But he run out of puff in the end. I just kept wrestling him and I was wearing him down. I was thinking, "No one treats me like that."

It broke up in the end and people pulled us apart. There was a cop standing there, even after Luke poked me in the eye. That's why I went and got the gun. I thought the two of them were working together. And I thought, "Aw, okay, got no help from him. I'll get my own justice if I don't get any help from a policeman that's standing right there."

Luke was standing in the shop gloating to everyone about the fight. And I said to him, "Aw, ya fuckin' wanker. Ya dirty bastard. You poked me in the eye, ya fuckin' cunt… fuckin' weak, bay."

He said, "I fuckin' gave you a good thrashing in front of everybody."

I said, "You fuckin' blinded me, ay, because I had the upper hand. And then you go blowing off to everyone about how good you are. But it's not finished yet."

"I'll be waiting."

"I've got the way to deal with you. I'll be back. Mark my words."

"I'll be waiting."

"Choice. I won't be long."

I came back with the shotgun.

"Aw, no need for that. There's no need for that, bro."

"Who's the man now? Who's gonna give who a hiding?"

He was pleading with me. "Come on, bro. There's no need for this. It's only a joke."

"I'm not joking. Who's joking?"

From the second interview with Luke: All that happened was I just went to town to get some stores and there's Hemi Toi Reuben and Hata. They were both walking along the road there. I went to turn into the supermarket and they yell out from the side there, "Ay, ya cunt! You fuckin' beatin' up the bros. You're all shet."

And I just ignored them. I drove in. I parked my car. And they walked back towards me. So I hopped out of the car and just walked up to them. I actually expected that there was going to be just a bit of a discussion. And then when they split, I thought then, "Aw, here we go." One went around the back of the car and the other stood in front of me. When Hemi Toi went around the back I thought, "Aw, this bastard's gonna come up behind me and…"

King hit ya?

Yeah, try and tag me from behind. So as I turned around and looked, Hemi Toi was suddenly on the other side of me. He moved pretty quick. So I just went to move into safe territory, away from Hemi Toi. And just as I turned back old Hata took a swing at me and he just clipped me on the top of the head here. So I into him. And I into him and I tried to get him actually between the bank and the driveway because it was a little bit embarrassing out on the bloody street. So I moved into that driveway and I thought, "I'll nail this bastard right inbetween the gate and the bank wall." As soon as he got in there he wouldn't be able to go nowhere and I was just going to deal to him in there. He did come in. And as he come in I just whacked him, plumb, bang in the face. I think actually, him and Hemi Toi, I think they'd been on drugs because they just seemed all hyped up and Hata's reactions were a split second too late. As I pulled my fist back, he wasn't moving. When I went bang, he woke up a bit. That's what happened. Then he just put his head down and charged into me. He went to put his arms around me. But I think I'm just a little bit bigger than him. He bloody bit me right on my arm here, mate. I mean, how many years ago? It's still there now. See, you can see it. Mate, he was in like that and he wouldn't let go. And you know when you're pumped up your bicep comes up like that. You put your teeth in there and then it pumps up. He just latched on and I couldn't get him off. So all I could do was just push him out and, mate, his head was here and the only thing I thought of immediately was, "Aw, I'll fuckin' gouge his eyes." So I went straight into his eyes. My fingers were underneath the lids…

Woo-hoo (high-pitched and cringing).

…and I was going like this, I was going like this.

Aw, farck.

I was in there as hard as I could, mate, and I was trying to hook his eye out.

Yeah, aw, fuck. Aw, Go-…

That there was just to make him let go. But he fuckin' wouldn't let go. So all I did is I just dropped my hand there, under his crotch, picked him up and I had him in the air like this and we just went bang, down.

Spear tackled him?

Fuckin' just straight into the ground, yeah. And he still didn't let go. Still didn't let go.

Bit of a bulldog isn't he.

He just held on like that. But to be fair he's only a little guy anyway. So it wasn't any problem picking him up. And at that time I was pretty young and I'd just come from playing football (rugby league) and stuff like that. So I was fitter than him. I just banged him on the ground. But when we were down on the ground my shoulder actually cushioned him. If he hadn't been biting like that I would have smashed his bloody head, broken his neck. And that is what happened. And when the cop came along, Matt Sillars, because someone had rung, he pulled up, and everybody was gathered around watching this, and he just said, "Okay, you two, break it up or I'm gonna arrest you." And Hata wouldn't let go. And my arm by this time had gone limp. I couldn't feel my arm.

Far out.

And I knew I couldn't feel it. So I had his hair and I was just going bang, like that, whack, whack on the footpath. And he just wouldn't let go. And my elbow, here, was being gouged out on the footpath.

Yeah, couldn't get him off. Jesus Christ. So how'd you get him off?

Sillars then came along and he grabbed me. I was on top of Hata. He grabbed me by the shoulder and he said, "Right, come on, that's it, Luke." Then Hata let go. And he stood up. His eye was bleeding. You could see where I must have broke the tissue.

He just up and walked away. Matt Sillars says, "Come back here."

He said, "No, fuck you," and went away.

And Sillars said words to the effect: This fighting in the street isn't on.

I said, "Yeah, okay, that's cool." And I walked into the shop. I walked into the shop and the lady in there gave me an ice pack and I put it on my arm. I was in there about five minutes and the adrenaline was still pumping. So I wrapped the ice pack around my arm and did my shopping. I went and got the milk and the bread and stuff like that. There was only about three or four items. And then I come out, paid for it, everybody was talking.

Aw, that's right, the reason that Hemi Toi didn't get in was because Roger Te Puni had come down because someone had said, "Hey, you're mate, he's in a scrap down the road." So Roger raced down there. He's got tattoos, Mongrel Mob. And he came down and he stood with the bunch. And when Hemi Toi was going to move in, Roger said,

"You fuckin' stay out or I'll fuckin' have ya." So that kept Hemi Toi. And that's why the fight was only really between me and Hata.

Well what happened with the shotgun?

When I come out of the shop I got to the door and then Hata was walking back in from the street, walking towards the shop and he was yelling out to me, "You wanna go, cunt? You think you're fuckin' tough?"

So I put the stores down and I thought, "Fuck, back into it."

Heh heh heh.

And just as I stepped off the thing there, fuck...

He pulled this gun out.

He pulled this gun, yeah. I didn't see it. I wasn't thinking of any gun or anything. He pulled this fuckin' gun up. It was under his coat. And farck, he pulled it up and he put it up to my bloody face.

Right under your chin?

Well, yeah, he whacked me in the head and said, "Right, how tough are you now, you cunt?"

I said, "Ooh, bro."

And when I said, bro, he goes, "I'm not your fuckin' bro."

I says, "Put down the gun then." I says, "If you want to finish this, you and I, we'll just go over the bank, just by ourselves. Fuck the cops. Just you and I go over the side now."

He said, "Na."

I knew he was frightened because I'd fuckin' waste him. And he put the gun down in my stomach, fuckin' whacked me in the stomach. He said, "Come on, how tough are you now?" And then, bang, up here again. And then Roger's standing beside me, Roger says, "Aw, come on, bro."

He whipped the gun over to Roger and says, "You! You, ya bastard."

Roger says, "Aw, come on, bro, we're okay."

"I'm not your fuckin' bro."

And then he turned over to me and I was thinking to myself, "Fuck, if that thing just wasn't so short." Well, the thing was there was an opportunity to just whack him into a headlock and break his arm because I've got a few years of martial arts and I could have quite easily. But there just wasn't enough length on the gun, on the barrel.

Sawn off, was it?

Yeah it was. Fuck, it was cut right down to about that, no more than that.

What's that? About twelve inches?

Twelve inches, yeah, fourteen at the most. It was cut right back to its absolute shortest. And I thought, "Na, I'm never going to be able to get that." So I thought, "I'm just gonna try and talk him out of it." So I said to him, "You know, you pull that trigger, you're gonna go away and do time." And I said, "Your kids? You know, you're never gonna see your fuckin' kids." Heh heh heh.

And he said, "Yeah, that's how much you fuckin' know. I haven't got any kids." (We both have a good laugh). I thought he had some kids. Yeah, he said, "I haven't got any fuckin' kids." And I said, "Aw, farck!"

He brought the gun down again, whacked me in the stomach, in the chest and bang under there again. My fuckin' head went back. I'm thinking, "Gees."

So are you shittin' yourself, or...

Aw fuck yeah!

Yeah, yeah.

You've got a fuckin' shotgun in your face. And I'm thinking about my kids. I'm thinking about my boy (Kiwi league star Jason Donnelly) overseas. And I'm thinking about trying to calm the situation.

It must be all slowed down, like a car crash.

Yeah, well it was. I'm saying, "Just, just chill out, you know, just, just cool it."

He says, "Don't fuckin' tell me to cool it! You ya bastard, how fuckin' tough are you?" And I'm just trying to keep him cool, don't let him fuckin'...

Pull the trigger.

...Pull the trigger. And then he whacked me in the guts again and he goes, "Get on your fuckin' knees, cunt."

And, fuck, I lost it. All these worries about my family and all that...

What did you say?

I looked at him and I said, "Ah fuck you. If you're gonna fuckin' shoot me, you fuckin' shoot me. I ain't gettin' on my fuckin' knees for you, cunt." I said, "You got any fuckin' balls, let's go to the fuckin' river, just me and you, just down the bank there, because I ain't gettin' on my fuckin' knees for you."

"Get on your fuckin' knees, cunt, or I'll blow your head off."

I said, "Fuckin' shoot. But you're gonna be shootin' me in the back you fuckin' arsehole." And I just turned around and I walked away.

And that's how it ended?

Yeah... ...He just backed away, kept on backing away. The Rastas that were in Hemi Toi's lime green Holden Kingswood had all taken off. So he just walked off down the street towards the park near the police station...

...The Armed Offenders got them the next morning about six o'clock because they were all doped out of their trees.

Matt Sillars says that after the initial scrap he went back to the police station. He was unaware of the altercation with the shotgun until after it had ended and he saw Hata Thompson walking past the station with the gun. He says he yelled out, "Thompson, put that gun down!"

But Hata just kept on walking.

Former Sergeant John Robinson: It was months and months before Hata came to trial. And the judge let him off very lightly. He said, "We've gotta put all the troubles in Ruatoria behind us." I think he gave him a suspended sentence or something.

Luke Donnelly: When they couldn't intimidate me directly, they'd try to do it through my family. Once my wife at the time, Elizabeth, was in town. She had our daughter Jesse in the car with her after school. And when they came to come across the last bridge just before you head up to the house, the Rastas were on the other side. And they crossed the road and blocked her in. She couldn't go anywhere and they got around her. There were about five or six of them on their horses. Chris Campbell wasn't there. But Cody Haua was among them. They wouldn't let her past and they were all up around the car and she was so terrified. She didn't want to put her foot down in case one of the horses fell on the car. That's basically what happened there. After they finished terrifying her for a couple of minutes they just let her go.

When my wife came home and told me I jumped in the car and raced down to see if I could find them. But they'd split.

You imagine any guy, if you get a bunch of gang types threatening and intimidating your wife... I was seething after that.

Apparently what they were saying is, "We're gonna get your fuckin' husband. His head is gonna come off." *Always* the threat of chopping off the head from those guys.

Luke: Another time, I heard that a few of the Rastas had turned up at the school asking people to point out which girl was Luke Donnelly's daughter. Why the hell did they want to know that? Jesse was only about six or seven at the time. You can only imagine what they had in mind for her to get at me. I was pretty alarmed about that. But that's the type of intimidation they used.

CHAPTER 6

MT HIKURANGI,
THE RASTAS' MT ZION (1)

January, 2000, this is an excerpt from how I wrote up the second interview of this whole project: *I'm in the Skyline garage at The Crossroads, Ruatoria, headquarters for the Rastafarians, with John Heeney and his wife Donna. Two more Rastas have turned up. They're introduced as Albie and TK. Albie stares straight ahead into his own world, and gives a start as if being woken every time you speak to him. TK reminds me of a jolly Maori Santa Claus with a full moko. Albie also has a full moko and long dreads. They seem friendly enough. It's raining outside. Joints and a little plastic water-bong are being passed round and round the table. You toke a joint and then a packed bong's in front of you.*

I haven't had as much as the others, but I'm not used to it. I haven't smoked for years so it's hitting me hard. And I'm remembering all the reasons I gave up in the first place. There are moments when I feel extremely uncomfortable. I feel as though I'm surfing the vibe all the time, trying to act as if everything's normal when suddenly my whole body's buzzing and my brain is fogging over and paranoia is seeping out of every pore.

John Heeney: Uprising. An uprising, that's how it began. It was an uprising because when you've got the sunrise as you're taonga, well every morning it's an uprising. Every morning we get an uprising.

East Coast, yeah.

And that's how it happened. But what's happened here - this is how we perceived it - when the sun shone, Bang, BING, the spirit from Ethiopia, Bob sent it to us through the ray of sunlight. Bing.

Yeah.

It hit us, ay.

Right in the morning.

And then, bang, bang, bang. We did all what we did. And then the second ray come out, over the top of Hikurangi, DOONG, to the next area.

Yeah.

Because to me when the spirit of God comes, it comes through here then it goes to the rest of Aotearoa. But it comes through Hikurangi first. Cos it comes like a current, a flow.

And it gets you guys first on the way there.

Yeah. Because "the lord loveth the gates of Zion more than all the other dwellings of Jacob." See, and Mount Zion is the mountain that cannot be removed.

Yeah.

And Hikurangi is a mountain that cannot be removed.

Is that what it means?

It means so much I could talk to you all year and you still wouldn't get through the start of it because there's so much. We're just talking on our little shed wall here, ay (pictures of "martyrs") but outside there's heaps and heaps. And it's all so intertwined and woven that you'd never be able to figure out the politics of anything, ay, because it's just so intertwined with everything. There's no separation or distinction. The only separation is this side of the river and that side of the river.

Mmm.

John tokes on a joint: But Luke Donnelly...

Mmm. (I'm starting to feel a bit uncomfortable).

I've always got him in my prayers to God when we go and ask The Man, ay. I pray for him. I pray for him.

Mmm. (By now, I'm so stoned, "mmm" is as intelligent as it gets for me).

You know. He came home and he was the man chosen by the baldheads to come back and deliver…

Mmm.

…You know, the psalm of death to the brothers. And he didn't bring life here. He came and brought death.

Mmm.

Silence (we're all stoned).

Maori Myth and Legend, Margaret Orbell: Eleven species of moa once browsed on trees and shrubs in Aotearoa… The tallest of these wingless birds were two and a half metres in height, and the heaviest weighed more than two hundred kilograms.

Moa-hunting reached its peak in about 1300, great numbers were killed in the century that followed, by 1500 they had become rare, and soon afterwards they disappeared completely.

A common expression, "lost like the moa", means "lost utterly and hopelessly". As well, moa appear in tradition as remote creatures with extraordinary attributes which live on the summits of certain mountains. A solitary moa that stood on one leg was believed to guard Hikurangi on the East Coast. Moa, such as this, were said to be similar in appearance to human beings but to feed only on the wind. So a person who did not eat very much or a girl in love who had lost her appetite, might be called "a moa that feeds on air".

The Gisborne Herald: A series of articles about the mountain by Colin Rex McLernon reveals Hikurangi as of historical significance to both Maori and Pakeha. McLernon wrote that Hikurangi had been the focal point of ritual, legend and waiata (or song) in New Zealand and in other parts of Polynesia. Even the Moriori of the Chatham Islands had a legend relating to Whakatau and his jump over the summit of Hikurangi. In Hawaiiki it was known as the holy mountain.

The god Te Manu-o-te-Ra, Bird of Day or Bird of Sun, dwelt on Hikurangi.

In certain legends relating to Tane, the mountain on which certain stars rested and displayed their light was called Mahikurangi.

And some people believed eternal life rested and death was unknown there.

The mountain has also been referred to as a haven or a place where no violence will be tolerated.

During his visit to the Waiapu Valley in 1838 the Reverend William Colenso recorded a sighting of a moa, which by then was known to be extinct. In 1839 the Reverend Richard Taylor also recorded seeing a moa. Both men lay claim to being discoverers of the moa. On both occasions they reported sighting the moa on Mt Hikurangi.

The geological aspects of the mountain have been the subject of much contention for about 140 years. It was first thought that Mt Hikurangi was some sort of volcanic rock. But that theory was thrown out the window two years after it was recorded.

Colin Williams (former owner of Pakihiroa Station, which includes part of Mt Hikurangi): I love that mountain probably just as much as any Ngati Porou person does. I've been all over it and I bet you I know that mountain probably better than most of them. I've been through the bush all round it, and climbed it.

You get up there on that mountain and there's no doubt about it, it's a very special place, as all those mountains are. I've been to the top of all of them except Wharekia.

When we owned Pakihiroa we made this road on Mount Hikurangi that goes right virtually to the end of the grass, as far as we could go. And that's where they leveled off this place and put all those big carvings there for the millennium. So it's not hard to get from there to the top of the mountain. About an hour and a half and you're up there.

Maori Myth and Legend, Margaret Orbell: It was believed in some regions that when the hero Maui was pulling up the fish that became the North Island, the first part of the fish that rose through the water was a mountain named Hikurangi. This was therefore the first part of the land that the light fell upon.

In another myth, the story of Paikea and Ruatapu, who were living in Hawaiiki, Paikea is about to travel to Aotearoa when he is warned by his demotic brother Ruatapu that at a certain time he will arrive at Paikea's new home in the form of high waves breaking upon the shore, and that the people must then run to Mount Hikurangi to escape the flood. And when these great waves come, the crowds upon Hikurangi survive the disaster.

In both these myths, then, Hikurangi rises above the ocean (which is a nonhuman realm associated with danger and destruction). In both stories it is a sacred mountain of great power, in the first because of its primacy and the light that falls upon it, in the second because it is a place of refuge and survival.

As well as existing in mythology, the name Hikurangi was given in reality to a number of prominent hills and mountains in different parts of the country. The best known is Hikurangi on the east coast, the tapu mountain of the people of Ngati Porou. They believed that their mountain was the first land fished up by Maui, and that his waka was still up there on the summit, turned to stone. At dawn the sun lights up this high peak while all around is in darkness – and this event repeats the first occasion on which the sun shone upon Hikurangi as it rose above the waters.

CHAPTER 7

A FIGHT WITH POLICE

Wednesday, November 21, 1990: There's a fight between Rastas and police at Whareponga Beach.

Tensions have been brewing for a while. About forty Rastas, including women and children, have been camping down at the beach. Chris Campbell is out of jail and back in Ruatoria. There is a new wave of devotees ready to follow his instructions. And there are fears that he'll revive the impetus of the Rasta movement in Ruatoria.

Landowners asked the Rastas to leave the beach two weeks ago. But they have so far resisted.

The trouble starts at 10.30am when the acting sergeant at Ruatoria, a constable and a civilian head down to where the Rastas are camping. There, they find a trailer, which belongs to the civilian, and a stolen car.

There are only three people at the camp when police arrive. But other police are called to help recover the car and trailer. They also seize a rifle and a large number of cannabis seedlings.

That's when a group of Rastafarians arrive home. The police are outnumbered and the Rastas become hostile and attempt to take back stuff the police have put on the trailer.

Scuffles develop and the police decide to withdraw to protect the property.

Rocks are thrown at the police vehicles, causing damage to one. The demeanour of the Rastafarians is described as being "fanatical".

District Commander Superintendent Rana Waitai says steps are being taken to deal with the offenders. There will be a police response. "It will be done in our own time, and in the manner we decide. We have several strategies in mind," he says.

Ed Te Rauna, former Rasta: We were just camping there. A lot of the guys were surfers and there was an endless supply of free food down at the sea. We wanted to live close by those resources and plus we had some plots up the hill and stuff. So we were just down there doing what we thought was perfectly fine, just camping on the beach.

Chris Campbell had just come out then. Some of the landowners, or some of the land-leasers I should say, had got together. These were the guys who were labeled the vigilantes. Luke Donnelly seemed to be in charge and he was probably the biggest, strongest character out of them. And he was just really aggressive. Man, he just wanted to go out there and just kill everyone... for his own reasons. He had his own reasons. Some of it was justifiable.

But what happened was we were notified to get off the land by these guys. It was all the farmers from around the place that were leasing all the surrounding blocks. They formed an alliance, I suppose, to look after their livelihoods and their backyards.

And we were down there doing a whole heap of things, you know. Some of them, like I said, were against the law. Some of them weren't very nice things, like killing their meat and that for barbecues, stuff we shouldn't-a done. Well, yeah, that's how that conflict began. And that's how they grew to hate the Rastas. And I don't blame them for that nowadays. Poor things. That's their futures we were tampering with.

So they came down and they notified us to get off the land by such and such a date. Chris Campbell told us to stay. He wanted us to stand our ground. We had kids in there. Like I was only a child myself. Charlie Turnbull had his whole family. He had his wife and kids there. Later on in that week as it was getting down to the deadline I think Chris probably came to the realisation that a conflict was too dangerous with the families about and agreed that we should move.

Chris Thompson, Hata's brother: The day the police came down, we had a big crash on the road. One of our drivers was driving in top gear down a hill and ended up smashing into a vehicle that belonged to the same faction, coming *up* the hill. And it was like a God-send that that happened because lo and behold not even twenty seconds behind us a whole team of police jeeps and that turn up with trailers.

I think they'd watched us leave town and they had the intention of getting the whole lot of us in one hit. They were coming down to bust us for all the stolen property. And all of that *did* go on. I won't talk any shit. It happened.

Now these cops, good public servants that they were, they offered to turn around and remove the vehicles off the road, and we could find our own way back to the beach. They went on ahead to the beach camp. We'd left a couple of minors, who were about fourteen or fifteen back at the camp. And, believe it or not, the cops served them with the search warrant.

Meanwhile, we all piled into one vehicle, thought we'd make the most of that. We whipped the front panel off and off we went. We got down there and it was actually a pregnant woman who was in the car that actually sparked the whole chain of events.

The cops had thrown everything onto these trailers, right down to the kids' bikes and they were declaring they were stolen. But these bikes weren't stolen. And this pregnant woman, Hilda Wharepapa, had receipts for all that she had bought. And she was saying, "That's not fuckin' stolen!" She gets up and she rips this bike off the top of the pile and says, "You're not taking this. I have receipts that prove I bought that."

Well a cop grabs the other side and starts yanking it. And it turns into a tug-a-war. She's going, "You're not going to take it." Well he goes and shoves it into her guts.

Then one brother gets out of the car and says, "You don't do that to a pregnant woman, you disrespectful mongrel."

Then a huge scrap broke out.

Chris Campbell wasn't at the fight. Chris, Hata and Diesel Dick had gone into town in the morning on horseback. But the cops must have thought Chris would be there.

One of the cops said later that he was stabbed in the forehead with a screwdriver. That cop was lying blatantly. I saw what happened there. It was like one of the brothers said, "Here, take a bow," and then the cop's head was smacked into the iron railings on the trailer, right at the end of the piping. And it lifted the whole front of his forehead. It was pretty. He just started crying. He was screaming like anything.

But while this fight was taking place there was a helicopter with a hang-man on it, a man on a line, lifting up (cannabis) plants. The cops ended up taking everything they could possibly take.

Monday, November 26, 1990: After being issued with a written eviction notice, the Rastas finally agree to move. They head as a group to Mangahanea Marae. But, before they can remove their belongings, two caravans belonging to the Rastas and two privately-owned baches, in which the Rastas have been staying, are burned down.

Chris Thompson, Hata's brother: So everybody decided to pack up and move and the day we moved, that same night was when the baches were torched.

And it wasn't just Luke (Donnelly) that went down to do the burning. There was a truckload of them that went down. It was mostly that team of vigilantes who were young and full of testosterone.

The faction weren't even living in all the baches. We were living in caravans and we'd just borrowed one of the baches.

ONE COP'S VIEW OF THE "RIOT"

Email from former Sergeant Nigel Hendrikse: At that time there were no Rastas there... they'd all taken off to a marae in Ruatoria after the "riot".

Briefly, I'd been driving down to Whareponga in the Police truck to talk to Chris by myself after he came out of prison (so there was absolutely no fear on my behalf about going down there). I think the Rastas respected in a funny way that I wasn't scared to drive down to the camp. I never took a pistol, just me and the truck. When the other goons would barge over to me and shoulder into me at the Rasta camp I'd just tell them to fuck off as I only wanted to speak to Chris. The funny thing is I can't for the life of me remember exactly what I was there to discuss with Chris... I was the go-between for my boss Rana Waitai and would communicate messages to Chris and tell Rana the reply.

Then one day I saw one of the Rasta cars hauling a trailer along the road in Ruatoria that I instantly recognised as being stolen from Stan Bryant, the owner of the Te Araroa Holiday Park. I'd been relieving Sergeant up there and had actually taken the complaint from Stan.

So when the Rastas were still camped at Whareponga, Russell Holmes and I headed down there with a search warrant to get Stan's trailer back. The early warning system was in place and a Rasta car racing ahead of us down the very windy road to the beach to warn the Rastas that we were on our way crashed head-on into a Rasta car coming out of Whareponga.

We came upon the crash and of course all the ropeheads were in a rage about the crash cos their cars were locked together. I think they thought we caused it cos they were speeding to keep ahead of us... anyway I stopped and even offered to winch the cars apart with the winch on the front of the Police truck but they weren't having any of it and were in a rage so we took advantage of their cars being smashed together to carry on down to Whareponga to do our business... all the while aware that they would eventually meet us down there, even if they ran the rest of the way. I am trying to say that there was only two of us and we weren't scared of them otherwise we would've headed back to Ruatoria. We were certainly wary, but not scared... we just were doing the job we were paid to do.

There is only one way out of Whareponga. So we got down there and got the stolen trailer and saw a number of stolen surfboards from Gisborne and a hot Austin 1300 that they were using as a dog kennel. Eventually the Rastas turned up in a blind rage, and completely by coincidence, and bad luck, a drug recovery helicopter and it's Police team arrived on the hillside above the Rasta camp... we had absolutely no idea they were going to be there as we were just the local cops doing our thing and they were doing their thing.

The chopper incensed the Rastas as they presumed they were taking their dope, which they probably were, and it all sort of turned to shit down at the camp. The ground crews working with the chopper came down to the camp. Actually, we may have called them to help us, because we wanted to haul the car away too and only had our truck, and it was all on for young and old.

The chopper team had rifles and pistols so it was pretty hard to hand-fight knowing that these guns were in their cars. I certainly didn't have a pistol but remember seeing a rifle on the back seat of one of the chopper guys' cars so it was a bit of a worry to look after the guns... the Rastas never came close to getting the guns but after Quentin Hollis got stabbed in the head we decided to clear out with our recovered trailer, which I think I had hooked on the back of the Police truck. Poor old Russell chased the dogs out of the stolen car and someone hooked a snig chain onto one of the Police trucks and we cleared out of there, with Russell steering the crippled 1300 full of dog shit through the river.

So the fight at Whareponga was upgraded to a riot by someone higher than me (not by me or Russell, or Rana, someone in-between). Russell and I had decided to call it a draw in true Coast Policing fashion. So the Rastas knew they were in the shit and we'd be back in force unencumbered by trailers, 1300's and too many guns. So they sloped off with their tails between their legs to a marae in Ruatoria. So the camp was empty.

CHAPTER 8

THE RASTA CAMP IS BURNED DOWN

Email from former Sergeant Nigel Hendrikse: I can't remember whether it was that night or the next night but the fire siren sounded in Ruatoria and we followed the fire engine down to Whareponga to find the flames only about 12 inches high and nothing left. I managed to get radio contact with the Nightshift Sergeant in Gisborne, Alex Bryant, and he advised that he had no staff to send us, I mean for a scene guard of the fire scene overnight. I had to consider that Russell and I were a long way from Ruatoria, unarmed, and on a dead-end road, with the likelihood of doped up Rastas hearing about the fire and coming down, and we had no other cops between Tokomaru Bay and Te Kaha. So I decided to leave the scene unattended and head back to cover Ruatoria for the rest of the night.

That meant that the scene had its chain of evidence effectively broken. I don't regret doing that. Russell and I were the Johnnys-on-the-spot.

I got to bed pretty late and in the morning was preparing a report at the Ruatoria Station for Gisborne when I heard that Rana was already at

Whareponga in a TV helicopter and recorded the words on TV that night along the lines of "the Lord acts in mysterious ways" in relation to the baches being burnt. Then I got it in the neck from Loss, the owner of the Manutahi pub, over what Rana said because her bach was burnt too and she was one of the good guys!!!

Of course, Rana didn't know that when he spoke to the TV. Rana's words certainly made me chuckle... A taste of their own medicine, I would say.

One of the bach owners, Jim Morice, says two vehicles were seen leaving the beach after dark last night.

"From now on things could flare up," says Morice. "It's ridiculous and unnecessary. The retaliation ahead may get worse and it will probably end up being worse than it was before."

Morice, who built his bach a year ago, says he's had no trouble from the Rastafarians. They'd broken into his bach two or three times to get cover from bad weather, but had not caused any damage or taken anything.

Morice says the trustees of the block of Maori land had recently requested that the baches be removed.

Senior Sergeant Roger Crawford says the dwellings were unoccupied for several days before the fires started. And while the tiny coastal settlement was the scene of a scuffle between the police and a group of Rastafarians last week, Crawford says there's no reason to believe the two incidents are related.

(It can be a small world in Gisborne and the East Coast. About the time this is set, Roger Crawford lived next door to my family in Chalmers Road, Gisborne. He had been a well-liked neighbour of ours for years. Judith Harrison would later own Crawford's house. She was one of the women who picked up Joe Nepe and Jason Keelan and gave them a ride back to Ruatoria, not realising that Joe had just beheaded Lance Kupenga. She was also a good neighbour, so well thought of that if she had lots of visitors, Mum and Dad would let the extras park on our lawn.)

Senior Sergeant Alan Davidson (retired): I think Chris Campbell was still alive when all this happened. It was when the Rastas were camped out in baches down on the beach at Whareponga. They were on property there that some of the local people wanted them off.

So what happened was some armed police went down to the beach where the Rastas were camped and a confrontation took place. One of the cops, Quentin Hollis, was stabbed with a screwdriver. That's when Rana Waitai, who was in charge of the Gisborne police at the time, gave me the order to get them out. Rana would make a decision. Yeah, fuckin' oath he would. And he'd stand by you. And it had to be legal.

I remember Rana said to me, "Get rid of them."

I said, "Legally or illegally?"

"What's the difference?"

"The price."

"Legally."

At that stage Luke Donnelly had come on to the scene. Until that point he had been a non-event. And also living up there were two Tauranga friends, Russell Holmes, who's now a constable in Gisborne, and Nigel Hendrikse, who later made headlines when Mongrel Mob member John Gillies stabbed him in the back with a screwdriver and left him a paraplegic. Russell and Jimi (Hendrikse) were long-term relievers in Ruatoria but they'd been having troubles.

So what happened from my perspective was we realised we didn't have many options. To get down there was going to be dangerous because the bush telegraph would have told them we were on our way. So we had to come up with something else.

Now at that particular point Luke Donnelly was making threats that he was gonna do this, this and this.

I flew up in a fixed wing plane a couple of times and did sweeps across the area to see what the situation was. I went in a fixed wing because I was concerned that if we went in a chopper they'd shoot at us.

Now they'd been seen in town at Ruatoria one day. They'd come in to pick up the dole or something. Whatever. They'd been seen in town. So I did a sweep over in the plane and flew back. I rang Ruatoria and said, "That, place, is, *empty*. There'll be a few dogs there. That's all. If anything was going to happen to that place, it would be happening *tonight*. If that place was to burn down *tonight, nobody* would be burnt." You know what I mean? "If somebody was to sneak down there for instance nobody would see them because nobody would be there." That's the type of *ifs* I was talking about.

"Oh, really?"

"Yeah. That's right"

Now I don't know if Luke Donnelly was a suspect or not. All I did was have a conversation with someone up there, I can't remember who. I know that they were having lengthy conversations with Luke. But Luke will tell you himself that if he went and burnt them down then it must have been his idea.

And I vividly recall going back the next day and chartering the same plane from out of Gisborne, flying back and the pilot going, "Jingoes! It's all burnt!" because he was the same pilot.

And I said, "Fuck, well fancy that. Come on. Let's go back to Gisborne."

CAMPBELL'S WARNING

Tape recorded note to myself after a conversation with Cody Haua: Chris Campbell wanted all the Rastas to get off the beach at Whareponga because he'd heard from Barney, his brother, even though Barney was out of the police force by that stage, that they were going to be burnt. I think it was Hata Thompson wanted everyone to stay. But Chris told everyone to get out and they left.

Email from former Sergeant Nigel Hendrikse: In relation to the Rasta baches being burnt, it didn't take a rocket scientist to make a shortlist of suspects... Proof is another thing!!!

Now, about Alan saying that he phoned someone in Ruatoria, it certainly wasn't me he phoned, as far as I remember...

...Now, to the reliability of our memories of that time. Some years ago Russell (Holmes) and I were yarning about the time we fought Dickie Maxwell out of a window he'd dived through at 1am while doing a burg in the Kiwi Tearooms, Ruatoria. I said, "And hell it was hard trying to choke him out in the pitch black night with those dreadlocks in the way and you pulling him back through the broken window by his ankles."

Of course Russell didn't know that I was pulling him out the window, and I didn't know that Russell was trying to pull him back in. Diesel Dick certainly knew there was one of us on each end as it was his bloody legs being dragged backwards and forwards over the broken glass in the window.

Anyway, during our yarn-telling Russell turned to me and said, "What do you mean you had his head? I was outside pulling him out and you were inside trying to pull him back in!!!"

Now I know that I am right because I can still feel the thick ropey dreads against my face... but Russell knows he is right too....!!!!!!!!!!!!!!!!!! We never did sort that one out. What the passage of time does to memories!!

I remember chasing a shadowy figure into the dark one night and only finding a greatcoat and some stolen rifles and heaps of dope. That night we caught Dick at the Kiwi Tearooms, Diesel Dick admitted to me off the record that it was him who'd run into the bush and how pissed off he was with me for taking the guns and dope. I read years later that he got murdered up at East Cape.

I remember once just after Chris got out of jail for Laurie's kidnapping, getting a call to say that one of the Rasta associates that we wanted to arrest was coming into Ruatoria in the Grey Ghost (EH Holden s/w with no front guards, the same one that they were in when Chris got shot). So I headed that way in a brand new Police truck (or more correctly as Chris called them "Steedless Chariots") that hadn't yet got its roof lights and I waved out for the Grey Ghost full of ropeheads to stop. And it didn't. So I simply turned the truck in front of them and took them in the side of the truck. And we got our guy. I remember Chris getting out of the Grey Ghost quite shaken from that cos I guess they didn't expect it to happen.

A short time later Rana Waitai said to me, "I heard about you and the truck and the Rasta car," (meaning, I heard about it, as you knew I would, and I approve). No paperwork required. That's how it worked. It was not like normal policing as we previously knew it.

I quite enjoyed my meetings with Chris Campbell at the Ruatoria Police Stn. He liked the fact that I was called Jimi Hendrikse. But he always chose to formalise my Jimi to James.

Tuesday, November 27, 1990: Dick Maxwell is in court today. His lawyer Phil Dreifuss says Maxwell has cut all ties with the Rastafarians.

Maxwell pleads guilty to breaking and entering with intent to commit a crime, possession of burglary instruments and two charges of driving while disqualified.

Police prosecutor Sergeant Peter Haines says Maxwell had jemmied open a window at the Kiwi Tearooms and then removed $140 worth of foodstuffs.

Police found Maxwell inside following a tip-off. When he saw police approaching he took a "running dive" through a closed window. He had to be forcibly restrained and a torch, crowbar and knapsack were discovered.

Dreifuss says Maxwell is now living alone in Ruatoria and has no association with any groups up there. "He is trying to stay out of trouble and currently is not receiving any income. He broke into the tearooms simply to obtain food."

Raewyn Rickard, early Rasta Beau Tuhura's sister, who was also the partner of Rasta Tony Tuhou: We had issues about all the baches and Rastas' homes at Whareponga that got burnt down.

No one really wanted to listen to uncle Tom Fox who was trying to explain to everybody about the Queen's Chain. That's the length of land between the low tide and the high tide mark. Anyway, she owns it.

And at Whareponga with everybody's baches there they would have more than likely come in and built a public toilet there so people could go in, stay there and enjoy the park. But none of the family wanted that.

And the only way it could be achieved was to burn all the baches down. So Uncle Tom got another cousin to go and burn the lot. They burnt everybody out. And he never got in trouble like everybody else did when he went and arsoned all the family's homes. A lot of people lived there. And yet that same cousin who torched those baches was the one who shot Chris. Luke Donnelly torched those baches because that was the fastest way that the uncle who told him to do it could see that we'd get around that issue of whether it should be a public domain down there.

In February 2010, I put the accusations that he was behind the burning of the Whareponga baches to Luke Donnelly. He just smiled and said; "Those poor Rastas ay. I'd love to tell you all I know. But I'll just say that whoever did it must have really had it in for them back then."

MORNING RAID AT A MARAE

Senior Sergeant Alan Davidson (retired): Anyway, after they were burned out of the baches at Whareponga Beach, they went and stayed on the marae. And Rana Waitai told me to "get'm off the marae". So I had to do an operational plan for that.

I went up in a plane and videoed the whole scene and I got sick trying to film while we were flying. So I filmed the entrances and accesses of all the houses on either side of the marae. Then we flew in people from out of town to add to our squad. And we put the pictures I'd shot onto our TV and did a briefing, showing where the marae was and the road access.

Chris Thompson, former Rasta: We even invited one of the policemen into the marae, under the sanction of the marae, and he left with a big smile on his face and said, "Yes I will tell them that you'll talk with them."

He came on behalf of the police to negotiate. They were after those who were involved in the scrap, which was everybody. Women were in there, too. It was funny really, when you think about it.

When that policeman left the marae that night, I was the last one to go to sleep, but I felt like eyes were watching me for some unknown reason.

Alan Davidson: Then that night we drove up and, rather than drive straight into Ruatoria, we stayed down some back roads in Te Puia and places like that. The armed offenders squad went in covertly a lot earlier.

Later, a few car loads of us hid behind one of the schools in Ruatoria because somebody had come screaming down the road, stopped off, looked into the school, then screamed off somewhere else. Obviously someone had seen a convoy of cars coming into town and they started looking.

Chris Thompson: Well the next morning we were awakened to, "Pigs! Get up. Get up, the pigs are here!" So everybody got up. The guy that was screaming that to us was standing in the doorway. He said to the cops, "You can't come in here." But they just grabbed him and tore him out of the doorway. There were young kids screaming. They even dragged outside innocent people who weren't at the beach the day of the fight. And these innocent people were identified as being at the brawl. If they thought you were there they just dragged you out. They were even dragging out minors.

One of our women was yelling out, "What are you doing? He wasn't there that day."

And I said, "Fuck up. Let them do it. If they take an innocent victim they're legally fucked. They'll be in Shit Street."

But it was too late, because one of the cops overheard what I was saying.

Tuesday, November 27, 1990: Police arrest six men and a woman in an early morning raid at Mangahanea Marae following last week's confrontation between police and Rastas at Whareponga Beach.

Mangahanea Marae is a hive of activity after the arrests. A Paul Holmes TV crew arrives in the morning and talks to members of the Rastas.

Meanwhile, Ngati Porou runanga chairman Api Mahuika tells a National Radio reporter he's optimistic about finding a solution. He suggests that Crown land could be either leased or given to the Rastas and they could build their own homes on it and make it their turangawaewae or place of belonging.

All seven arrested Rastafarians are remanded after appearing in the Gisborne District Court. Some of the charges relate to the scuffle with police at Whareponga last Wednesday and others to the police raid this morning.

Senior Sergeant Alan Davidson (retired): Anyway we cleaned out the whole marae. One of the policemen who'd been involved in the confrontation down at the beach said, "There's one, there's one, there's another." And he pulled out the guys who'd been involved in the fight at the beach. We locked up about a dozen of them.

Chris Campbell was out of prison at that time. He was living with the Rastafarians. But he wasn't there that night. He was not on the marae. Chris had a girlfriend and he may have been with her. He was not there that day although I expected him to be.

Wednesday, November 28, 1990: *Hata Thompson's mum, known by most people on the Coast as Aunty Ga-ga, says she's taken the Rastas to Mangahanea Marae because they have nowhere else to go.*

But, although they've been welcomed by marae elder Nazi Awatere, the community is asking them to leave.

"The people around town don't want us here, but they can't move us because we have strong blood ties to the marae," she says.

The Rastas lost most of their clothes and all of their blankets in the arsons at the beach.

"At the moment we are playing a waiting game to see and hear the reactions from the community."

Aunty Ga-ga says the Rastafarians are using the marae as a sanctuary because it's "the last place of mana for Maori".

She says traditionally all differences would be settled on a marae and no one would be allowed to leave until matters were resolved. That's how Aunty Ga-ga and the Rastafarians hope to achieve some sort of answer.

She says one of the main reasons the Rastafarians chose a marae to stay in was because they feared for their safety.

"One of my sons who is a Rastafarian (Hata) was attacked in the Ruatoria main street by one of the so-called Neighbourhood Watch Group (Luke)."

She suggests that situation could have re-ignited if the Rastas had not decided to take refuge on the marae.

Hata Thompson says the marae is the only home open to them. "We forgive those for what they have done to us. We don't hold any grudges, but I just hope they don't touch our children," he says. "We can still be Rastafarians and hold on to our Maoritanga at the same time."

Thursday, November 29: *The man who owns the land at the centre of the current Ruatoria troubles is angry. Tom Fox says the media has given more sympathy to the Rastafarian group than to those whose rights are being affected.*

Tom Fox is chairman of the Paiitaua Incorporated Blocks at Whareponga Beach, near Ruatoria. He says he's disgusted by the blatant bias towards a group of Rastafarians on TVNZ's Holmes show last night.

He says the programme glossed over the fact that the group had been illegally camped on Fox's family land. Buildings had been put up on the land without building permits and there had been substantial stock losses.

When a request to leave was ignored he had asked the police to accompany him to serve the group with trespass notices.

The television programme had largely ignored these facts and Fox's rights as an owner, and placed more emphasis on the cries of the Rastafarians that they had nowhere else to go.

"That's utter rubbish," he says. "These people, like me, have their own homes and their own family lands – some of those boys have family lands just down the road from mine. Some have Housing Corporation houses of their own in Ruatoria. They have somewhere to go but they want to be together. The problems would be resolved if they went back to their own family homes – there should be no need for them to squat."

MARAE WATER "POISONED"

I interviewed Laura and Chris Thompson almost by accident. Laura, known as Aunty Ga-ga, is Hata and Chris's mum. I didn't take a note of when I interviewed them. But I know I interviewed Hata in July 2001 and it would have been just before that. I had been trying to get an interview with Hata for a while. Despite some pleasant conversations on the phone, we were struggling to hook up. He was quite elusive. On one occasion he told me to meet him at his mum's place, just south of Ruatoria. When I got there, his mother told me he'd gone out surfing with a mate. I had a chat with Laura and Chris and, in true Ruatoria fashion, they asked me if I wanted a cup of tea. I did, and eventually asked them if I could get their perspective on things and tape record the conversation. Laura explained why she took the Rastas to Mangahanea Marae after they were burnt out of Whareponga.

Laura: I had recently lost my husband and I had a daughter and three sons in the Rastafarians.

So I had to do something for my children as well as the children of the community because in Maoridom we believe that every other child that's related is your child. So what could I do when they were under and we were all under stress. The only thing for me was to turn around and gather us up and take us back to the marae. Then the cops came and tried to move us off Mangahanea.

Chris: This is how low things got, how low the tactics were. Before my actual true blue involvement in the movement I was up in Auckland and I returned with a couple of friends. And one of my friends, Jason, actually reacted to the water at the marae. When he was taken in it was said there was a certain element in the water that was toxic. How it got in the water we don't know.

Q: Someone had been sticking stuff in the water?
Laura: Yeah.
Cyanide or something?
Laura: Well we don't know what it was.

Chris: We don't know what it was but it caused irritation of the skin. My mate blew up. He actually reacted quite badly.

Swelled up and everything?
Chris: Yes. And that was just from an external exposure to the water. It just happened to react on him, thank God, before it did on everybody else because he decided to take a shower in the middle of the day, being a city boy.

So what happened once he blew up? What did everyone do? Everybody just got out?
Chris: No, they didn't move.

Laura: We said, "Don't touch the water. Don't cook with anything like that. Don't wash. Go to the river to wash." We had to think of our safety.

So who do you think would have been doing that?
Chris: I don't know. Cody was a part of the group then. So was Hata. See, there was a tight few at that time, very tight. Hata and Chris were very tight. And it goes back to that academic mind and that naïve mind. Chris was trying to influence those who were younger who he considered lacked empowerment and the same capacity of intellect.

But he was a remarkable intellect full stop though wasn't he?
Chris: Well he had a diploma in law. I don't know where he got it. All I know is that he'd acquired a diploma before death.

Laura: And there was another thing worrying me when Jason reacted to the water. He had to be taken into hospital and we didn't have a car. Luckily there was another woman friend of ours who had one. But he could've died on our hands.

How bad was it?
Laura: Quite bad.
Chris: The brink of death.

It could have been lethal?
Laura: Yes.
Did anyone ever find out what it was? Did the hospital know?
Chris: We never asked for a toxicology report.

Laura: We didn't follow it up because we knew it had to be in the water. And we knew we had to look at our safety.

Chris: We knew that the attack must have happened the night before. Mum was very well hated, hated like in a nasty manner, like threats on people's lives. At that particular time this is how bad and how hateful the situation was. She was called a black bitch plenty of times.

Laura: Ha ha ha.

Chris: Aw no, black queen. They called her black queen.

That's not too bad, black queen, though.
Laura: Ha ha ha.
You could take that as a compliment.
Ha ha. Oh yeah.

Chris: We got a nasty letter, telling us all to wake up.

Laura: Or we'll get you.

Chris: At the end of the day it shows who's gutless and who isn't. And where are those people today? Tomorrow's arrived and now their kids are doing exactly the same as what they didn't like us doing back then. The thing they hated about us has evolved in their household.

Their kids have ended up in the Rastas or the gangs?

Chris: It's happened to some of the most militant vigilantes, people who would order you out of a public hui and blatantly shout at you and put you down and abuse you. You had two forms of vigilante. You had the young guys full of testosterone, nothing more, nothing less, no brains, the guys with bad attitudes who thought that bashing the hell out of the Rastas would beat some sense into them. Then you had the second team of vigilantes who were older and wiser, the guys of Bob Kaa's school who, even though they were against what the Rastas were doing, were also against the strong-arm tactics of some of the more extreme vigilantes.

But tomorrow has come upon some of these fullas and their own children have paid them back for their dues. What they judged the next man for yesterday, has arrived today for them.

Laura: I think it goes right back to the public meeting we had at the Hikurangi clubrooms when I said to the whole community that they had no right to oppress the children how they were. And I said, "Tomorrow you will bury your head in the sand and won't be able to look at me for what you are doing to me." And most of the people who were in that room have come back and apologised.

But the ones who had written their threatening letters cry about it when they're drunk. They say, "Did you receive that letter? I was part of that."

But I just look at them and I think, "You're only saying this because it's happening in your household now." It may not be Rastafarianism. But there are drugs out there on the scene. And they're getting involved in them.

Chris: And what they've realised is that the drugs have actually changed, ay.

The drugs are stronger or the scene's more dangerous or what?

Chris: It's no longer now just dak, as it was back then. It's gone to coke, P, tripping, pills.

Tuesday, July 2, 1991: The trial of five Rastas charged with rioting at Whareponga Beach last November finally gets to court. Robert Haua, Anthony Kaihe, Jonathan McClutchie, Nehe Reuben and Tony Tuhou – all plead not guilty.

This is Crown prosecutor Denys Barry's version of events. The police arrive at the camp with a search warrant looking for a stolen trailer. Constable Nigel Hendrikse asks Detective Sergeant Mark Templeman to stand by with other police. When Hendrikse enters the camp the people present are passive and co-operative. The trailer, a suspected stolen car, a number of surfboards and a large quantity of cannabis are found.

Detective Sergeant Templeman, waiting outside the camp, arrives with his officers and arrests Robert Haua, charging him with cultivation of cannabis and receiving the surfboards. Police take possession of the stolen property and seven hundred and fifty cannabis seedlings. They're about to leave when a station wagon, driven by Kaihe and containing twelve Rastas, arrives at high speed.

They jump out of the vehicle – Nehe Reuben shouting, "Jah Rastafari" - and charge at the police party, yelling and screaming. The men try to get the surfboards from the trailer. Some of them are yelling, "off with their heads" and "get their scalps". Police are assaulted and rocks are thrown at their vehicles.

Templeman says he saw Constable Quentin Hollis held from behind by Haua and one other while Tuhou punched him in the face.

Templeman tried to put Haua in a headlock and grab the other man but they fell over and an unidentified person then assaulted the officer.

McClutchie was seen throwing rocks at police vehicles. And McClutchie, Reuben and others made attempts to get the cannabis from the recovered car.

Templeman says, "I heard McClutchie shouting, 'This is our land. You can't take our herb... get their heads.'"

McClutchie, Kaihe and Reuben tried to remove the surfboards from the trailer.

Eventually, the police were forced to retreat under a shower of rocks and had to leave behind surfboards, and cannabis growing on the hill.

Wednesday, July 4: *In his closing address, Barry describes the Rastas as being in a frenzy, saying that Jonathan McClutchie and Nehe Reuben were literally spitting. The violence happened and the defence doesn't dispute that. Police went to the camp with a search warrant for the trailer and had every right to take it. They showed restraint during the incident.*

"Restraint my foot," says Denis Kohn, counsel for Robert Haua, in his closing address. "Police decided they were going to look for the trailer so they mounted this massive operation with armed officers and a dog."

Police knew that something was going to happen, that it was likely to blow up. "They walked into it with their eyes open. They blew it."

Kohn says the police acted grossly in excess of their authority with regard to the surfboards and a child's bike that was also placed on the trailer.

"You can spit and rant and rave, but it's not violence," he says.

Each lawyer comes up with a new argument or a new point.

Ray Hovell, for Kaihe: The only evidence against his client is that he removed a board from the trailer.

Phil Dreifuss, for McClutchie: The definition of a riot is six or more persons, acting together, using violence against persons or property that causes alarm to people in the neighbourhood. "There is no evidence of six or more persons using violence" And on his client:

"McClutchie did not strike anyone. The worst things he is accused of doing are spitting and throwing stones."

Vicki Thorpe, for Reuben: "He did not strike anyone, despite having ample opportunity to do so. I suggest to you that these men are here because the police knew their names."

Doug Rishworth, for Tuhou: "No one is above the law, not even the police." The search warrant gave police the authority to search anywhere in New Zealand rather than mentioning a specific place. "It was the most unusual document."

The jury finds the five Rastas not guilty.

"TERRORISTS ROAMING THE COUNTRYSIDE"

Email from former Sergeant Nigel Hendrikse: What says a lot to me is the review comments (for Volume One) like the one from Cath Hallinan in that she'd never heard of the Rastas before. So many people I've talked to over the years knew nothing of it, and normally when I would start to ramble about it their eyes glazed over within 25 seconds and they started talking about rugby. I hate talking about rugby...

Whether it is a denial mechanism or plain ignorance I am not sure but I also got glazed looks from people in the mid to late 90's when I would talk about this dude O B Laden (having been to Afghanistan myself in 1992... long story). I was taking an interest in what was going on pre and post Taliban. They thought I was fucking nuts... I had/am having the last laugh I guess.

Often during those times of the Rasta stuff I would think, "Fuck, we've got terrorists roaming the countryside and is it possible that nothing is being done about it at very high levels?" I would like to think there was lots of other stuff being done covertly that, of course, I wouldn't have been told about at my peon level. But if there was, it didn't work.

Hughie Hughes, Ruatoria electrician: I'm a nomad really. I was born in New Zealand but my parents were English and Dad worked on the railways so we transferred a lot.

And Ruatoria's okay. The people are good. You feel safer here than you would in most other places. *But* you wouldn't wanna leave anything lying around.

During the time of the fires, burglaries were also rampant. Burglars almost emptied the shop of everything of value one night. They busted in through the back door. One of my staff had come in late and left the alarm off. And the thieves smashed in the back door.

No one lived in this area except Eddie Harrison who ran the pub at the other end of the street. So anybody could do whatever they liked down this end without ever getting caught.

In the five years to July the 14th, 1990, my shop got burgled twenty-seven times. The 14th of July is the day we started sleeping there. The same week we put up roller doors. Now me and two other guys take it in turns to sleep at the shop. And since then we've built a flat in the back.

But it was a very stressful time. All the burglaries were sending me broke and at the same time I was going through a marriage bust-up.

While it was all happening you had this churning in your chest. The feeling was one of absolute despair. Like every time I was burgled I had to pay the insurance company fifteen hundred dollars. That was the excess on every claim. Well, the burglars might smash a window worth four hundred dollars and just steal something worth twenty. There's no point in putting in a claim. So you've just got to wear the loss.

I stood here one night, heard the smash of windows just down the street from another shop, rushed to the door, saw the guy running out with an armful of cigarettes and stuff and I rang 111 and asked the police, "Can I shoot him?" I used to sleep with a gun in those days.

They said, "That wouldn't be a good idea."

But I yelled and it frightened him off.

From 1990, when we moved into the shop, things got better. But a year ago we were building this flat at the back and we hadn't jacked up the security for it and that particular night there were no vehicles there and we were living on this side of the shop. Well they took the window out and quietly robbed the place. The one of us that was staying here slept through it.

We moved into the other side of the shop the next day and haven't had any trouble since.

CHAPTER 9

MT HIKURANGI,
THE RASTAS' MT ZION (2)

Sue Nikora (early influence on the Rastafarians): A long, long time ago the stories were told to us. But we didn't have anything to verify them until we started doing our research and we saw these things and they became a reality. But they told us that at certain times in certain years they used to sit and wait at Te Aowera (at the bottom of Mt Hikurangi). They'd have a special spiritual hui at the marae. And they had these two discs which were special receptors on the bottom ends of the two barge boards or facing boards that came down the line of the roof. They were the receptors though they didn't tell us at the time that they were the receptors. And at certain times they'd sit and they'd pray. They'd pray to the gods. They'd pray to Tangaroa (the father of the fish and creatures of the sea). They'd pray and pray and pray until such time that the light would come out of Mount Hikurangi in the shape of a fish. And when it came out the lines would come from there, straight out towards Whareponga, towards the sea. Now no lines are straight, ay. Lines of light bend. That meant the lines crossed paths. And where the lay lines cross, if you happen to be under that crossing, you can have a full force of energy, which they call blessing. You have the full force of the blessing. And it would happen during that time they prayed, for good harvest or good whatever. And funnily enough when they did this the oranges and the lemons would grow beautifully and they'd have huge pumpkins and watermelons. Scientifically and technically they didn't know why it happened. But it did and they kept working with it.

And the Maori of that time was known as Tunui a te Ika. The Maori is the life essence. Tunui a te Ika was the life essence of Mount Hikurangi. It responded to the prayer as a light in the shape of a fish rising up out of the mountain.

Colin Williams (former owner of Pakihiroa Station, which included part of Mt Hikurangi): A great friend of mine, who was probably one of the world's top geologists, a guy called Colin

McLernon, who I think was born and bred here in Gisborne - he's dead now - anyhow he worked overseas with oil companies in North America, and he just loved coming back to climb these mountains. And he set a record I don't think was ever equaled. He started at the shearers' quarters at Pakihiroa, he climbed to the top of Hikurangi, he came down along the ridge up to the next mountain which is Wharekia, down and up the next mountain, which is Taitai and ended up at Matahiia homestead where Jeremy lives, in a day.

Sue Nikora: We have in our possession an aerial drawing of the North Island, drawn by one of the old people. It's pre-European. It was drawn in carbon by charcoal or something like that on a piece of parchment. It may have been dog skin or something like that. But the thing about it is he drew it to specification. The thing is: how could he have drawn it? The only way he could have drawn it like that was if he was looking down from up in the sky. And there weren't any aeroplanes in those days.

Colin Williams: The interesting thing about those five mountains up there is that they stick up and the geology of them is all upside down.

There's a big fold in the rock that's come from somewhere else and these have all been dumped upside down and just worn away over thousands and thousands of years.

The geology of all of them, according to Colin McClernon, and I'm sure he's right, is all upside down. They've come from somewhere else. They don't belong to the geology of the East Coast at all.

There's a Maori legend that touches on that sort of thing.

A Maori princess was in love with a prince who lived round the mouth of the river. Anyway she used to trot down there at night to see him. But if she got caught by the sun before she got back to Hikurangi, she'd be turned to stone. And she is standing in the middle of the river. She got caught by the sun.

I've ridden past that stone plenty of times and I'm pretty sure there are shells in that rock. So where the hell that came from, goodness knows. I hope it's still there. The river bed's risen so much.

Sue Nikora: I had a personal experience which helped me develop a theory on how that person was able to make an aerial drawing of the North Island all those years ago.

Our father died on the 4th of July, 1973. My father's name was
Joseph Teaorare Keelan. They rang us up at about six o'clock in the
evening and said, "Sorry, Dad's passed away." He was a very religious,
very spiritual man and a tohunga (Maori priest) in his own right. He
died and of course we were terribly distressed about it. But we got ready
to go back and put our stuff into the car and all that. And then we had to
take our son to my husband Noel's brother's place for the time we'd be
away, about four or five days.

So Noel and I and our daughter went back home to Ruatoria. We
had a fairly new model Cortina and it was running in excellent
condition. It was a bit rainy when we left from Gisborne at nine o'clock.
And we expected to be at Te Puia Springs at about half past ten to 11pm
at the latest.

We got to a place they call Busby Hill on the top of Tokomaru Bay.
Normally, in the daytime, you look down from the top of this hill on the
way in to Tokomaru Bay and you see the sea. Anyway, Noel was
driving this night and when we got to this point I said, "Stop!"

I could see these waves coming to us up the hill towards our car.
And you know that sensation you get when your car is being washed at
a car wash? It was the same sensation. I was quite aware of the
situation. The waves were like white foam. And I was thinking to
myself, "How can the waves from down the bottom get up here?" And
when the wave came over the car it started to shake it and that's when it
felt like being in a car wash. And I said, "Stop!" So I started praying. I
thought, "Hell, let's pray." Noel knew something strange was
happening and felt the car shuddering. But I was the only one who saw
the white foam. Our daughter, who was twelve at the time, was asleep
in the back seat. After a few moments I said to Noel, "Right, start the
car but go very, very slowly."

We drove at a snail's pace but it didn't seem to take long at all for
the wave to pass over the bonnet, over the roof and off over the boot of
the car. But by the time it had passed it was daylight, the car lights were
off and we were almost at Te Puia Springs.

So anyhow we went down slowly to Te Puia Springs. We got to the
hospital and it was seven o'clock in the morning! We know because the
nurses were changing their shift. So somewhere along the line we lost
about nine hours. And we have no recollection of what happened in
those lost hours.

Anyway we got to the hospital and my niece Wiki Tibble was there and she said, "Oh Aunty, what is wrong with you? You look so pale. I'll go and get you a cup of tea."

So she made me a cup of tea and I said, "Oh dear, I think our car broke down." That's exactly what I said to her. "I think our car broke down. But we need to go back to Tokomaru Bay to get our keys for the house at Hiruharama."

And she said, "Aw, here you are uncle, here's my car keys. You go and get your keys from Tokomaru Bay." But she never *asked* how come we came past Tokomaru Bay, because as far as we know we didn't even go through Tokomaru Bay. We weren't aware of that at all.

So anyhow, Noel went back, got our key for the house at Hiruharama, brought it back. And I said, "Okay, let's go," because we needed to get our father's clothes so we could dress him at the morgue and take him back to the marae.

So we went out to the car and I turned the key and it started straight away. There was nothing the matter with it. So we drove on, got the clothes, went to the morgue, put the clothes on him, waited for him to be all dressed and nice and we took his body to the marae. At that time our uncles and aunts were still alive. And everything simmered down after the call onto the marae. And I was sitting down beside the coffin and I said, "Uncles, aunties, guess what happened? We left home at nine o'clock. And we didn't make it to Te Puia Springs until seven o'clock in the morning. Do you know, no one heard me saying that. No one heard. Nobody made a comment. I thought to myself, "It's insignificant."

So anyhow we had his tangi, buried him. Then our cousin died. We stayed on, buried him, then we came back to the shop here in Gisborne, the Mill Road Dairy, and got some bread and milk from Mrs Forsyth, the old dear who owned it. And as I came to the counter I saw the Woman's Weekly. And I love the Woman's Weekly. I still love the Woman's Weekly. So I picked it up as I came past with the newspaper and bought that, too.

Then we came home and I said to Noel, "Ah, put some tea on. Let's have a cup of tea."

And then I sat down on the settee to read my magazine. And *you know* I just opened it up and there was this woman, her husband and two children and their car. They were standing in a paddock. This happened in England or Scotland or somewhere like that. And I thought, "Huh! What the hell are they standing in a field for with their car?"

So I read the story and blow me down, it said these people found themselves standing in this field and they believed that they had been taken up by a UFO and dropped in the middle of the paddock. And they had lost five hours.

I got up and I said to Noel, "Look at this. I'm sure this is what happened to us."

But we never told anyone what happened. What we should have done is have the car examined. We were so worried; we didn't want to say anything in case people thought we were stupid or crazy.

But when I put two and two together and after researching what we know now, I'm quite convinced that we were taken up by a UFO. And I believe its batteries or power source were charged at that mountain, Mt Hikurangi.

I reckon it was quite a normal thing in those old days for the pick-up to be done and for things to happen. I don't think it could have happened any other way for that aerial drawing to be done of the North Island.

And I'm quite convinced this whole thing is to do with the lake on Mt Hikurangi. I reckon that's where this UFO is coming from rather than from the tip of it, that alpine region. It's coming from the lake. And the water comes out all the time from there into the two rivers. And it's tied up with the moamoa stones. That's why the moamoa stones on the mountain have such healing power and it's why the Maori, Tunui a te Ika used to come out of the mountain and formed the lay lines when the people prayed.

See Mount Hikurangi is the point where Maui fished up the North Island. Legend has it that Maui's canoe is supposed to be fossilised up in that lake on Hikurangi. But the canoe is supposed to be a spiritual canoe. I call it a spiritual canoe because it's symbolic. It's symbolic of how the land was formed. It's not real. Maui *is* an ancestor from whom we descend but the canoe is a symbol.

I haven't got any proof, but I'm convinced the fossilised canoe in the lake is really Tunui a te Ika, the Maori or life essence of Mt Hikurangi, and that it goes out at certain times each century. It must take about twenty-five to fifty years for it to charge its batteries before it's able to come up out of the lake.

I'm quite convinced that the waka is really a UFO. And it's in the lake. The Maori is in the lake. It's probably some sort of craft because Tunui a te Ika is a manifestation of a shape. It's not just a light that comes out. It has to be something physical.

My theory is that our car would have been taken up into the hold of a craft and we would have been taken up for nine hours.

I don't know of anything in the local history which suggests there is a UFO up there other than that there is a powerful energy that comes out of the mountain. But this has been a personal experience. I relate this because it actually happened to me and Noel.

You might think that Sue Nikora and her husband Noel are the only people in New Zealand who believe there could be a link between the early Maori and UFOs. But there is at least one other, whom I stumbled upon while on holiday in Northland in late 2002. While waiting for my dinner one night at a fish and chip shop in Warkworth, I started reading an old copy of the Truth newspaper which was among the stack of reading material. The headline – Maori flew to New Zealand writer claims - caught my eye because of my previous conversation with Sue. So I sneakily tore out the story and stuck the clipping in my pocket.

Kris Wills, The Truth: Forget the waka – some Maori FLEW to New Zealand during the great migration a new book claims.

The Hawks are Talking is the first in a series of books by Hokianga writer Joan Leaf.

In it Leaf claims that Nothland was populated by Maori who came "through the air as a bird flies" and not by waka as other Maori did.

A rural area called Mitimiti, just north of Hokianga, became home to the "bird people" about 1000 years ago, according to Leaf.

However incredible they may sound, Leaf insists the claims are based on symbols and incantations memorised and passed down through the generations.

And her book has sparked renewed interest from UFO researchers who believe some early Maori may have had contact with aliens.

"It is extremely interesting information for researchers," says UFO expert Bob Valkenburg.

"This type of claim is not alien to me at all.

"I have heard things like this before from Maori people."

"Not alien to me at all." That's very good. Nevertheless, Te Aowera Marae secretary Sarah Sykes said there was an Indian healer who came up the Coast once. Someone asked him about Mount Hikurangi, if he got anything off Mount Hikurangi. Apparently he said the UFOs would be interested in the energy at Mount Hikurangi. That's all Sarah said about it. (I'm not even sure if she meant an Indian from India or a Native American). But it ties in with what Sue Nikora believes. Anyway, I'm not saying it's possible or impossible. I'm just noting the connections in what people have said.

AERIAL DRAWING

Question to Sue Nikora: *Back to that ancient aerial drawing of the North Island. I've had this experience and my mother has too of being lifted out of your body. It can happen to you naturally in times of intense stress. You're up high and you're looking down on yourself. I've read that the Scottish Highlanders used to do it through meditation. They called it riding the wind. And they reckon you can basically go anywhere you like. Is there any Maori tradition or stories about riding the wind or astral traveling or anything like that?*

Sue: There was this old lady who stayed about a kilometre away from our home. Now a person had to cross the river, come down Whareponga Road and cross the bridge to get to our place in Hiruharama. It would normally take about half an hour. Well the old lady rang and said to my mother, "I've got a very, very sick boy with a cough. Have you got any cough mixture?"

My mum said, "Yes, I've got some cough mixture here."

I was standing there, as a kid. I would have been about seven or eight. But I can always remember the woman said, "Right I'll send Moana to pick it up."

And Mum said, "All right then," and she put the phone down – knock on the door, immediately. I personally opened the door and Moana was there. She must have been about thirteen. I couldn't believe it when I saw her.

And my mother said to me, "Oh, don't stand there. Go and get the cough mixture."

I was flabbergasted. Mum had just finished talking and then there was the knock on the door. But Mum seemed to have understood how Moana could be there in two jiffs.

So I went to get the cough mixture, still wondering, "Hell, how did this happen?"

I gave Moana the cough mixture. She thanked me. And I closed the door and I said to Mum in Maori, "How was she so quick?"

And she said to me, "Because her friends brought her." She was talking about her friends in the spirit world. Nowadays people would call it astral traveling. Lots of Maori people could do that.

Ruatoria is a town where, according to many of the local Maori, the natural and the supernatural coexist. Someone there once told me that Ruatoria has more churches for more different religions per head of population than any other place in New Zealand. I don't know if it's true but it wouldn't surprise me if it was. One morning early in the year 2000, my teenage nephew Daniel and I stopped outside Sarah Sykes' house to ask a young man for some directions. He was Steve Haereroa, a relation of Sarah's. We got to talking and within minutes he was telling us the following story.

Steve Haereroa: Seven o'clock at night. Looking across to that marae, Te Aowera Marae. I saw someone holding a candle light at the front of the marae, ay. It was like a man figure, this blue flame just walking around this marae. Then it started walking around the marae and I thought they were doing a prayer, ay.

There was an old house next to the marae too: big, brown old one, real old. And this blue flame went through the house and out through the front door. I thought, "Aw yeah, Rastas, doing some prayers."

Then it came over the fence. It was standing in front of the marae and it went up twenty foot in the air. Then within thirty seconds the light turned into a big blue ball of flame and was just hovering there. I went, "Shit!" There were four people inside Sarah's house. I thought, "I'll grab one." I brought one person out. Joshua was his name. And I asked him if he could see it. And he said he couldn't see it. And I could see it, ay. It was there. I said, "You can't see it, bro?"

He said, "Na."

And then he said he could see it.

So we added a couple of more on, two more people. They pushed out the window from that sitting room there. And then they had a look at it and it was just a big blue ball of flame now, ay. It was no bigger than a man. But it was bright yellow in the middle with blue steam coming round the outside of it. It was beautiful, ay, beautiful.

It was there, but then it started going around the marae. And then it started going around the marae again, and then it went around the marae in one second. And then it could go through the whole place, through that old house and everything in one second. I was, "Shiiiiit." Then it hovered right up in front of the marae and then shot right up and just blew up, no sound though, but just a big explosion.

And that's true, ay, a true story.

Sarah wasn't home. Then she just turned up and we told her. She had four of us telling her and she just looked at us sideways. But an old kuia heard the story and they'd seen it when they were small. And when they told other people, they'd been looked at sideways, too.

One of the people who saw it was Sarah's daughter. She don't like that sort of thing, ay. She don't believe in ghosts or Lord or Bible. But after I saw that, make me a little bit more faith in believing in the old Lord.

If I'd seen that on my own that night I wouldna told anyone. But I had three others with me who saw it. We were between the ages of sixteen and twenty-five at the time. It wasn't a UFO. You know how you see a lightning, ay? It was like lightning but... It was like a falling star but it wouldn't fall.

PART 9
STUCK ON A COLLISION COURSE

CHAPTER 1

THE INTIMIDATION OF AN OLD MAN

From the second interview with Luke: I don't go looking for trouble. I've never gone looking for trouble. But if trouble comes looking for me I won't back off. And if it goes looking for my family and friends I'll always be there to help them out. But it's always gotten me in trouble because people have taken advantage of me, I think, and of the fact that I was able to help them out if things got rough. The thing is, I never used to look at it this way.

Binnie was Prince Ferris's second wife. She was Tom Fox's sister. Anyway, she rings me up and she says, "Luke, can you help us?"

I say, "Why? What's wrong?"

She says, "Aw, these boys they've threatened to cut Moss's head off. They're threatening they're gonna kill'm."

I say, "What's going on? What's the matter?"

Well, apparently, Hamana Brown went to steal Moss Ferris's horse. And the horse has, you know, saddle on, bridle on, and Hamana just walked into the paddock, just below the house, and just takes the horse and leads it away. And Moss had been drinking and was pretty drunk. And suddenly he spotted Hamana. Well he grabbed his 22 and he steps out on to the porch and he says, "Leave that bloody horse alone."

Hamana apparently said to him, "Na, fuck you, you old cunt! I'm taking this horse."

So Moss put a shot, bang, straight over the top of his head. The horse, jolted by the sound of the shot, ran away and Hamana took off down the road and dived into the drain and was yelling out from in the drain, "You wait! We'll fuckin' get you and cut your fuckin' head off you old bastard."

Well, the house is reasonably close to Binnie. And Binnie's in the kitchen at the sink and she can hear exactly what's happening. Hamana's oblivious to Binnie being right there. And she can hear all the profanities and all this.

She's getting all terrified. She's behind the curtain. And she decides to ring me and I say, "Well ring the police."

She says, "I have. But they said they can't do nothing. They say there's nothing they can do until the Rastas do something."

So I said, "What can I do?"

I thought she was going to get me to go and see Hamana and just give him a bit of a clip on the ear. But she says, "Oh, I was wondering if you could just come over." I think she thought my presence might be good and make her feel a bit safer.

I said, "Look, I can't come over until later on."

She says, "But they're coming back tonight. That's what they said. They're coming back tonight and they're gonna chop Moss's head off."

"Okay," I said, "I'll organise my family and I'll come over tonight." I said to my wife, "They're a bit older. They're a little bit uptight. They're a bit afraid. I'll just go over there and just sit with them." I had a Dobermann dog and my cousin was staying with me, so I knew my wife would be safe at home.

I went to see Binnie first and she said, "Aw, he's up there. Just go up."

So I went up to Moss's place and knocked on the door and he wouldn't answer. Actually, he was frightened. Everything was locked up. The lights were off. I said, "Moss?"

And then I heard, very softly, "Yeah?"

"It's Luke."

He says, "Aw, okay then," and he opens the door. I went inside, turned the light on. He says, "No, no, no, those fullas, they'll know that I'm home." And he'd been drinking, ay, all that day, all that night. He was just barely able to speak and keep his eyes open.

I said, "Look, go to sleep. Go to bed."

"No, no, no, if those bastards come here I'll fuckin' fix them." But he was frightened. He was terrified.

I said, "Look, just go in there and sleep. If anyone comes I'll wake you up."

"Aw, okay," you know, slurred speech. So he goes into the bedroom and after a few minutes, bang, you could hear him snoring his head off.

So I'm sitting in the lounge and I'm thinking of things to prepare myself in case they do come through the door. I decide, "I'll keep the ranch slider right open. I'll open it right up so if I get thrown through the window I won't get cut or anything." So I did little things like that. I put the gun right in the corner of the wall so I knew where to fall if push came to shove. I had a baseball bat and that's what I was going to use. But if anyone was showing a gun I was going to just grab mine.

So I'm sitting there. And I could see in a straight line about two k's to Ngarimu Hill and then this car, about three o'clock in the morning, starts coming down the hill slowly. And I thought, "Aw, gees, this one's late."

And then, next thing, it comes up the road. It's coming up slowly and it gets to Moss's gate and it stops. I'm thinking, "Aw, fuck, here's a go."

I could see they were smoking dope. I could see the glow the moment they lighted up. And it was just glowing. I mean, I don't know for sure if they're smoking dope or cigarettes. But they smoke two or three of these things. And it glows over here, then it glows over there, like they're passing it around. So I assume they're smoking dope. Then the car door opens. In the country you can hear everything, especially at that time of the morning. Also, I knew it was their car: a light blue '72 Falcon XC, I think it was.

You can hear the murmur of their conversation for a while then, next thing, someone calls out slowly, "Hey, Moss." Then quiet... Then, "Hey, Moss." They're trying to intimidate the old fulla. They don't know that I'm there. They're yelling out, "Hey, Moss, your head is gonna come off, Moss," and all this sort of talk.

So here I am with this carload of guys outside and I'm starting to hear things. I'm freaking out. I honestly thought I saw a guy run past the window. Well, immediately, I picked up the bat and walked back to the kitchen and I'm looking out the window because it's totally dark and I'm aware that I can see out but they can't see in. And then I hear this, "Mo-o-oss," and this goes on for about five or ten minutes. And then they started laughing like it was a big joke. The car starts and they just drove off. And that was the end of it. It was just intimidation for the hell of it, a bit of fun, a big fuckin' joke.

But my point is these people took it seriously, the old people. They were just so petrified, so frightened. My mother, before I went home, she said to me, "Look, I want you to come home. There's trouble here."

She knew I'd look after her if I was there because I doted on my mother. If anyone ever dared to hurt her, that was it, it fuckin' would've been a bloodbath.

So I just looked at the effects they were having on the old people, the fear the old people were suffering. And that's the thing that was coming across. It was nothing for them to feed off the fear they were generating. So to me it was terrorist activity in that sense, mind games. They weren't going around putting bombs everywhere but the thing is if you go and burn down a few homes and buildings, thirty-two I think it was in total, that's a form of terrorism.

PHILOSOPHY "NEVER MADE SENSE"

Jeremy Williams, Pakeha farmer: Their philosophy never made sense to me. It never made sense at all. Why would you want to ride your horses six abreast down the main street and hold all the traffic up? You're only going to aggravate the situation. Why do you want to hassle Moss Ferris, an older Maori guy in the Whareponga Valley, steal his horses and all that sort of stuff? Why do that? What are you achieving? Moss was harmless.

I couldn't understand why they burnt that marae down, or the churches. And I couldn't believe that they'd go and burn down Bob Kaa's garage while he was at his mother's tangi. That to me is a bloody no-no. But it seems that any rules or normal form of behaviour went out the window.

It's almost like a bad dream. It wasn't very pleasant at the time. But it's amazing how time heals things.

Excerpt from an interview with former Senior Sergeant Alan Davidson: *So were business people and the police involved in bringing Luke Donnelly to Ruatoria?*

Alan: They were. I have no two ways about it. But Luke thrives on that. He began to believe his own publicity. And that's fatal. Yet he thrived on it.

He was sitting up there on that farm at Makarika. I don't know. *He* said it was his.

He would have been encouraged by the police going and talking to him, by all means. Aw, for sure.

Of course Luke was being encouraged by local business people. How else was he surviving? He was always going around borrowing money. Whether or not they were calling in debts, I don't know.

I approached Luke Donnelly with the various conspiracy theories about how he acquired his money at that time. He asked if I'd heard the one about him being a drug dealer who was trying to take over the Rastas' business. I said that seemed far-fetched even by the Coast's standards. He said people wondered how he was surviving and why he kept disappearing for days on end. But he was actually just starting to study law and that often kept him away from Ruatoria during the week.

Luke explained that he'd got $127,000 from the sale of his house in Hamilton. Then he bought the ten acre block with his mother Sophie's house on it back from the local council for $40,000 after putting down a $4000 deposit. He said it was a low price but he argued with the council that it should be doing all it could to give the original Maori owners the best chance of retrieving their land and accused them of being racist. He suspected the council decided to accept his low offer instead of buying into a fight about racism.

Luke also took over one two-hundred acre block in Makarika, just south of Ruatoria, and another one-hundred-and-ten acre block across the road that had the Rasta pad on it (he torched the pad).

He bought five-hundred breeding ewes and nine black-faced rams and he organised a $100,000 mortgage with his bank so that he could buy cattle. He had dreams of becoming a big-time cattle rancher. The cheque from the bank was due to arrive on Thursday, December 6, 1990. But two days before that he shot Chris Campbell and all previous plans had to be changed.

Lyn Hillock, former Gisborne Deputy Fire Chief: The Rastas hang around outside people's fences, outside their gate. Kids are scared to go to school. The wives up there are just a regular bloody mess.

It gets to the stage like people in Gisborne with the Mongrel Mob. They cross the road so they don't have to walk too close to them. It needs someone to walk right through the middle of the bastards. If you've got a carload of Mungies parked outside your house looking over your fence, it doesn't take long for people to start wondering, "What the hell do these arseholes want?" That's what it's like with the Rastas and that's all they need to do and they do it. Their presence outside someone's house was an effective form of intimidation.

We fuck up one night. What they do is they ride up over the bridge and up past Denis Hartley's place and turn left to go up towards the forestry blocks. They have these fibre-glass Pultron shepherd sticks. And they hook the top wire of the electric fence, so that when you open the gate in the morning you get a fuckin' hua of a clout. So we strung a length of deck cord along this fence and pull the electronic detonator up so that when they earth it everybody in town knows the bastards have been there.

We want to put two hundred and forty volts onto the fence. But Laurie Naden says, "Aw, don't be fuckin' stupid. It's a man trap and you'll get done for it." Laurie and Hemi and Thommo (Mal Thomas) and those guys, they keep us on the straight and narrow.

CHAPTER 2

FAMILY FEUDING

On Friday, July 6, 2001, I went around to see Luke Donnelly at his home in Childers Rd, Gisborne. It was across the road from Bella's Dairy, which Luke and his wife ran at the time. I'd arranged the interview the previous Saturday when we'd bumped into each other having breakfast in McDonald's in Gisborne. I knew Luke from the early '90s when I was the rugby league reporter for the Sunday News. Luke was the dad and manager of then Kiwi winger Jason Donnelly. We'd talked on the phone a lot and he'd popped into our newsroom to say gidday once or twice when he was in Auckland.

Anyway, Luke didn't want me to tape our interview but as soon as I got home afterwards, I repeated into a mini-cassette recorder as much as I could remember and later transcribed the tape verbatim.

Here's a thumbnail sketch of Luke. I'd guess he's about six foot three in the old measurements and probably about a hundred and ten kilograms. When I last saw him he still looked extremely powerful with big shoulders and hands. He has short-cropped curly dark hair and a strong jaw. And I remember his eyes as being a bit like mine except brown instead of blue: they tend towards a squint; and the more he squints the more he's summing you up. But they're not piercing eyes. In my experience they weren't eyes you needed to dodge for fear of invoking a challenge. He was an easy guy to have a conversation and maintain eye contact with. I've always really liked Luke. But then again he's a talker and I'm a listener. And that usually works.

I read in a New Zealand Herald article, dated May 1992, that he doesn't smoke or drink. "As a kid I had a few drinks and woke up the next day and couldn't remember what I'd done, that was that, I swore off it."

There's one thing we discussed that day that I'll save for later and that's about how shooting Chris changed his life. But this is the rest.

Tape of myself after interviewing Luke Donnelly: Luke was telling me how he fits into the Campbell family. Now, his mother was a woman called Taewa. Becky Taewa, I think. And she was married to Tom Donnelly. That marriage later split up. And, for whatever reason, Luke was brought up by his aunty, Sophie Taewa.

The Taewas have land alongside the land the Campbells live on. The land the Campbells live on, according to Luke, actually belongs to their close relations the Haereroas.

Sophie Taewa married one of the Haereroas. Now that Haereroa was Luke's adopted dad. But he died and Sophie stayed on that Haereroa land. And the Campbells always felt she had, through marriage, acquired their family land.

So in a European way of looking at things that land would be hers. But maybe in a Maori way of looking at things it should have gone back to the Campbells. I'm not sure. I don't know. But there was a bit of conflict there.

And now when Luke eventually came back there was definitely conflict because Willie Campbell, Chris's father, was letting the stock into Sophie Haereroa's land. According to Luke, he was letting his stock through willy-nilly. Now before, that had been fine because Syd Campbell, who lived there before Willie, would pay the rates on Sophie's land so that he could graze there. And he'd look after the fences and stuff like that. But, according to Luke, Willie didn't do that sort of stuff. So there was a bit of conflict there that Luke came back to.

And Luke said that in about 1987 there was an incident with Barney Campbell.

What happened was Willie had come home to look after the farm and as Willie was letting the stock into Sophie Haereroa's land, Koro and Barney, Luke's two brothers, were opening the gates and letting the stock go out on to the road. Now the Campbells were getting very annoyed with this. They couldn't see why the Haereroas couldn't just let the Campbells' stock graze on their land and they were even more upset that their stock was being let out onto the road.

So Barney Campbell turned up in his police uniform. And he confronted Koro, who was there with his two kids. Now Koro had a heart problem at the time. But Barney had this piece of black hose. And he kept prodding Koro back with it. One of the kids had gone away, but one of them was still there and saw this. Koro was a hard man, who'd worked all his life in the coal mines. But he wouldn't hurt a flea, according to Luke. Anyway Barney was prodding him with the black hose, and saying, "If you keep doing this I'm going to arrest you. Don't you ever do this again." He kept prodding him, prodding him, until Koro fell down backwards and Barney just kept on prodding him with the black hose. And apparently he gave Koro a really bad scare. Now this doesn't sound like the Barney Campbell I met. So maybe Luke exaggerated in the telling of the story. I don't know.

But anyway, Luke was back there soon afterwards and one day he saw Barney with his father Willie. And they were having a discussion about some fence or something like that. And Luke went up there and things got a bit tense. Luke said, "Look, Barney, you frightened my brother, Koro, who wouldn't hurt a fly and who has bad health problems. If you want to take on anyone in this family, take on me. We'll see how tough you are then."

He said, "You may be a cop and your uniform may intimidate a lot of people. But you don't intimidate me and I'll take you on right now if you want. Right now. Me and you. Come on."

And he said that Barney did as most people would when they've had it put on them. He said, "Aw no, don't worry about it Luke. Don't be silly," and just shrugged it off, which sounds much more like the guy I met.

Now Luke was saying that when he was young he'd always been a bit of a tough guy. Tougher then than he is now, he said.

We were talking about people who'd stood up to gangs in court and got protection and whatnot. And he said, "Well, I stood up to a gang in Christchurch once."

There was a gang in Christchurch called The Epitaph Riders. And one of his friend's little brothers had a Triumph and when The Epitaph Riders were riding along in a group he'd come up behind them and weave in and out of them and overtake them and take off. This guy was a Harris; apparently a cousin of the infamous Harris gang.

Anyway, one of The Epitaph Riders, a guy known as Blondie, went round to this guy's mother's house and kicked the door in, scared the kid's mother and caused a bit of damage.

So this kid's older brother rang Luke and said, "Hey, do you reckon you can sort out this guy for us. Do you wanna see if you can do something?"

So Luke went round to The Epitaph Riders gang headquarters in his little Prefect car, parked it up outside. He said they were all lying around on the lawn. There were about seven or eight of them. And Luke saw Blondie. He walked up to him and said, "You know that little kid whose house you went round to?"

The guy goes: "What's it got to do with you?"

Luke said, "Well, you don't go near him again."

The guy said, "What are you gonna fuckin' do about it?"

And Luke said, "I'm gonna cut your ears off. If you go near that kid again I'll cut your ears off." He looked round at the guy's mates to see if they were gonna do anything. He said, "Now, your mates (nods to them) you can all have a go now. But I don't care how much they hit me, cos you're the one whose gotta watch out. You're the one I'm gonna come back for. And I *will* come back for you. And I *will* cut your ears off."

And the guy says, "Okay, mate, okay."

So Luke walked off, jumped in his little Prefect car and chugged off into the distance. So he's a pretty full-on sort of character.

I asked him if at any stage he was scared of or frightened by the Rastas.

And he said, "I wasn't frightened; I was more excited, just like in the last few minutes *before* a league game and the first few minutes *in* a league game. Your muscles are all flexing and you're all pumped up and you're all hyped up and the adrenaline's running and you just wanna get into it." He said he's not the type of guy who hangs back and waits for someone else to throw the first punch. He loves to get in first and whack in first and hard. He said, "He who hesitates is lost." He said he always liked in the first few minutes of a league game to get in and really rip into someone, just really whack into them and he said that's how he felt with the Rastas.

I said I'd talked to a lot of the Rastas and they didn't seem like fighting types of guys, they didn't seem like fighters. And he said, "Yeah, well, I suppose I was the only one doing the fighting." He said, "I fought Willie Campbell, I fought Chris Campbell, Joe Campbell, Ike Campbell, a guy Edmonds, who was one of the Rastas, and Hata Thompson." He fought various people. He said he'd given them all a hiding at one stage or another. So he's not very well liked by the old Rastas.

He said that he'd always been the one in the family where if there was any trouble, they'd ring him up and he'd sort it out with his fists. And he's still really solid.

Luke was saying that one time he was working on the fence between his and Joe's properties. And Joe's Rottweiler came *charging* over to him, barking away like mad, and basically dove at him *through* the fence. But luckily Joe had a bit of netting on his side of the fence so the dog got caught in the netting. While the dog was there, old Luke, who'd been tightening the wires on the fence, took the wire-tightener, got it clear of the fence and *whacked* the dog in the face with it as hard as he could. So the dog went off yelping: "Ro ro ro ro ro ro ro ro."

So he managed to save himself from the Rottweiler. But he said Joe was going to charge him for vet's bills.

Luke was talking about one day he went to see Ike Campbell. He was talking about this scrap he had with Ike, who, again, doesn't strike me as a fighter actually.

But he said he went up to see Ike and there was a fence up the top near the plateau between the properties. They'd made up some new boundaries so the Campbells had access to the roadway.

He went up to see Ike and they talked for a while. Then Ike went to pull out his knife. Luke reckons Ike was yelling at him, "I'm gonna gut you! I'm gonna gut you!" which doesn't sound like Ike to me but, anyway, that's what he said. But as Ike was pulling out his knife he got it caught on something. And in that moment, as Ike glanced down at the knife, Luke whacked him. And after the third time he whacked him, Ike just collapsed down on the ground, totally unconscious. He said he whacked Ike so hard that he did something to his eye and Ike had to go to hospital for a couple of days to get fixed up.

I think in Ike's version of this story, Luke kicked him in the head.

A HAKA TO LUKE

Tape of myself after interviewing Luke Donnelly: What else was he talking about?

Apparently, Joe told Luke at different times that Chris had said from jail, "Leave Lukie to me. Leave Lukie until I get out. I'll handle Lukie."

So he was telling me about this time when Chris had *just* got out of jail. Luke said it was a sunny hot quiet afternoon. "All you could hear were the birds tweeting and the stream twinkling through the brook."

Luke's daughter was playing on the trampoline out the back. She must have been about five at the time. And suddenly she cries, "Daddy, what's this?"

Luke looked across and coming round the corner, really slowly, were eight of the Rastas on horseback. Now you can hear the slow steady clip-clop of the horses' hooves on the gravel.

But what they didn't know was that he had a gun with him. He loaded his .303 rifle, walked over to the fence, stuck the gun down by his feet and waited for them. And they were all staring at him. Chris was giving him the evil eye. They stopped outside his house, just looking at him. And he was thinking, "Aw well, if it comes to anything, I'm ready. I've got this .303 rifle all loaded. I've got a loaded shotgun in the house. And I've got another gun in the house with about fourteen shots in it. So I'll be okay." And he was ready to have a go at the whole lot of them.

Luke told me about an incident two days before he shot Chris. He said he looked out of his house and he could see Chris and Joe and Reece Bolingford out on the front lawn of Joe's place. They were doing a haka towards Luke. He felt they were declaring war on him. He said

88

that to them maybe it was a declaration of war. But to him it was just three guys acting like a bunch of idiots.

So anyway after they'd done their haka they got on their horses and they came round to Luke's place. And they were mouthing off and Luke said, "Come on, Chris. Come over here. Come over this fence and we'll sort it out."

So Chris rode up. And Luke was leaning on the fence. And Chris was nudging into the fence with his horse, trying to get his horse to nudge into Luke. Luke was slapping the horse out of the way. Chris kept nudging it forward.

And Luke reckons the first thing he said to Chris was, "Chris, let's see how big your balls are." And he goes, "Me and you. You come over this fence and we'll sort it out."

And Chris was going, "Na, you come over this fence. I can't go onto your property because Rana Waitai (the Gisborne police chief) said I can't go onto your land. He says if I go onto your land I'll be sent back to prison."

And Luke said, "Rana Waitai can't tell you whether you can go on my land or not. I'm the only person who can tell you whether you can come on my land. So you come over here." Luke said, "You know what your problem is?" He pulled down his zip and pulled out his penis and his testicles and said, "You haven't got a good set of these. You haven't got a good set of balls. Your balls aren't big enough." And he said, "People see you going into the bush with all those young boys, Chris, and they think you're going to get that herb. But I reckon you're going in there and you're rootin' the arse off these boys."

He said Chris was going *berserk*. He got his knife out and he was *slashing* at Luke. "Aaah, ya bastard, I'll kill ya!"

And Luke was going, "And I have it on good authority that when you were in jail a long time ago the Mongrel Mob used to give it to ya. They used to use you as their bitch."

And Chris was going berserk. "You don't know what you're talking about!"

And I asked Luke whether any of this was true or not and he said, no, he'd just made it up. He'd just made it up because he knew it would piss Chris off. And you take any advantage you can get. He just pissed him off so he knew that Chris wouldn't be in control if it came to a violent confrontation.

Anyway, he said he pulled his prick out again and was going, "This is your problem, Chris. Your balls aren't big enough. You haven't got a good set of balls. You're not brave enough."

Anyway, it all sort of ended and that was that without too much hassle. But two days later Chris went down there and Luke shot him.

CHAPTER 3

JOE BOOTS' CONSPIRACY THEORIES

Senior Sergeant Chris Bunyan: The funny thing is that as time went on when I actually talked to Chris Campbell when he came out of prison, when I talked to John Heeney, they didn't know half these guys who had joined the Rastas. While Chris was in jail a lot of these guys came along, grew the dreads and smoked the dope and called themselves Rastas. But Chris didn't even know them.

A lot of the pressure that built up for him was, "You wait until Chris gets out." And a lot of this was building up before he got out. He just walked out straight into it.

About a week before Chris died, we were up in Ruatoria doing inquiries. I was in the CIB in Gisborne by that stage. I had a chat to him. And he basically told me that he wanted to shift to Kawerau, that he didn't like the whole scene he'd come out to, that the pressures were on him. It wasn't what he was into any more. He was more into the philosophical side of things. And he said the pressure that was on him from these people that he didn't even know was incredible. They saw him as the answer to all their little altercations they were having with people.

They built this up with Luke Donnelly, too, particularly Chris's brother, Joe. See, Joe was very easy pickings for Luke. I think Luke had physically donged every single one of the Rastas at one stage or another. That's just the way Luke did things.

Detective Sergeant Gary Condon: Chris Campbell was totally different from the rest as far as I was concerned. I never interviewed him on a specific offence. But as far as I was concerned he was far better to talk to than the rest, mainly because he was more intelligent. Well you *could* talk to him. But you couldn't talk to his brother Joe. He was an example of what happens when you smoke too much dope.

I don't claim that the comments made in this next recording are factual. They are included to give an example of the stories that are told about Chris Campbell's death in Gisborne and the East Coast. The events have become part of local legend. And Gordon Sutton and I were just the latest players in a game of Chinese whispers.

Angus: Okay, this is a recording Angus and Gordon are making on the way home from a trip to see Chris Campbell's brother, Joe. I should mention that Gordon Sutton is an old neighbourhood friend of Joe, Chris and Ike Campbell. He's also related to me in that he's my cousin Linda's ex-partner and they have three beautiful kids together. It's almost dark because we had a bit of trouble getting away from Joe and it's absolutely pissing down. But Gordon's four wheel drive should handle the road okay. And I'll try not to distract him too much...

...Joe lives in a white fibrolite house on the corner of a back street in Ruatoria. There's a wire fence around the back yard and a warning sign on a metal farm gate. A couple of little bull terrier dogs were tied to an old car sitting up on blocks. They didn't look very pleased to see Gordon and me.

There were more brown baby bull terriers peeping out from under the house...

...Joe had a full moko with the Rasta colours across his forehead. So what was he talking about?

Gordon: He started off about land issues when we first got there didn't he. That was the number one issue. Then he started going on about that conversation he had with this guy who came to visit him one day. This guy said that he knew a woman who had overheard something at a marae at a hui back in Gisborne. She overheard someone saying that there was a person who was about to be released from jail and that when the prisoner returned to Ruatoria, there would be an attempt to get rid of him.

That's right. And the woman who overheard this forgot about it. But she was doing the dishes one day when she heard on the radio that Chris Campbell had been killed and suddenly she remembered what she'd overheard and she thought, "Oh no, this is what was meant to happen."

He was also talking about the land issues. According to Joe, Chris had researched his own land claim, and he'd sent it away to the Waitangi Tribunal and the Crown. And he sent Joe a letter two months later saying he'd received correspondence acknowledging his claim and by 1984 he'd done the research and had his claim all prepared.

Joe believed that the death of Chris was connected with his land claim.

Strongly connected.

And he said it was a big land claim; mountain to mountain, he said, ay?

All the land that's all around the Coast to Tokomaru Bay. So it's a big issue.

It was a much more intense and ambitious land claim than the one his brother Ike's been working on. Anyway, Joe reckoned Chris's land claim went missing. And also his lawyer made inquiries into what happened to that claim and was told that there was no such claim and no record of such a claim.

No record.

Did he talk about anything from the day Chris died?

He talked about threats from Luke Donnelly.

That's right. He was living next door to Luke Donnelly. Luke was living at the corner of Makarika Road and the main road into Ruatoria. There's nothing there now but a white water tank and an old gate. It's all overgrown with weeds now. The Rastas burnt down the house after Chris was shot. Joe was living next door and heard the gunfire when Luke shot Chris.

And there was a mate of Joe's who told him he'd wanted to drive his wife down to Gisborne to the hospital; she was pregnant.

That's right, and the cops were there. They were blocking the main road to Gisborne.

And they told them that no one could go through there at that time. So they had to go back.

Before the shooting this was.

And in the lead-up to that day, Luke Donnelly had been hassling him. He used to threaten him on a daily basis. On one occasion he said that Luke was yelling and ranting at him, yelling out, "Joe Boots, Joe Boots! Yeah! Come out, Joe!" So Joe goes out. He's dressed in shorts and he has bare feet, so obviously not in the right attire to be getting into a scrap. Luke's kicking the fence going, "Yeah, Joe, Yeah, Joe." He just keeps kicking the fence with his hobnail boots and then he came over the fence.

He started walking up the drive to Joe in a real intimidating way. He was scraping his hobnail boots up the drive and kicking the mud off and carrying on.

Until Joe picked up an iron bar and said, "Right. Fuck off." And he left. That was Joe's version anyway.

The other one was Luke Donnelly came up on his horse. He came up the driveway on his horse didn't he?

That's right.

And he wasn't holding his gun but he had his gun strapped to the horse and he said, "If anyone messes with me..." and then he patted his gun. Joe says that he mentioned that to Hemi Hikawai, but Hemi didn't use it in evidence against Luke. And he says he had an argument with Hemi at the trial and he asked, "Why didn't you use my evidence about Luke hassling me and threatening to kill me?" Hemi said he didn't think it was important.

Also, Joe's partner saw that incident with Luke on the horse and she took it to mean that Luke was gonna shoot Joe. Their kids were there too.

Michael Valintine, who was a journalist on the Holmes Show, had an interview and lunch with Tom Fox and his son-in-law Boxy on November 27, 1990, seven days before Chris's death. Tom and Boxy were members of Luke Donnelly's vigilante group and Luke turned up at the lunch.

During Luke's murder trial Valintine testified about his conversation with him that day.

"He said they (the Rastafarians) were the cause of the problems in Ruatoria and that the problems in Ruatoria would never end until they were got rid of - out of the township... ...He said that they should be driven out of town... ...Well on separate occasions he suggested at one point that they should be beaten out of town...

*... "He told of an incident in Ruatoria where he'd been
threatened with a firearm by a Rastafarian (Hata Thompson). And since
that time he now carried a firearm with him wherever he went... ...He
said if he was threatened again he would use the firearm.*
"He was much more reserved on camera."

**At Luke Donnelly's trial for the murder of Chris Campbell, P W
Cooper, for the prosecution, questions CIB Detective Chris Bunyan
about an incident at the bottom of Luke's drive on the 28th of
November, six days before Chris's death:** And did you become aware
that when he (Donnelly) rung the police station about those people
being present that he had held his telephone outside his house window,
so that the shouting could be heard by the person talking to him on the
telephone?

Yes, I remember that taking place.

So that the telephone call was made as the incident was occurring?

Yes.

And during the course of your conversation with Mr Donnelly, did
he say that he had been threatened?

Yes he did.

And the nature of the threats that he was reporting to you were
what?

Threats of death. Arson. And reference to his mother's grave. And
the dissecting of his body and burying body parts with his mother.

And did he tell you the names of the persons that he said were
saying these things?

Yes he would have.

And do you recall the names?

Yes, there was Campbell and I think Bolingford.

... And what was the first name he gave you?

From memory, without me referring to my notes, I'd say
Christopher. Chris Campbell.

**At Donnelly's trial, prosecutor Bruce Squire questions Joe
Campbell:** I want to ask you about some events which occurred some
days before the 4th of December 1990. Was Chris Campbell at your
home?

Joe: Yes. I presume you're talking about an incident a couple of
days before the shooting.

Who was involved in the incident?

Myself, Reece Bolingford and my brother Chris.

Tell us what happened in relation to that incident?

Well it wasn't long after some baches that were occupied by the Ruatoria Rastas were burnt down. I know who did it. I knew who did it...

... What happened then?

I saw Donnelly and I yelled out to him, "I know it was you who burnt those baches down at Whareponga." He replied, "Yeah, so fuckin' what, up you," and gave me a sign (demonstrates with his right arm)...

... Where was Chris Campbell?

He was inside my place having a - oh, he was drinking water. Drinking water...

... After Mr Donnelly made the gesture that you've just shown us, what happened?

Well my brother heard us yelling so he came out and he yelled out to Luke to fuck up and fuck off.

Luke replied, "Yeah Chris, come up here and I'll give you a bloody thrashing."

What did Chris do?

Oh he got on his horse and he went to Donnelly's driveway, at the bottom out on the road. Just him.

Where did you go?

Oh I stayed at my place.

When Chris got to Donnelly's place on his horse, what happened?

He was telling Luke to come out onto the road.

What did he say?

"Come out onto the Queen's highway and let's do it."

"Let's do it."?

Yes. Yes. Not with a gun.

Did Luke Donnelly say anything?

Yeah. He told Chris to come up to his house.

Did he say anything else?

Yeah, he told him he was all shit, if he was a man he would go up there. To that effect. We knew that Donnelly didn't have the makings to come out on the road.

Chris didn't go up the drive to Donnelly's house?

No.

What did he do?

Stayed out on the road...

...How long did Chris stay out on the road?

Oh five, maybe 10 minutes.

Where was Luke Donnelly when Chris was out on the road for these five or 10 minutes?

He was up at his place and he had ripped his shirt open and he had one leg up on the fence and he was saying, "Yeah, come on Chris. Come on Chris."

Did he stay in that position very long?

Yeah, well what I remember, yeah.

After the five or ten minutes had elapsed where did Chris go?

He didn't go anywhere, from there he went back to my place.

Did you see what Luke Donnelly did?

Mr Donnelly said he was going inside for a cup of tea.

Under cross examination by lawyer Les Atkins, Joe Campbell says that by the end of the five or ten minutes he and Reece Bolingford were also at the bottom of the drive and the three of them left the scene together.

CHAPTER 4

COUNTDOWN TO A KILLING

Sarah Sykes, secretary of Te Aowera Marae: Chris Campbell's time was up. The tipuna (ancestors) had had enough. And they were taking matters into their own hands. They felt so strongly that it was his own mother who got the dream. That was a sign of how serious the tipuna were. Chris's mother dreamt that Chris was going to die. She told him that he had to stop what he was doing immediately. But I think it might have gone too far. He was dead within a few days.

Katarina Paterson, friend of Chris Campbell: Chris wanted to go horse riding with me. He hadn't been out of jail long. He took me to the place where he was supposed to have kidnapped the cop, Laurie Naden. He said he wanted to tell me what really happened with the Rastafarians. He said he wanted someone to know the truth because there'd been so much bullshit written and he wanted the truth to come out one day. He said he needed to tell me in case something happened to him and the story died with him. He was scared that he was going to die. We spent two days riding around the hills and he told me everything that happened. A few days later he was shot dead by Luke Donnelly.

Tape recorded note to myself: Ian Sykes (Sarah's husband) said that one day he was mustering with Luke Donnelly. And Joe Campbell started yelling abuse at Luke. So Luke grabbed him, wrapped his dreadlocks around some barbed wire on a fence, so he couldn't move, and just started laying into him… whacked him over. With his dreadlocks wrapped around the spikes in the barbed wire there was nothing Joe could do but take it.

Detective Hemi Hikawai: Luke Donnelly was putting out a challenge to the Rastas. When Campbell and Heeney and Cody Haua and Hata Thompson went to jail, you've got to remember that the hard core of them were suddenly all inside. Donnelly arrived while those guys were inside. So things had settled down to a certain extent in the minds of the police who prior to that had been up and down the Coast all the time. That's obviously not how Donnelly saw it or how those who were supporters of him saw it.

The Rastas were still cutting fences and stuff like that. But it was more or less the mopping up after the battle.

Luke occupied a property right next door to the Campbells. Luke was adopted so it was his family land. He'd come from Hamilton back there, see, to move onto that farm. It wasn't big enough to make a living from. He had his views and his thoughts on the matter and he went about doing things his way. That didn't gel with some of those people there and soon we had the problems flaring up all over again.

On one occasion prior to the shooting, the Rastafarians had been camping down at a beach called Whareponga. Their huts and all that got burnt. They'd been warned to move off the land but they refused to go. And then suddenly they found themselves on the receiving end of a bit of their own medicine and were burnt out. I think Luke and his sympathisers set the huts alight. They called themselves the Ruatoria Rangers. You had what they called the vigilantes, who had the police backing. Then you had Luke Donnelly coming in and setting up his group, who were running around in camouflage gear.

Tape recorded note to myself after a conversation with Cody Haua: Cody said that Chris Campbell had a dream when he was in prison. He dreamt that he had a confrontation with Luke Donnelly and that one of them died. Chris knew that Luke was going to kill him because he saw himself lying on the ground with a tear in his eye. And then he saw his face sinking into the ground. Chris told Cody about this dream when they were staying at the beach at Whareponga.

Cody reckoned that the morning that Chris had his final confrontation with Luke he prayed down by the sea and sprinkled water on himself with his hands.

PART 10
HEAD-ON COLLISION

CHAPTER 1

TUESDAY, DECEMBER 4, 1990

Sarah Sykes's husband Ian is supposed to be moving some sheep with Luke Donnelly today. But just as he's about to go to work he starts feeling very heavy. He can't even lift his legs properly. His arms feel like lead weights, his head like a demolition ball. And he has to lie down. Suddenly he's asleep.

Cody Haua's nephew, Wiki Haua, says he was supposed to be in the car with Chris that day. He was just a teenager at the time, one of what's often referred to as the second generation of Rastafarians. And growing up among the Rastas meant he grew up hard.

"Nanny Punky had seventeen children of her own and five adopted children. Well, four adopted children actually. The fifth one just turned up one day and she took them in, too. I was one of the four kids who were adopted. There is a story that at one stage she had forty-two children staying at her house and she fed the lot. She was an amazing woman.

"On six occasions, between the age of ten and fifteen, I had guns shoved in my face by cops. One time they came up and raided our house, about ten of the Armed Offenders Squad, guns out, chests pumped. I was about twelve. And one of them was opening the potato bin. I asked him what he was looking for. He reckons Hata Thompson. And I said, 'Well he's not going to fit in there.' The dude was pissed off with me. He turned the gun and pointed it at me and asked if I wanted to be a smart-arse. Funniest thing is, I wasn't scared and just smiled at him.

"Another time I got shot in the leg by a local only because they didn't know who I was in the dark. It just skimmed my calf so I was lucky."

Chris Campbell had always had a soft spot for Wiki. "One time when I was eleven I asked him to teach me to play chess. He was a master. He took me to a room at the Crossroads and we played for two hours. Then he sent me out and told me to play and beat John Heeney's brother Mike, so I did. Chris had an effect on me from an early age."

So why wasn't Wiki in the car with Chris the day he was shot?

"Chris and the others were going to kill a meat," *Wiki recalls.* "And I wanted to go with them because I liked hanging out with Chris and I wanted to learn how to kill a meat. I hadn't done it before. But before they left Mangahanea Marae, Chris told me to hang in there because my Nan wanted me to stay away from the Rastas for a while. He had great respect for Nanny Punky and he told me to listen to her and stay away. I often wonder what Luke would have done if I was in the car with Chris and them that day."

On the morning of December 4, Reece Bolingford was working at Chris Campbell's father's place, killing a sheep and cutting it up for

*meat, when Chris, Bill Kaihe, Joe Ward and Harley Te Hau turned up
in the Rastas' station wagon, the Grey Ghost. After chatting for a while
Bolingford jumped in the car and they all went for a swim.*

Bill Kaihe: The day started just like any other normal day. We just decided to go for a ride in the vehicle to have an early morning swim at the Makarika River. We started heading back into Ruatoria along the main road and Chris Campbell noticed Luke Donnelly on his property gesturing us to come up to his place.

In court, Bolingford says that Chris Campbell rode up part of the driveway on the bonnet of the car.
Kaihe says Campbell sat on the front but the car stalled soon after that so he jumped off and walked the rest of the way.
Campbell was wearing black sunglasses, a blue fishnet tank top, a dark blue tank top, black tracksuit pants and boots.
Witnesses say Luke was wearing a white T-shirt.

Joe Ward cross-examined by Donnelly's lawyer Les Atkins at the murder trial: Did Chris Campbell tell you to go up?
No, we just followed.
He didn't tell you?
Nah.
Did Chris Campbell say to you in the car at any stage, "Follow me up"?
Ah, yeah, he said, "Come up." We drove him up some way. He started walking. We pulled up alongside him. He jumped on the bonnet, then our car stalled, and he walked up, carried on up.
And did he say, "Follow me up."?
No we just followed him up.
Well, did he, at any time, use the words to you, "Follow me up."?
Yeah, in the car.
At the bottom of the drive?
Well he never said, "Follow me up." He said, "We'll go up."...
...And you didn't hear him say anything to Donnelly about the house being burned, or Donnelly being "wasted"?
Ah, the only lines I heard were, "Go and see what this fella wants."

Bill Kaihe: And when we got up to Luke's property, he wasn't there for a couple of minutes. And then he come around the corner. I'm not sure how many shots he fired at Chris. But most of his shots found their target.

Things just happened so fast I didn't have much time to think about what was happening.

Once the first shot was fired everyone was just diving for cover. But I was still stuck in the driver's seat.

Luke fired a shot at the car and shattered the front windscreen. The shot hit the windscreen at the top left corner as I was looking at it. I got about half a dozen shotgun pellets in my shoulder. At first it was just like a sharp pinprick and after that I didn't feel anything. There was no pain, no nothing. I thought it might have just been broken glass that had embedded into my shoulder.

Luke also shot the front tyre.

The other guys all moved to a safe distance after the first shot and Chris and I were just left there.

His wife wasn't on the scene. It was just Luke.

Luke told me to get out of the car and to come up towards him and to lie face down on the ground. He also told me not to move or he would blow my head off. I was fearing for my life by this stage. He was already in the process of taking someone else's life. He'd already shot Chris. So I felt that to take another man's life would be *nothing* to him.

Before the police arrived Luke managed to get a couple of boots to my head. He kicked me in the mouth and he made my nose bleed.

I didn't say nothing and I didn't even try to get away, not with him reeling the gun around.

Prosecutor Bruce Squire questions Harley Te Hau during Donnelly's trial: The shot hit the window of the car, the front window was it?

Te Hau: Yes.

What did you see then?

The whole window just shattered - it was all white. We couldn't see.

When Chris fell to the ground... did he remain there?

Te Hau: Yes.

At that time did anybody say anything that you heard?

Yes, Chris.

What did he say?

He said, "I'm down, brothers."

Did he say anything else?

He said, "Come on, Luke, let's talk about it."...

...Did Luke Donnelly stay in the same position or did he move somewhere else?

No he moved from side to side up the top of the hill from the car, pointing the gun at us , the three of us that were behind the car, on the ground.

Do you recall whether anything was said by anybody at that time?

Yeah, Luke Donnelly said, "What are you doing hiding behind the car? Come out." And he had the gun raised like he wanted to shoot us again.

And again, you're holding your arms up at shoulder level, left hand extended, right hand just below the chin, and you said he was moving the gun?

Yes, he was walking from side to side of the car. At which direction was the gun pointing?

At us, lying on the ground.

When you saw that happening what did you do?

Got up and ran. Reece ran first. He ran down the hill. I followed behind him. Joe Ward was behind me.

As you ran down the drive did anything happen?

Another gunshot went off.

Do you know where that gunshot was aimed?

No...

...When you got to the road, where did you go?

Straight across the road. After we ran across the road we ran down towards the river.

During the trial, Joe Ward tells prosecutor Bruce Squire that he got up about ten seconds after Reece and Harley took off and ran halfway down the driveway. He ran past two trees on the right and then dove over a bank. He could see Donnelly pointing the gun at him as he dove and he dislocated his arm when he landed (having to go to hospital for treatment later). Ward jumped up and continued running - hearing a shot as he ran - down to a stand of willows at the right of the intersection of the drive with the main road. He climbed over two fences until he was out on the road and flagged down a Ministry of Works truck. Then a courier van came along and he waved that down too and got a ride with the van to Kiriana Bartlett's house on Makarika Road and rang the police. From that house, he could also see Luke still standing over Billy and Chris. After that Ward went to the Mangahanea Marae. Five minutes later he was picked up by some of his mates and they went to the Makarika Turnoff, where they were spoken to by a policeman, Rangi Walker.

Prosecutor Bruce Squire questions Bill Kaihe at Donnelly's murder trial about what happened after Kaihe got out of the car:
What did Luke Donnelly say to Chris?
     I can't actually remember what he said. I only remember parts.
     Tell us the parts you remember.
     "I could blow your heart out."...
     ...Do you remember whether Chris Campbell said anything?
     Yes.
     What did he say?
     "Let's talk about it."
     What's the next thing that happened after that, which you saw or heard, Mr Kaihe?
     Chris Campbell yelling out in pain...
     ...What was the next thing that happened?...
     All I heard was, "I've been hit."
     Did you recognise the voice?
     Chris Campbell.
     What was the next thing that happened?
     Luke Donnelly told me to walk towards him.
     And did you?
     Yes.
     Whereabouts was the gun that he had when he told you to walk towards him?
     In his hand.
     How was he holding it?
     He had it pointing at me...
     ... How close did you get to Mr Donnelly?
     Face to face.
     And when you got face to face with him, what happened?
     He told me to kiss the dirt.

When he told you to get down and kiss the dirt, did you do anything?

I got down.

What position were you in?

Lying on my stomach.

And in what position was your face?

I was face-down.

When you got close to him... ...did you see the gun?

Yeah I saw the gun.

What sort of a gun was it?

It was a shotgun.

... What was the next thing that you remember happening?..

Luke Donnelly just told me not to move.

... After that?...

Luke Donnelly told his wife to go inside to grab the gun-belt, handcuffs, and another rifle.

...What was the next thing?...

I turned my head to one side.

And did you see anything when you did that?

No.

Did you hear anything?

No I didn't hear anything.

What was the next thing that happened when you turned your head to one side?

Luke Donnelly kicked me in the face.

What happened after that?

Then he stood on my head.

Did he keep his boot on your head or did he stand on your head and take his foot off?

No he kept his boot on my head.

What was the next thing that happened, that you saw or heard, after he put his boot on your head?

More shots.

... Do you know in which direction they were fired?

Down the driveway.

How do you know that?

Because he was facing that way...

... What was the next thing that happened after that?

I felt the barrel being pointed to my throat.

At that time, what position were you in?

Still lying on the ground.

What happened when the barrel was pointed to your throat?

Luke Donnelly told me to keep still or he would blow me apart...

...Was it before or after Mrs Donnelly handed the other gun to Luke Donnelly that the gun was put to your throat and you were told to lie still?

It was after...

...Are you able to tell us how long he kept the barrel at your throat?

A couple of minutes.

What happened after he took the barrel away from your throat?

I heard his wife say that he was wanted on the phone, someone was wanting to speak to him...

...What happened when his wife said that to him?

He told me not to move and then he disappeared...

... Well, what did you do after he disappeared?

Stayed on the ground.

When did you get up off the ground?

When the police arrived.

At Donnelly's trial, Ruatoria Police receptionist Leonie Walker says the first call she received about the incident was from Donnelly's wife Elizabeth at 2.35pm. Detective Rex Harrison spoke to her. Then Harrison left the station. At 2.45, she received a message from Gisborne Police that they'd received a 111 call from Joe Ward and that she was to ring him. Then she received a message from Harrison asking her to arrange for the attendance of an ambulance. At 2.50 she advised him that the ambulance had been dispatched. Then at Harrison's request she rang the Donnelly house. She got Elizabeth Donnelly to bring Luke to the phone. She asked if Detective Hikawai could go up and see him. He said, "Yes, tell him to come up."

Bill Kaihe: The cops must have turned up about five or ten minutes later. One of them asked me what I was doing up there. He must have thought I was a spectator or something.

Luke had waved us onto the property. We had no intentions of going to see Luke in the first place. We were just on our way into Ruatoria.

Luke might have said he was afraid for his safety. But he killed an unarmed man. There's no justice there.

It wasn't until later on that afternoon that I felt the pain return to my shoulder.

And then I found out when I got to the hospital that I had pellets in there. They managed to get one out but the rest are still in my shoulder.

I was back at Mangahanea Marae where we were staying when we got word that Chris had gone. We got a phone call.

Former Detective Hemi Hikawai: We'd got a call to say that the Rastafarians had gone up to Luke Donnelly's house causing trouble. So myself and two others head over there and I'm thinking, "Aw no. Here we go again."

And as we were en route to the place we got a report that there'd been a couple of shots fired. And we were unarmed. And I was thinking, "Aw God, what the fuck do we do here?"

Ike Campbell, Chris's brother: I was on top of this building in Sydney, scaffolding, carrying these big bits of steel, and my legs gave way on the top storey. They're quite high the buildings in Sydney, very high. This was Sydney Central. My legs collapsed, just out of the blue. My knees gave way. And I knew something was wrong in the family. I didn't know who or what, but I knew something was wrong.

Hemi Hikawai: So we drove up on to the property. I was sitting in the back seat. I saw Luke standing by the gateway to his address. And that's all I saw at that stage. He had a shotgun and a 3-O.

The other Rastas have scattered on foot by now. Luke's immobilised the car by putting about three or four shots into the radiator, into the windscreen, into the tyre. So they've all scarpered and I haven't seen Chris yet. I've just got out of the car and I'm thinking, "Fuck, someone could get shot here."

Across the way to my left I can hear these voices, yelling and screaming that they're going to fuckin' kill some bastard. "You're gonna fuckin' get it, Donnelly!" they're shouting.

Anyway I manage to get Luke to put the guns down. And when I'm yelling out to Luke, I hear this voice call out to me. It's saying, "James… James… Help me, James." I turn around to my left and I see, "Fuckin' hell, there's Chris Campbell." And he's all huddled up by the fence line down below the road.

I say, "Lie there, Chris, stay there." The other guys from the car are still not far away yelling, "We're gonna fuckin' kill you, we're comin' back," and all the rest of it. And I'm thinking, "Shit, we're gonna get caught in the cross-fire here. We'd better be careful."

I yell out to Chris Bunyan, "Run down and have a look at Chris." Chris Bunyan and Rex Harrison were the two cops with me...

... Campbell had been warned by the police to stay off Luke's property because we knew the confrontation was coming to a head. So Campbell, as a rule, never went on to Luke's property. In fact on previous occasions he'd invited Luke out on to the main road.

But Campbell reckons Luke had invited him up to the property, waved him up. "Come up, let's see how good you are."...

... Luke reckons that he didn't invite them. He says the Rastas came up and were yelling and screaming that they were going to kill him. They were going to kill his missus and everything else. And so fearing for his safety he ran in and got the gun. I don't know how Campbell was going to kill him. With his finger? They never had any guns.

Luke came back out with a gun and started shooting. Then he yelled to his wife to bring the other gun and shot Chris three more times with that.

I manage to get Donnelly back into the house, which was the safest place to be. I've got no fear that they're going to shoot me. If they're going to shoot anybody it's going to be Donnelly. But they're such piss-poor shots I don't want to be out in the open with him.

"PIECES OF HUMAN FLESH"

Prosecutor Bruce Squire questions CIB Detective Chris Bunyan (a former schoolmate of Chris Campbell) at Luke Donnelly's trial: Did you then walk down the bank to where Chris Campbell was lying?

Yes I did.

Describe the position that he was in, please?

He was lying in what I would call the recovery position. By that I mean he was lying on his right side with his head towards the boundary fence. His right arm was stretched out with his head rested on his shoulder. His left arm was in a 'v' shape, over toward his right arm, and his legs were drawn up toward his upper body.

P W Cooper, for the Crown, questions Bunyan about the state of Chris Campbell when he saw him: Were you able to detect any pulse?

No...

Did you notice whether he was still breathing?

Yes he was breathing, slowly but rhythmically.

Did you identify yourself to him?

Yes I did and he recognised me.

Did you let him know that medical assistance was on the way?

Yes.

Did you note the injuries that he had?

Yes I did.

What were they?

He had an open wound in the bottom side of his right wrist which was showing exposed sinews. There was no blood coming from this wound. He had an injury to his right knee and the clothing in that area was wet with congealed blood. He had an injury to his left knee and there was a lot of congealed blood in the clothing of that region as well. He appeared to be in shock. He was cold to the touch, and his lips were showing a greyish discolouration.

Did he appear to be in pain?

Yes he appeared to be in pain and he later told me he was in pain. He rolled over to his left onto his back. I actually told him he'd be better staying how he was, but he rolled onto his back.

Did you then notice something else about the state he was in?

Yes, he had vomited when he'd been lying in the other position and it wasn't until he rolled over that I noticed the vomit on the ground. He then asked me if I could assist him by moving his right leg, which I did, and he acknowledged that he was feeling more comfortable in that position. He then vomited but was able to turn his head to his left and clear the vomit.

At 18 minutes past 3 did an ambulance arrive at the scene?

Yes it did.

Did that ambulance park behind the police vehicle?

Yes.

And did it carry a doctor?

Yes.

Were there other people round about the scene who were injured?

Yes, there were two other persons who received attention at the ambulance - Mr Kaihe and Mr Ward.

Did you then assist the medical staff in the treatment of Campbell?

Yes I did.

Chris Bunyan, interviewed by the author: We were investigating the burning of the baches at Whareponga. And one day there was a domestic dispute between Luke Donnelly and Joe Campbell. Luke rang up and you could actually hear Joe Campbell yelling and shouting in the background along the lines of, "I'm gonna kill you, I'm gonna cut your heart out, I'm gonna bury your body in your mother's grave," and all this sort of stuff. "Your house is gonna burn down, you're fucked, you've had it, you're gone," all this sort of stuff.

So I think Hemi and me drove out there and we sorted it out. This was several days before Chris Campbell died.

Well we were finished our inquiries and we were due to go home on the particular day Chris was shot. And it was getting into the afternoon. We were actually helping Thelma Plews, the health nurse, shift some gear into her new premises. We were only moments off going home.

And Rex Harrison drove over from the station, which was on the next door property, and was out on the side of the road. He opened the car door and said, "Aw, I need a hand guys. There's another domestic out at Donnelly's."

We didn't have our notebooks or anything. We just jumped in the car and thought, "Righto." We thought it was along the lines of what had happened a few days earlier.

Well we would've been on the Hiruharama Straight when we called up Leonie Walker at the Ruatoria Station and said, "Look, can you get us a few details about what's going on." And next thing the call came in. "A couple of people have been shot. We don't know who's fired the shots or what's going on." So we basically stopped. And just waited. And not long after that it came back, "Look, it's all clear. You can make your way up there. Luke Donnelly will wave to you when you get there." So we proceeded forward, not knowing what the hell had taken place, who was where or anything. We didn't even know that Luke had done the shooting. The extent of the message that had come through was that something had happened on Luke's property, a couple of people had been shot but Luke was okay and that we were okay to go on up.

We parked at the gate at the bottom of his driveway. And he yelled out, "It's okay!" or something to that effect. And because we'd actually dealt with him the previous week we had a reasonable rapport with him. We didn't feel threatened by him and didn't feel that he had a beef with the police. But we didn't know what had happened. We didn't have a bloody clue. So we started wandering up the driveway and quite literally on portions of the driveway there were pieces of human flesh as you walked up the driveway. Pieces! Pieces! And having worked in the freezing works before I joined the police I knew it was definitely meat. And as it transpired it was Chris Campbell's flesh.

And we wound our way up the driveway and it dipped off to one side and down in a little hollow here's Chris Campbell just lying there.

And actually Luke Donnelly had another guy on the ground, Billy, with his foot on his head, saying, "I've got one of my own fuckin' whanau here," sort of thing, "and he came to get me."

You didn't know where anyone else was. You felt totally bloody vulnerable and obviously Chris Campbell's been shot, Billy Kaihe's lying on the ground up there. Luke was holding a firearm and Hemi grabbed that off him. And I said, "Right, I'll look after Chris."

And I went down there and man he was a mess. He had long pants on and they were just full of blood all around his knees. And there was blood on the ground. And he was lying there. He had a hole in his arm and lying there quite still. He was pretty pale, pretty grey, and I spoke to him and I said, "Look, you know who it is?" We'd been in the same class all through school.

He says, "Yeah."

"Are you all right?"

He says, "No, I'm fucked."

I didn't go into what happened or anything. I just said, "Okay, mate, the ambulance is on its way. Just hold tight."

Other things were happening in the background. We'd called in cops from Te Araroa and Tokomaru Bay. They were armed and started setting up a scene to protect the evidence. I removed two people from the scene. One of them was Cody Haua. Chris was still lying there. And by this stage an ambulance had arrived and was up the driveway. And Cody was just absolutely lathered up. And I got quite stroppy with him.

I physically removed him from the immediate scene. And then another cop with a rifle took Cody off the property.

My biggest fear was being shot. On at least one occasion I went into the house where Hemi was talking with Luke and I said, "Look, I'm really concerned. I feel totally bloody vulnerable." Hemi's in the house. Rex is up relaying all the information on the radio to the Gisborne station. And I'm stuck right on the scene on my own with Chris Campbell. And there's Rastas on horses by this stage yelling out, "Utu!" and all sorts of bloody things. Having worked there for a couple of years I know those guys, when they get lathered, you just don't know, they're unpredictable bastards. I said, "Look, I've got a feeling we might have to use these guns." I was really, really concerned.

At one stage Chris asked me to move him and I turned him and, fuck, his leg was just like jelly. From the knee it was just as loose as. The bones were all smashed. And there was like a huge hole in a portion of his arm. Down on his wrist area you could see the sinews and everything. You could see the entry wound and then the exit wound where the bullet basically came out. He vomited a couple of times and I managed to just clear his mouth. I didn't administer probably the best first aid I guess because he was in such a state and I was a little bit shocked by it all. But he was conscious. He was aware of who I was. He basically told me he was buggered. And I think the most he might have said about the incident was, "Luke shot me." That was it.

Excerpt from Doctor Kenneth Thompson's post-mortem report on Chris Cambpell: The right thigh showed on its medial aspect 14cm below the groin an oval entry wound 11mm in diameter, with an area of abrasion beneath it and medially. Small fragments of foreign material were present. Dissection of the right medial upper thigh showed a bullet track extending deeply into the medial musculature with considerable associated haemorrhage. Buried within the muscle some 10cm from the surface was a lead bullet which was slightly deformed.

"LIKE A BLOODY BATTLEGROUND"

Detective Rex (Wene) Harrison (retired): As Hemi will tell you, we were only three minutes away when Chris Campbell got shot. We were up investigating those bach fires at Whareponga, down by the beach. To the best of my knowledge it was Luke's lady friend who made the first call to police. But she was acting on Luke's instructions.

So Hemi, Chris Bunyan and me started driving down to Luke's. Halfway there we stopped and Hemi got on the radio and got the receptionist to ring Luke and make sure everything was okay. We didn't want to go walking into an ambush. Luke said, "No, it's all clear. Come on down."

We went down to the house and it was like a bloody battleground, with shells lying all over the place. You feel very wary when you walk into a scene like that, much more wary than scared. It's like that old adage, "Run to a fire, walk to a fight." You have to be very cautious. You fine-tune yourself. And you've got to take into consideration where you are and you don't take any bloody stupid risks. What's the use in becoming a bloody dead hero. It's amazing what thoughts go through your mind: family, wife, kids, what happens to them if something happens to me. It's far better to deal with the whole situation professionally instead of charging in because, knowing what they were like, we were just baldheads to them. We were just another enemy. So I was very bloody careful.

Bill Kaihe was on the ground and Luke had his boot on him. So Bill wasn't going anywhere. But where were the others and were they armed? They were my main concerns because we were open targets.

Hemi looked after Luke. We ran the operation all that afternoon.

I honestly didn't think Chris was going to die. I was talking to him as per normal. It was a bloody shock to hear later that he'd passed away.

During Luke Donnelly's trial, prosecutor Bruce Squire questions New Zealand Police firearms expert Robert Ngamoki.

He asks Ngamoki to look at a photograph of a small hole, an entry wound 5mm in diameter, in the leg of Chris Campbell's dead body.

Ngamoki confirms that the wound is too small for a shotgun slug and too large for a shotgun pellet. Ngamoki says the wound is in keeping with a bullet from a .303 rifle.

Then Squire shows him another photograph of a wound on the opposite side of the leg.

"Now I'd like just to assume, for the purposes of the questions I'm going to ask you, that that is the exit wound..."

"Yes."

"In the course of your duties as an armourer have you encountered .303 bullets, either with soft lead points or the tips of which have been filed?"

"Yes I have."

"And are you familiar with the kind of injuries that would be sustained or that are sustained by living tissue when hit by bullets either with soft lead points or tips which have been filed?"

"Yes."

"And characteristically what kind of exit wounds do you expect from cartridges with soft lead points or the tips of which have been filed?"

"Very destructive wounds. Very similar to the one in the photograph."...

... "When the tips of .303 bullets are deliberately filed, what is the purpose of that exercise?"

"It's intended to cause the projectile to break up or expand as it's passing through, basically flesh."

"With what consequence?"

"A more severe wound than would normally be expected."

"IT'S NOW A HOMICIDE"

The scene examination starts at 5.48pm. It's hot and humid, there's high cloud overhead and it's expected to rain.

Chris Bunyan: Before long the AOS turned up in a helicopter all tooled up in their gear and they then set up guards all around the scene. The doctor arrived in a helicopter and they took Chris out of the area by helicopter.

Rex asked me to do the scene. And the weather report was that the weather was gonna deteriorate. Now further up the driveway by a little fence was a Holden station wagon and it was riddled with bloody buckshot and there was a big hole in the front guard and through the wheel and the windscreen was whacked and obviously it was there to stay. And I thought, "Gee, that's one of your main exhibits." So we photographed everything and just started doing the normal police things from there. We located all the bits of blood and stuff, pegged out an area where Chris had been, and just started noting things down and going through the scene. Because of the threat of rain we actually uplifted those things. And there were a number of shotgun cartridges expelled onto the lawn. So we uplifted all of those as well.

We finished work that night at ten past ten and we went out onto the road and Rex Harrison came up to us and said, "Aw look guys, basically it's now a homicide. Chris Campbell's just died." And that really, really shocked us because Dr Sepp from Te Puia Hospital had come back to the scene by helicopter and said, "Hey, just thought I'd let you guys know that the man is in hospital in Gisborne. He's sitting up talking to one of your guys." That was Dave Neilson.

We had a briefing and worked out what was gonna happen the next day and then went home. I finished work at half past midnight and at 6.30 the next morning we were back in the station.

CHAPTER 2

LUKE'S VERSION OF WHAT HAPPENED

It's Wednesday May 12, 2010. Fifteen days ago Luke Donnelly gave me the elusive third interview I'd been asking him for. And he did what he never had to do in court and what he didn't do in any of our previous correspondence: he talked about what happened the day he shot Chris Campbell.

I met him at a pub in Northland. He was with a woman friend and a mate, who I knew from Gisborne. We had a bangers-and-mash lunch, which he shouted because I was embarrassingly broke.

Anyway, here's his version of what happened.

Luke Donnelly, Tuesday, April 27, 2010 (on the events of Tuesday, December 4, 1990): I was being interviewed by a New Zealand Herald reporter by the name of Ron Taylor. He turned up about 10 o'clock… About four hours later, he goes to leave and says, "Shall I shut that gate at the bottom?"

I said, "No, don't worry about it," cos when I looked down about a dozen of my sheep had gotten out on the road. So I said, "No, leave the gate open. I'll go down and get those sheep in."

A BREAK IN PROCEEDINGS: Luke Donnelly chats to a mate through a window of the Gisborne District Court.

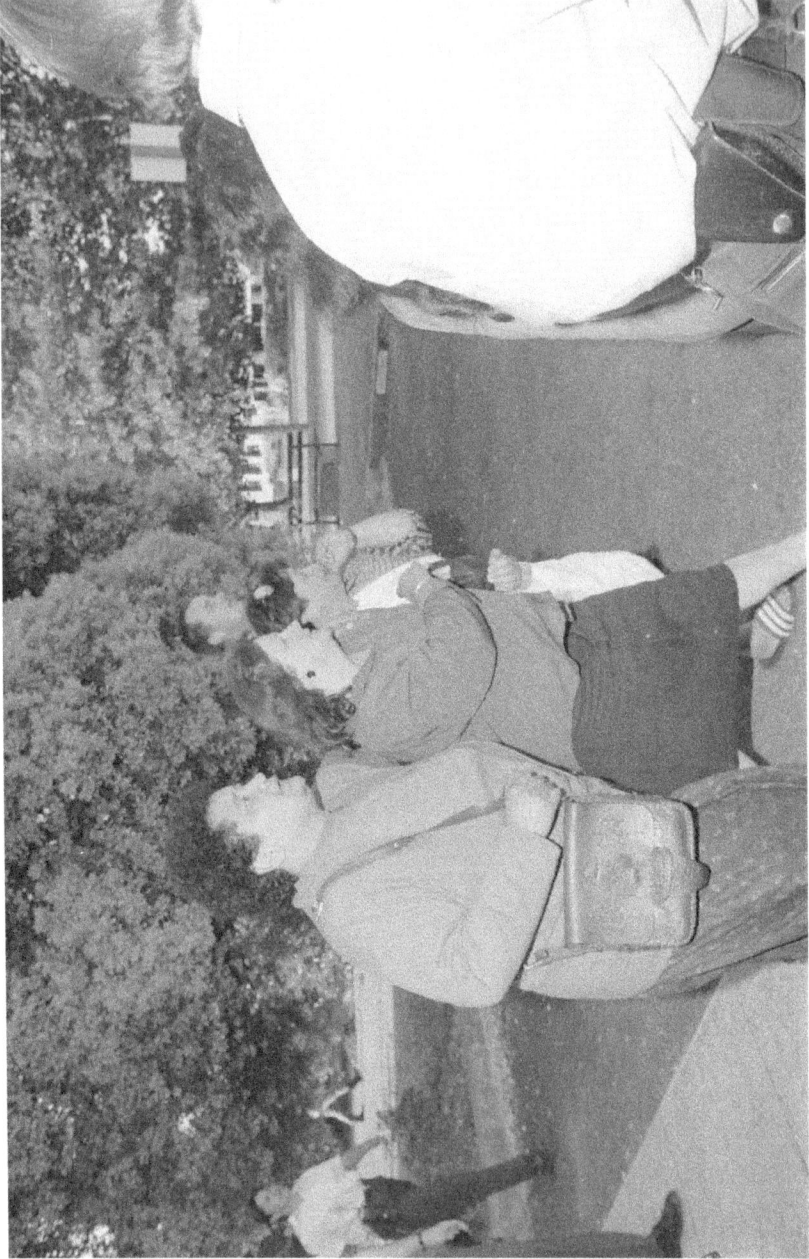

AN ARM AROUND THE SHOULDER: Luke Donnelly's wife at the time, Elizabeth, is supported by a friend as she walks into the Gisborne courthouse.

HANDCUFFED: Luke Donnelly is walked from the courthouse to the back of the police van.

JOHN (HONE) HEENEY: Chris Campbell's right hand man in the Ruatoria Rastafarians' original 12. These days he tattoos the moko for the brethren. Photo courtesy of Maro Kouri.

CHRIS CAMPBELL: Seen by some as deluded, by others as an outlaw prophet who would have been more at home among his warrior tipuna.

He drives out. I walk along the road. And I bring these sheep back. And just as I get in and close the gate, I look up the road and from where my gate is I could see coming down Makarika Road this thing, all dust and that. I could see it coming, the Grey Ghost, the Rastas' Holden 64.

I'm starting to walk up the driveway and it's about seventy metres to walk up to the top. And by the time I get about fifty or sixty metres, I'm still walking and I turn around and see the car parked at the bottom there and they're giving me the fingers. They hop out and they're all yelling out, "Aw, you bastard. You're gonna die you bastard. You're fuckin' head is coming off. We're gonna bury you with your mother," cos my mother's grave was nearby.

So after about five minutes I thought, "They're not gonna go." So they're seventy metres away. Their words are carrying enough for me to hear them. But it's still a fair way away. I just put my hand up and do the same thing… I put my hand up (he gives the fingers) and, "Get fucked! Fuck off you dickheads," and tell them to piss off.

And this is where the confusion comes. Was I giving them the fingers or was I waving them up? They reckon that I was saying, "Oh, come up." Heh heh. I can't quite remember exactly what I was saying. I believe I was just giving them the fingers. That's what I believe.

You didn't say, "Why don't you come up here and try that!"?

(At this point Luke's mate, who's having lunch with us, says, "No!" on Luke's behalf.)

Luke takes the interruption on board, then continues: I don't recall that. It was more likely I was just giving them the fingers and I'm quite satisfied with that.

But the next thing is they reverse back and then they come through the gate. They just cruise up slowly and I'm standing in the gateway there. They drive up. They stop about five metres away from me. I used to carry a machete. So I'm holding on to this machete. I used to have a lot of thorn and stuff that I used to just clear as I was walking around. So I've got this machete. And Chris gets out of the car. And I remember him saying, the first words he said were, "Come here you *cunt*." (Luke impersonates Chris, making him sound like a king talking down to a lowly subject.) He said, "Come here you *cunt*."

And the first words I said to him were, "Fuck off you fuckin' idiot."

And I'll always remember this. Just to his left was this spot down near this little lake where I shot one of their horses.

Luke spends a long time explaining that as he was standing there he thought about how he shot the horse and the odd way it died. It was a beautiful white Arab cross – "what they call a bluey-white" - that someone had told him was Chris's prize horse. Luke shot it in the head because it was in his paddock. He used a huge slug in his shotgun, which blew one side of its head clean off. The horse collapsed straight down with all four legs splayed so that if you wanted to you could still sit on it, as if riding it.

Luke continues: Chris had his shirt on and he opened his shirt out as if to say, "Okay, she's all on," and started to approach me, saying that he was going to deal to me and my head was coming off, same thing they used to go on about.

And I had a shirt on. So I opened that up to let him know we'd be mixing it. And I was all cool with that. Oh yeah! And just as I was moving forward to get into it, he turned around and said, "Cut his fuckin' head off."

He said that, yeah, "Cut his fuckin' head off." Oh, "and burn that fuckin' house down."

My wife was standing in the window. That's why I changed from going to use these (Luke holds up his fists). That's why I said to him, "You just changed the fuckin' rules."

I turned around, went and got the shotgun, came back and he was still standing there. I had the shotgun in the scabbard with my arm inside the scabbard too.

And he said, "You're all full of shit. You're like the fuckin' rest of them (meaning the community). They're all full-a shit."

I brought the gun up like that and pointed it at his head. He said, "You won't shoot. Come on. Try it. You ain't got no fuckin' bullets in there." This is real brave stuff, you know. And I knew he'd done it before with Gordon Shirkey. So I already knew that that sort of stuff didn't frighten *him*. So all I did was kept the gun in the scabbard and I said, "Is that right," turned the gun on the Grey Ghost and BANG! Blew the radiator. BSHSHSHSHSH! Steam's shooting up everywhere.

"No bullets ay."

BANG! Blew the headlight off the car.

Popped a tyre. PSHSHSHSH! (It's a higher-pitched sound than the radiator).

One shot went through the windscreen. That's when Billy (Kaihe) got it in the neck and in the shoulder. There were these guys sitting in the back seat. It went between them and out through the back window. They just folded straight down at that point and let the two dogs out, two big pit-bulls.

Chris had shut up by now. I brought the gun back up and put it to his head. And I said, "Now fuck off. Go now. Fuck off."

Then I saw the dogs coming. And they were coming at me so quick I only had time to just point the gun down and fire. It caught the front dog on the ear and tore the ear off and tore through the shoulder. The dog just jumped in the air, spun around and as it was leaving I could see it was dragging its leg along underneath it. And when the gun went off - BANG! - the other one just took off. They both did, down the driveway.

And Chris is standing there and he's still pretty defiant. And then the next thing I think the ricochet took over.

The "ricochet" is a theory put forward at Luke's trial. The defence called a firearms expert who claimed that all of Chris Campbell's injuries could have been caused by ammunition that ricocheted off the ground. I guess the inference was that Luke would have missed Campbell if it wasn't for the pesky ricochet. It sounded to me like a defence lawyer had dreamt it up. I said to Luke that if he was sticking to the ricochet theory then we'd resume his version of events after Chris had received his injuries.

Luke: Chris was lying on the ground. And I went over with the gun. Like, he's rolled down the hill. And he said to me, "I'm sorry, Lukic."

I said to him, "Don't fuckin' say sorry to me. You say sorry to Ruatoria. That's who you fuckin' need to say sorry to. Not me."

And, mate, even though he was turning purple, he just lifted his head and, as if there was an audience out there, towards Ruatoria, he just blurted out, "I'm sorry Ruatoria!" That's what he said.

I don't know what you can make of that. But to me it gives a little bit of credibility back to him. To me it says that he has done wrong and it is the community that he affected. And maybe he'd been brought to his knees and forced to confront the hell and the terror that he's been responsible for.

Maybe it was the start of a confession… or of conscience, I don't know but those are the words he said.

At this point Luke's mate moves away from the table to talk to someone else in the room. Instantly, Luke's face adopts a twisted, slightly-ugly expression.

He says: And um, I was just about to bash him in the head with the gun.

Surprised, I burst out laughing very loudly. (I laugh because I feel he's been lying but as soon as his mate moves away, he tells the truth.) Luke nods. My involuntary and probably inappropriate laugh seems to spur him on. And he's still got that twisted expression.

He got that out just in time because at that point I had resigned myself to going away for life. And I thought, "I'll fuckin' bash your head in. I'm not going to get any less or any more. I'll get the whole whack whether I just fuckin' smash your face in." That's what was going through my mind at the time. "I've come this far. It don't matter to me any more."

I laugh again, just as loudly. I say, "It's just as well he said it then." And Luke says: So it's just as well he said it because I was just a split second away from…

Luke describes what happened when the police turned up: Joe Campbell and all these other Rastas were over at my uncle's house about four hundred metres away and they heard all the shooting. They jumped in their car and drove over near the marae. So I was watching this carload of Rastas. Then the next thing the police rang through. My missus, she answered the phone and yelled out to me. I'd already got her to ring the police before that anyway because I had a feeling things were going to get heavy.

So they said, "We hear the Rastas are there at your house."

And she said, "Yeah. There's been some shootings. A guy's been shot." And they said, "Who was it?"

And she said, "Aw, talk to my husband."

And she called out to me, I went over, got the phone, and Rex Harrison says, "Kia ora, cuz, what's goin' on out there?"

And I told him. I said, "These bastards have come up here threatening to cut my head off."

And he said, "What's happening?"

I said, "Chris is on the ground. He's been shot. And the others are just lying in the van and they're just staying put." I said, "Billy's wounded his neck. And he's lying against the fence."

He said, "Aw, who's got the guns?"

I said, "I've got the guns."

He says, "Well, put your gun down."

I says, "No, I'm not puttin' it down. There's a carload of Rastas." And I remember saying this… I said, "If anyone shows or points a gun this way I'm gonna fuckin' let 'em have it… from here."

He says, "So what-cha got?"

I said, "I've got a 303 and it's fuckin' loaded," because I'd already emptied the shotgun. The Rastas had knives. They had two knives.

So after I'd hung up from Rex, Hemi Hikawai rung back a bit later. He was eight hundred metres away by the bridge and Rex and Chris Bunyan were coming up onto the property. And Hemi said, "Can you see Wene (Rex)?"

I said, "Yeah, yeah, I can see him."

He said, "Well, don't shoot. Don't shoot. Just be careful. That's two of the guys coming up. Nobody's got any guns. Just be calm."

I said, "Well, take those Rastas out over the other side because if I see they've got guns I'm gonna let them have it."

Next thing I see this red Falcon screaming past my gate. It was Malcolm Thomas, the detective. I think he had been helping the guys move that furniture earlier. He sped past, to the turn-off. And he pulled up just short of those Rastas. I saw a cop roll out of the car, into the drain and come up with a gun. And then Malcolm carried on past and then whipped around and came back and pulled up front-on to this Rasta car. The Rastas were locked in. They all came out and put their hands up.

So Hemi said, "Luke, that's taken care of. We're coming up now. Is that all right?"

"Yeah."

So they all came up.

Wene Harrison said, "Look, it's just me, cuz."

I put the gun on the ground. Chris Bunyan started to look at the shells. He said, "Is that empty?" pointing at the 303.

I said, "No, it's still loaded." So I picked it up and took the mag out. I had no problems with the police.

When Hemi came up I said to him, "We're not going anywhere for a while. Let's go inside. I'll get Liz to make some scones." So I said to Elizabeth as soon as we got inside, "Liz, I think you should put some scones on."

And Hemi said, "All right, sit down here."

I said, "I'm gonna have a shower first." So I just walked in, had a shower. They stood outside the door while I had a shower. And when I finished, came out, we had a cup of tea, hot scones. We had apricot jam on them.

Elizabeth was in shock. But to her credit she whipped up those scones, hot scones. I wasn't in shock. It was just like another day at the office. I was totally prepared and accepted that I might have to go to jail. And I was already making plans in my head as to what's going to happen and to make sure my family was safe.

And Hemi said, "Don't say a word to me. Don't say nothing to me." And he said, "Now, here's a number. Phone it. But I don't want to talk to you about anything."

So I phoned the number. Tony Adeane (then a lawyer, now a judge) comes on the phone. I said to Tony, "Look, I got this number to call you, Tony. I was just involved in a shooting down here. Chris Campbell's been shot. So I've been told to call you and get your advice."

And right from there, he said, "Right, this is what you say. To the police, whatever they ask you, this is all you say, nothing more…"

And he told me what to say and that was it. We went from there. It was just one sentence. And I can remember it to this day. He said, "The only statement you make is this: What I did I did to protect my family and myself." Twenty years later I can still recite it without even having to think about it.

*During the trial, Hemi Hikawai credits Donnelly with saying that line **before** he rang Adeane.*

Hikawai: The accused then asked his wife to make a cup of tea. The accused then said to me: "Hemi, I'm telling you this – what I did today I did to protect my wife and myself and my house. That was the only reason. Those bastards came up here threatening to chop my head off, drag me out and burn my house down. I warned them to stay away but all they did was say, "Cunt, we're going to drag you out now, chop your fuckin' head off and burn your house down. That fuckin' Chris Campbell was doing all the talking and those other bastards were backing him up."

At this point, I cautioned Donnelly. I told him, "You are not obliged to say anything. Anything you say may later be given in evidence. Do you understand that?" He said, "Yes." I said, "Do you wish to speak to a solicitor?" He said, "Do you think I need one? I suppose I should."

At this point a local solicitor, Mr Tony Adeane, was contacted and he then spoke with the accused Luke Donnelly. Following this conversation Donnelly said to me, "Hemi, I've got nothing to hide. However, my advice has been to say nothing more than what I have already said. I was acting in self-defence to protect my wife and myself, just like I told you."

Luke recounts how he heard that Chris had died: I wasn't in the cells because they were just holding me in custody at that stage. Then about 9 o'clock that night, they changed the charge. The first charge was just reckless discharge of a firearm. Wene (Rex) Harrison was in there with me at the Gisborne Police Station because we'd been helicoptered right out on the day.

Denis Hartley flew me out. There's a joke that Denis went the long way to get Chris to the hospital. He went sightseeing around Hikurangi Mountain on the way. People have a little laugh about that. That story's even grown legs. It's so true now that even Denis believes it. The legend's become fact.

But I remember at the time Rex said, "You better sit down."

I said, "What's happened?"

"We've just got a report from the hospital."

"How's Chris?"

"Aw, he's just died. The phone call's just come through."

And I thought, "That's not good."

Chris and I were family. And there was never any stage where we thought any different. We know what our connections are. We've got very *close* connections. And the odd thing about it is this and I've said many a time that the wrong Campbell got shot. The one that I think should have got shot is someone else. It should have been the other brother, Joe.

He was the one that kept telling me to wait until Chris got out of jail and kept telling Chris what was happening back in Ruatoria. And Chris said, "Leave Lukie to me."

That fuckin' idiot Joe is of no value to no one. Chris could've been turned around, I think. But, Joe, you can't turn that idiot around.

Luke's decision to stick with the ricochet theory caused me to wonder about other aspects of his story. For instance, I found it hard to imagine Chris saying, "I'm sorry, Ruatoria." And it bugged me. I mentioned this while on the phone to former Rasta Dion Hutana. But he seemed to think it was a possibility.

Dion Hutana, Wednesday May 19, 2010: This was before me and Eddie Kotuhi went up for our High Court trial in Gisborne for the burning of the Ngati Porou Marae. And what happened was I used to go into Chris's cell at the Hawke's Bay prison and I used to feel powerless because I could see he actually was crying. And when I walked in he'd try to be brave and stop himself because he didn't want me to see him crying. But there were just times he couldn't help himself. And it would be just flowing out. And then every now and then he would just say things like, "I've retired, Brethren. I'm retiring when I'm getting out." It was almost like he knew what he had to do. He said, "I want to go and spend time with the old people."

He felt responsible for a lot of the problems that had happened in Ruatoria and I believe that's why he was crying.

He was trying to bring a whole new direction to his Rasta movement. But he felt he was stuck on a path and it was too late.

When I would see him crying, I would want to help him. I wanted to hold him and tell him it was all right, "It's all right," because he was really, really worried for *my* life after the marae burnt. At any given time a vigilante or whoever could have just blown me away. And he realised that. And I think he took some of it on board and blamed himself.

So anyway when I was on trial, I called Chris in as a "McKenzie friend" (a layperson who assists a defendant in court). And in Gisborne the police shop was full. So they celled him up with me. And for some unknown reason we both woke up at 3 o'clock in the morning. And we did our Ringatu prayers together. So he'd say the first verse, I'd say the second. And we both noticed how free-flowing it was, no breaks. Then it was followed by a gentle silence. It wasn't a heavy silence.

Then Chris said, "Brethren, you know there's a bullet waiting for me out there?" *(Dion's inflection suggests it was half question-half statement, Chris was basically asking if Dion knew what Chris already knew.)*

And my heart sunk. I thought, "Oh no." Because I realised he was telling the truth. And I've always wondered if that bullet was meant to be for me.

I believe that the marae burning changed it all, ay. Besides all those other fires, even the churches, that one was just the biggest blow to the people of Ngati Porou.

And I suppose there had to be a pay-back. A life had to be taken, I would say. And I think the brother was more than happy to give his life, if that's what it was going to take.

I think that's another reason why I became psychologically suicidal with myself after Chris's death because I blamed myself. You know, "*I* shouldn't be alive either."

*You reckon that he took **your** bullet?*

Well, I don't know if he took *my* bullet but he *took* a bullet. I felt like, "Should it have been me?" because there was a great Ngati Porou leader's life that was lost. And I'll say it like that: he was a great Ngati Porou leader. Well, that's how I saw him. I felt that because of my actions, the Ngati Porou people had lost one of their great leaders.

And I went through that. I prayed to God every night for two years of my life to *take* my life. That's how fucked up I was. I didn't want to live any more.

There had been mention in some of the testimony in court that Chris Campbell had said sorry to Luke, but no one had mentioned him saying sorry to Ruatoria and this was still niggling. I decided to ring Bill Kaihe again. Remember, Bill was lying on the ground with Luke's foot on his head and his shotgun pellets in his shoulder during the standoff. So I figured he would have heard it if Campbell really did apologise to Ruatoria. Bill had moved away from the East Coast but I tracked him down to Waipukurau in the Hawke's Bay, where he was working in the freezing works. I read him extracts of Luke's version of events and he pretty much disagreed with everything. He said there was no apology from Chris. Why would he apologise when he was the one being shot? He said there were no threats to cut off Donnelly's head, no knives in the car and no dogs in the car either. He said there was a rumour about there being a dog in the car that surfaced at the trial and that had always confused him. Unfortunately, he may still be confused because at the trial he talked about a dog sitting in the back seat. Reece

*Bolingford did too, a bull terrier-Staffordshire cross that belonged to
Jonathan McClutchie.*

*After Bill's comments I went through the trial notes again. There
were two references to Chris saying sorry...*

Joe Ward in the depositions hearing: "He had a shotgun with
him. He came out aiming it at us and said not to fuck him around. Chris
was saying things but Donnelly wouldn't listen. Chris said he was
sorry."

Prosecutor Bruce Squire questions Joe Ward: You heard
Chris say he was hit?
Ward: Yes.
Do you remember what words he actually used?
"I've been hit."
Did he say anything else?
He just said to go and get help.
Just before the shot was fired which actually hit Chris, do you
recall anything that was said between Mr Donnelly and Chris
Campbell?
Oh Mr Campbell was saying sorry to Mr Donnelly just before he
was shot.
Do you recall whether Luke Donnelly was saying anything?
No he wasn't saying nothing.
Had you heard any earlier part of the discussion or know what it
was about, why Chris was saying sorry?
No.

*... And there were two references to two wooden-handled
butcher's knives being found in the car.*

**Donnelly trial notes, Constable Quentin Hollis, about items
he found on December 7, 1990:** At 11.09 I took possession of a
wooden handled knife from the left hand passenger's side of the station
wagon... At 11.14am I took possession of another wooden handled knife
found on the right hand side, the driver's side, of the Holden station
wagon.

The knife on the passenger's side was underneath some stuff on the floor. The other was underneath the driver's seat.

Detective Chris Bunyan questioned by P W Cooper for the prosecution: If you look at that photograph of the side of the seat can you see the seat-adjuster lever?

Yes.

Was the handle of the knife sticking out underneath the seat, just below that?

Yes...

...Was that knife able to be easily removed?

No.

What was the situation there?

It was reasonably tightly wedged in that position, and took some effort to remove...

... How would you describe that condition?

Old. Rusty. Dusty.

CHAPTER 3

QUESTIONS AND ANSWERS

Email from author to Luke Donnelly on Sunday, June 20, 2011:
Hi Luke,

I know it all happened a long time ago and the memory can get hazy, but I just wanted to check a couple of things.

When you told me the story, you mentioned you were clearing thorns with a machete. When I was reading it back I found myself asking, why did you go for the shotgun when you had a machete. I figured readers would be wondering why you just didn't approach the Rastas with the machete?

You mentioned two dogs. At the trial only one dog was mentioned. Are you sure there were two dogs? It's a small point but worth checking.

And in your version it sounds like you put the gun to Chris's head from close range, but in the trial notes it sounds like you were quite a way away from him. Neither version is all that clear. Can you clarify that for me please?

Also, I won't send volume three just yet because I'm still reading through it. And I'd want to factor in what you say in these answers, too.

Cheers,

Angus

Email from author to Luke Donnelly on Monday, June 21, 2011:
Hi Luke,

There are two other things I need to put to you. There are two elements that, to me, don't ring true in the story. The first is that Chris Campbell issued an immediate order for the Rastas to chop your head off. The two knives in the Rasta car don't seem like they would have done the job. It seemed like the Rastas didn't even know they were there. One was old and rusty and dusty and had been jammed in under the seat for years. I can imagine it's possible that they issued threats to cut your head off, but the immediate order just sounds a bit clunky.

Also, from what I've read and heard about Chris I really can't imagine him shouting out, "I'm sorry, Ruatoria!" I accept that he said, "I'm sorry." But the whole bit about, "I'm sorry, Ruatoria!" seems out of character.

I know how these stories change over the years in your mind. I love telling a story about getting the breaking news about the death of Osama Bin Laden on TV as soon as possible and I find myself embellishing it in every telling. I know you were telling me the story that you probably tell all the time. But cast your mind back to what exactly happened.   Was there an immediate order or just a general threat? And did Chris actually yell out, "I'm sorry, Ruatoria."?

I know this is a hassle but I just want to get it as close as possible to the truth.

Cheers,

Angus

Email from Luke to the author on Tuesday, June 21, 2011:
Dear Angus,

I am attaching a brief in response to your email as a gesture of good faith due to my valued friendship with your dad and your brother John for whom I have the highest regard.

For a seasoned "wordsmith" I sense a level of doubt by you, in my integrity to remember what happened on that fateful day. I feel you're bent on how it should be is at odds with what I am saying.

I'm sorry that you are having doubts as to my version of events and disappointed that there is an undercurrent of disbelief by you. Though you have not been brazen enough to suggest that I have "embellished" the events to some degree, my read between the lines suggests that you are doubtful of my recollection of events.

Nevertheless my friend, I will still send you the attachment herein but this is the last time I will discuss this matter or any more of the events to do with your book.

When I received your first email yesterday I analysed your queries and almost chose to ignore it, but today's email from you confirmed for me the discomfort of what I felt yesterday. So here is most of what you wanted and I don't think it matters what I say, you have your perspective of how it should be and I know the facts as to what happened that fateful day. Only I know, not even the other Rastas who were there, with their noses in the dirt or hiding away, can recall the detail that I know, even the trial didn't bring to the fore anymore than 40% of what happened.

One thing for certain is this, they weren't so fucken brave or as noisy as they were 5 minutes earlier once I stood my ground and made it clear I was not going to run or hide away waiting for no fucken police to come.

Cheers,

God Bless your whanau and yourself,

Luke Donnelly

Attachment:

Luke Donnelly <u>recollection</u>

Hi Angus,

Machete

1.	No I didn't say anything about clearing thorns with a machete, I wasn't out there that day for that reason.

2.	I always carried a machete in the event of the need, while out on the farm, to chip out ragwort, bracken, thorns, etc.

3.	I told you that I had just finished an interview with Ron Taylor from the NZ Herald.

4.	I told you that I walked to open the gate at the bottom of the drive, and then walked on further towards the Makarika Turnoff to drive some sheep back.

5.	On getting the sheep back through the gate, off the road, I was walking back up the driveway when I saw their station wagon coming down the Makarika Road.

6.	Elizabeth was hand feeding the horses when they went past the gate yelling out profanities shaking their fists out the car window, general acts of arseholes, etc.

7.	I gave them the fingers, you know the usual piss off stuff and they backed up to the gate and drove up my drive. This is all documented in the trial notes.

8.	When the car got up to where I was, Chris got out and walked towards me, threatening and ranting about me bashing up the bros while he was in prison, now he's back to sort me out, all that big time hero gonna sort out Luke Donnelly.

9.	Angus, I told you that I thought it was going to be a one on one fight.

10.	I took my shirt off and the machete at the same time.

11.	I never thought of using the machete as a means of defence at that point, I didn't need to, I thought it was gonna be just him and I.

12.	I remember thinking at the time, "You arrogant prick, thinking you can do what the fuck you want, and shit on whoever you want," just roll up and think everyone's gonna just bend over and be fucked over by him.

13.   I thought, "Ok you fucken cocky bastard, let's see how fucken good you are."

14.   I knew I was going to kick his head in, and I had no doubt that if it was a one on one scrap, that he would lose, I was fit as, I was training and used to run up the hill behind the house at least 4 times a week after working, and just survey the beauty of the valley. Our fucken valley that these bastards turned into shadows of hate.

15.   He was trying to be a big shot while he had mates around him to give himself backup.

16.   For a moment I feared they were all likely to mob me but the chance to smash this bastard over real good was there on a plate.

17.   He was frothing at the mouth and full of tough talk, gonna do this, gonna do that.

18.   I just told him, "Well here's your fucken chance, you piece of shit", "let's do it".

19.   I moved towards him when I had my shirt off and that is when he said to those fuckheads, "cut his fuckin head off",

20.   Then to me, he said, "I'm gonna bury you over there with your old lady," meaning my deceased mother, over in the family cemetery.

21.   When he encouraged them to get involved I had a feeling he was fucken uncertain of his chances of any victory over me.

22.   So there it is Angus. Print that if you want, I don't give a fuck mate whether it rings true or not. That's about the gist of what happened and as for the "sorry Ruatorea" that is fact, what he said.

Dogs

1.   There were 2 dogs in their car,

2.   When Chris told them to set the dogs on to me, the white bull Staffordshire ran towards me and I told you that I didn't even have time to line it up in the gun sights, when I pulled the trigger.

3.   It's not hard to shoot and hit a dog that is within a couple a metres of you when the bullet is pellets spread.

4.   Only one dog got shot in the side of the head and shoulder, when the white injured dog ran off the other one just followed it.

Gun at Head

1.   My version is my version.

At this point, my correspondence with Luke took a dramatic turn for the worse.

My next email to him started: "Jesus Christ Luke! There are always going to be different versions of stuff. It seems to me you won't be happy unless you're portrayed riding into town on a white steed with a white stetson on your head!"

And he came back just as hard. It would be unfair to repeat some of the more full-on bits. But I'm going to quote two excerpts. Luke's comments may give the reader an opportunity to pause and question the veracity of everything I've written – and they've read – so far. I started to subedit Luke's grammar because usually his grammar is pretty good, but in the end it seemed more authentic to leave it as he'd written it because he was obviously just belting it out in a stream of consciousness sort of way. (The John referred to is my elder brother).

Luke Donnelly: *If i was dealing with john, he would never have got us into this position cos i know that john would have come clean on his views, whatever they were, from the outset.*

Its you that didnt come clean with me in the first place, choosing to hold back what you really thought of me. It appears now that the real motive and your true feelings were to get me to spill my guts.

You continued to befriend my decency and when you thought you had exhausted what i had to contribute, then you scrolled away your real thoughts about where you placed me. It is clear that you see me as a murderer, while a whole jury of my peers think otherwise. I had a fair trial and i didnt ask for no favors from no one, i didnt beg for any special treatment when i stood trial, i was fastidious in my resolve and i instructed my lawyer from day one, quote "i want no favors Les, i will take whatever comes, i stand by what Ive done and i will take whatever the penalty (good or bad) when it comes. I shook his clammy palm and he was shaking uncontrollably at the time.

Luke Donnelly: If my child or wife or family are at risk , then i don't give a shit, they will need to go over me before i run for the hills mate. Angus I just hope you or your children, wife or someone close to you doesn't ever have to make that same decision i had to on the day. If they ever do, remember how you have treated me my friend, what will your approach be, given that you know the history may be similar to what i had to decide on.

At times like that , whatever your decision is , needs to be decided in a matter of seconds. That day was always going to be a fateful day for one of us Angus, I know now that one of us would die that day. I think i was mentally prepared for that cos i spoke with my wife about the possibilities of it. but i also know that i was physically prepared to fight to the death, if only to protect myself and my family.

My 6 year old girl Jesse would have been home 15 minutes later, and to this day i wonder about alot of things , including her crying over my dead mutilated body had i been a weaker man and tried to turn the other cheek. Who knows, you may have been interviewing Chris by now...

CHAPTER 4

CHRIS'S VERSION OF WHAT HAPPENED

*Of course, it's too late for me to interview Chris. But Detective Dave Neilson interviewed him in the Accident and Emergency Department at Gisborne Hospital, while he waited to go into surgery. The interview was ruled inadmissable as evidence in Luke Donnelly's trial because Neilson believed he was interviewing the victim of an **attempted** homicide, not an actual homicide.*

I made all sorts of efforts to get hold of this interview. I asked police and wrote to court staff in Gisborne urging them to look through their archives, to no avail. I wrote to the Ministry of Justice, but they couldn't help. I was wondering whether I could consider this book complete without the interview and I had a really uneasy feeling about it. But I wasn't even sure whether a copy of the interview still existed. I was about to ring Dave Neilson to see if he still had a copy when I thought I'd have one last look through some big plastic containers full of files, documents and clippings I'd amassed over the years. There, right at the bottom of the last container, was a copy of the interview! I can't even remember who gave it to me.

Detective Dave Neilson's hand-written notes of his interview with Chris Campbell just before Campbell went into surgery:

4/12/90 1848: Speak with Chris Campbell Gisborne Hospital A & E Dept.

I.S: Who shot you, Chris?

H.S: We were driving past Luke Donnelly's place and Luke was waving out for me to come up to his place. We had just been for a swim at the swimming hole. Luke was waving at me to come towards him.

Wednesday (Rex) Harrison said a driveway was a public place so I decided to go up the drive to see what he wanted. At the top of the drive Luke wasn't there so I called out, Luke, where are you?

Luke then came from the back of his house. He came out with a shotgun and shot the window of the car, the front window.

He said he should kill me for starting all the fires and troubles at Ruatoria. Luke then shot me with the shotty in the left leg. I fell down kneeling. He also shot me in the right hand/arm.

I fell down and he shot Billy Kaihe in the shoulder, I think. I think Harley got hit and Joe Ward.

Then Luke yelled out to his missus to bring the 303. She brung it. He called out to her to Bring the Belt.

I was down kneeling. I had one hand in the air.

He shot me in the leg with the 303.

He then shot me in the right hand before that with the shotgun. When I was hit with the 303 my leg gave out and I fell down the bank behind the car that I was sheltering behind.

He said to me, What if I shoot you in the foot.

I said, Do me a favour, shoot me in the head.

I fell down the bank and the chopper picked me up.

He then started on Billy.

He said to Billy, What the fuck are you doing here? You're my whanau.

Billy said that he was just driving the car.

I could hear him kick Billy in the head. He's a bad man.

I.S: Did you threaten Luke at any stage when you went up the drive?

H.S: No.

I.S: So when you were driving past Luke's place you said you saw him in the driveway.

H.S: He was at the bottom of his drive waving at me to come towards him.

We had been swimming and when I saw him gesturing me to come here I drove on, got Billy to drive up the drive to his house. When we got to the top of the drive he wasn't there. I then got out of the car and called out, Luke, where are you? And that's when he came out and opened up with the shotgun. The first shot hit the windscreen and then he shot me in the leg.

Note: At this stage Campbell lapsed into unconsciosness. Had lost a lot of blood. Became delirious.

Campbell stated that when Luke had shot him he said to Luke, Let's finish it here. I'll forgive you what you have done. We won't involve the police. I'll forgive you for what you have done to me and we'll end it. This was said while lapsing in and out of consciousness.

Chris said that Billy Kaihe was shot in the shoulder.

I.S: Have there been any threats made by either one of you, you or Luke.

H.S: We had a bit of a row the other day and the cops turned up.

I.S: What was that over?

H.S: Domestics, I think.

I.S: Did it have anything to do with the buildings down Whareponga that got burnt?

H.S: Yea, that and the land down there and he reckoned that I had started all the trouble in Ruatoria. I told him, How could I? I've just come out of jail. He then told me that I take it up the arse and that's what got me going.

I.S: Did that make you angry when he said that, Chris?

H.S: Yea.

I.S: Where did this incident take place?

H.S: At my brother's place.

I.S: Joe Boots Campbell.

H.S: Yea.

I.S: Was he at his place when this incident took place?

H.S: Yea, when I got there him and Boots was having an argument.

I.S: When you were shot, how many shots did Luke fire?

H.S: The first one went into the windscreen. I was the only one out of the car. The others were still in the car. Then I got the next shot. Then I think he shot Billy. Then the next one was me again in the hand and then I got the 303 in the leg and that was me finished.

I.S: What happened next?

H.S: I think there was a couple more fired and then he fired some at the brethren running away.

I.S: Are you prepared to come to court to give evidence against Luke after what he has done to you?

H.S: I'll have to think about that. Actually, I think so because he's becoming a bit of a danger to the whanau.

I.S: So the first shot got you in the left leg.

H.S: That's right. I was on my knees. He shot me from about 50 feet away. He told me to put my hands in the air. I had my hands in the air and he shot me in the hand. I went down holding my hand and more or less straight after he shot me in the leg with the 303.

You guys better lock him up for his own good because someone will be going to take a pot shot at him.

I.S: Who, the Rastafarians?

H.S: There will be a few upset people after what's happened to me, not only the Rastas but the whanau as well.

Campbell taken to theatre 1950 hours.

1950: Take possession Campbell's boots, go to theatre to obtain possession of Campbell's clothing from theatre staff. Campbell lying on top of clothing he was wearing.

Theatre

2045 hrs: Receive from Pam Morrison, nurse manager, Campbell's clothing.

Return to Gisborne station with Campbell's clothing.

Advise D/Snr/Sgt Kane of Campbell's injuries & details of what Campbell said.

2140: Mr Iain Kelman rings to advise that Campbell has died under anaesthetic.

Mr Kelman was asked if he could comment or ascertain what Campbell died from. Mr Kelman states that he is not prepared to speak about the matter to police at this stage as a hospital inquiry will be conducted.

2235: Secure Campbell's clothing exhibits in CIB exhibit room and retain key.

2320: Arrive Gisborne Hospital. Speak with security officer Laurie Ford re securing Chris Campbell in hospital chiller.

Obtain key to hospital mortuary.

2325: Place Campbell/Chris in small police mortuary chiller. Secure chiller door with padlock and retain key.

2335: Leave hospital.

Kelman wouldn't speak to Neilson because "a hospital inquiry will be conducted". But David McLean, who was general manager of the hospital, was later quoted saying, "There was no inquiry whatsoever." He said the circumstances didn't warrant any inquiry.

About the same time Neilson was talking to Campbell, a reporter from The Dominion Sunday Times spoke to the duty doctor at Gisborne Hospital.

The reporter asked about Campbell's condition and was told it was stable.

Question: So there's no chance you will lose him?

Doctor: No, no chance of that.

CHAPTER 5

REACTIONS TO CHRIS'S DEATH

Sarah Sykes is on holiday in Kawerau. She hears on the radio news that a Ruatoria farmer has shot a Rastafarian leader who was coming on to his property. "Oh no!" she thinks. "Luke's shot Chris! Ian was supposed to be working at Luke's today. I hope he's all right." She picks up the phone and starts to dial.

Gradually, Ian realises that the phone ringing in his dream is actually a phone ringing in his living room. He drags his consciousness awake and glances at the time. Shit! He's lost hours. Luke will have already moved the sheep. He won't be happy. And fair enough. Ian picks up the phone. It's Sarah. And it's obvious she's never been so overjoyed and relieved to hear his voice. She tells him what she heard on the radio. Jesus! It's a shock. But then again, things have been simmering so long.

Sarah asks why he didn't go to work at Luke's and Ian tells her what happened.

"You lucky man, Ian Sykes," she thinks. "You were taken out."

She says, "You were stopped from going there."

"Whadya mean?"

"You were put to sleep by the tipuna because you weren't meant to be at Luke's today. That's why I'm in Kawerau. We were kept out of the way."

Laurel Hillock, former nurse at Gisborne Hospital, wife of Lyn Hillock, Gisborne Deputy Fire Chief: There's a pre-Christmas party up at John Kyngdon the surgeon's place. I'm working for him at the time. That's the night Chris Campbell's brought in.

He's brought into Gisborne Hospital A and E and then taken to theatre. John Kyngdon isn't the surgeon on call. But we're up at his place having this party and he gets called away. It's actually a small party so there's only a few of us there. So when he comes back Lyn asks him, "Aw, how'd it go?"

And, of course, he can't say too much. But he says, "Aw, it's not good."

Later we find out that he actually died on the table.

Lyn Hillock: When I hear Chris Campbell's died I go back up the party at John Kyngdon's place. John comes in and says that Chris has sort of stepped off the planet and I'm just, "Yahoo!" and I hook into another beer.

The funniest thing is when Denis Hartley radios in and asks if I can give him a hand to clean up the helicopter because there's a fair bit of blood about. I say, "Yeah, not a problem." So he lands it in the backyard of the fire station.

I take the old stretcher out of the helicopter, then I go straight back into the station and get a couple of big bottles of Janola. And Denis says, "What are ya doin'?"

And I say, "Well this bastard's got Hep B, HIV, God knows what the arsehole's got. I'm not cleanin' this helicopter unless I'm using bleach, mate."

So the helicopter ends up stinking of Janola for about three days. It's the best cleaning job we've ever done.

Ike Campbell, Chris's brother: If you ask me the police used Luke. But he's so dumb he didn't realise. But sooner or later he'll spill the beans. Give him enough rope and he'll hang himself.

Former Rasta Dion Hutana: I remember the day he was shot. We were all in Mangaroa Prison. And we'd heard that someone had been shot on the news. We wasn't sure who, ay. But out of everyone, I knew it was Chris. Because everyone was saying, "Na, it wouldn't be the brother. It wouldn't be him." But in my heart I knew. I was saying, "Na, I think it's the brother, Chris, bros."

So we all got locked up that night and I felt it, ay, as I was lying there. I knew Chris was dead.

We all got unlocked the next morning cos every morning we used to go to John Heeney's house and have a prayer session. We used to pray together. And they unlocked John and then John came around quickly and told us, "Aw, I got some news to tell you."

So we all went in the room and John says again, "I've got some news to tell yous."

And when he told us I was already prepared. John Heeney broke down as soon as he told us that the brother had died on the operating table. Everyone broke down and cried. And I was the only one who didn't. I was the only one who didn't cry. I actually stopped them. I said, "Hey, I think we gotta stop this, ay, because I think if the brother Chris was alive or if he's up there, I think he would rather us carry on and be strong." And I think there was a lot of resentment towards me because I didn't cry and because I said that.

But John Heeney said, "Bro, you're right. He would've wanted us to carry on as if he was right here with us."

I said, "Exactly."

I'm only talking from my own experience, but it seemed there was such an emptiness for all of us.

Chris had passed over the leadership of the Rastas to John Heeney before he got out. I can tell you this cos Chris told me that he did that cos when he got out he just wanted to retire. He didn't want to be involved in any of the things any more. All that stuff that had gone on before, he didn't want any of that to happen any more. Like, he was out. And he felt the best way for that to happen was to just retire and go live peacefully by himself somewhere. The sad thing about it is he was only out for forty days and he was murdered.

I don't believe for one minute that Luke Donnelly acted in self-defence. I don't. Even though I wasn't there and I didn't see nothing, I can only go by hearsay, but I know deep in my heart it was his intention to kill him.

You just have to look at the interview that was on Holmes the week before that happened. Luke Donnelly was on TV and if you could read between the lines you could see that he intended to do something to Chris.

Rasta John Heeney: The biggest moment of that whole time for me is the moment of greatest hate. When I think about how Chris died I realise how much I hate those things we're up against. Everyone wants to go the way of the pale face. They're prepared to see their culture go down the river just so their bank account can go up to the roof, I suppose.

Because there's a compromise. With this way of life you've got to compromise and weigh it all up and say either yea or nay. You go this way or the other way. That other way of life, that's a nine to five sort of a thing.

But I and I just close the door on them. "Na." Disconnect. Want out of that. I don't want to be part of a system that does ugly things to people like that (beating and killing Rastas) and get cleared off and everyone forgets about it. Our brothers' lives ain't that cheap.

So when those things do happen it just makes us more dug in there, more entrenched because there are more things hung on the hearts, pictures of our wars in our hearts, pictures of our brothers are building up and they're still calling out. But you know what for? They want justice. But it can't be like Abel, when he got murdered. And his blood called out to God, "Give me a chance cos my brother murdered me and got away with it." And he was wanting utu, he was wanting revenge, Abel. But like Chris when he dies and his blood gets spilt he's talking forgiveness, ay. His blood gets sprinkled to forgive. He wants peace. He says he has to take on the role of peacemaker.

That's what he says when he gets out of prison. And what's he been in there for? Armed robbery, kidnapping Laurie.

Donna Heeney (John's wife): Actually, I reckon he's still the same when he gets out of prison. He's worse actually.

John: Yeah. He is. Hee, hee, hee, hee, hee. He's a full-face warrior when he comes out. He wasn't a full-faced brave when he went in. When he comes out he's deeper, ay. He's met a lot of important men in prison, from inside and outside. All the big-wigs from Maoridom were coming in to Pare to, "Bro, te mea, te mea." And the funny thing was a lot of the old people were saying to a lot of the inmates, "You people should get what that fulla got on his face. Get one of those things what he's got on. Put a moko on. And stand up and go hard."

He got the moko from a junkie. No one wanted this junkie to do it cos he was shaking so much. No one trusted him on the face. But he did a masterful job. You couldn't fault one line on Chris's moko. And if you look at all that guy's other work, beautiful work, ay. His spirit came through and the spirit of the moko came through and guided him because a man's blood is being spilt, the sword is going through his house.

But with Chris, after he died, if we'd charged straight in they would have blown us away too. And what good is it if we're all dead? See? They would win. They would have it their way. They would have got rid of the main big mouths, ay. And we couldn't afford that because if Chris wanted us to do that he would've come out with the theme of war from the start.

Hemi Hikawai: If Luke Donnelly's to be believed then, mate, with the awesome reputation that they had, he could well have been fearing for his own safety and the safety of his wife. You got to bear in mind that they'd already beheaded one of their own crew and that also they'd nearly killed another person, also they'd cut all these fences and killed so much stock. They were just a law unto themselves. If he genuinely believed he was in danger and if it was as he said it occurred then you can't blame him. But as to who you believe retrospectively...

But there was little sympathy for the Rastas. That was demonstrated at the trial when, despite the fact that Campbell was shot several times and there was evidence he was unarmed, they still let Luke go. The public of Gisborne had frankly just had enough of the Rastafarians and it was virtually open season on them.

It was terrible the way Chris Campbell died. But things have been relatively quiet in Ruatoria since then. Campbell's gone and a lot of those main characters are still up there. And there are no more fires. There are no more fences cut. As far as I'm aware, since Heeney did that spell in jail he hasn't done anything else. And you look at guys like Cody Haua, since he came out of jail for that kidnapping; never been in jail as far as I'm aware after that… because they were long spells that they did inside.

Wiki Haua, Cody Haua's nephew: Chris's death was out of it for me. I took it well considering how much I looked up to him, not for the incidents that he was involved in but more for his strength and the respect he treated me with, like I was his son. There was more anger because in my mind he was set up. But at the same time I somehow thought that it was bound to happen sooner or later so I wasn't entirely surprised. Things went a bit quieter for a while for us. I think that had a lot to do with Uncle Cody pulling back a bit. He lost his best mate among the brothers so he pulled away a little. I heard that uncle had some rough times with some of the Rastas a few years after the death of Chris. I haven't heard the exact story yet but one day it'll come out.

Gordon Sutton, childhood friend of Chris's: I was in Gisborne when I heard it on the TV news that Christopher Campbell had been shot and rushed to the hospital. And there was a lot of controversy around that as well. Like, what the hell are they doing letting him bleed to death? The guy's been shot a few times. And there are all these delays to treating him. And he's still bleeding. Like it's, Hey, what's going on here, mate? Are you guys waiting for him to die? Is this a set-up? What happened in the start? Questions are asked. The eyebrows rise. Why did Luke shoot him? Who organised this? Who's given old Luke a few dollars to shoot our mate? That's the sort of stuff that was being asked by people who knew Chris and were close to him. There was controversy all over the place.

Former Detective Sergeant Laurie Naden (Chris had been jailed for kidnapping Naden): I never saw Chris when he got out of prison. I was on my way to Wanganui the day he got shot. Gary Condon and I had gone over on a police bowls tournament and we heard it on the radio in a Dannevirke pub. We were having a beer in there and we heard that Chris had been shot.

I've gotta be honest, when I found out how he'd been shot I was pissed off. I know he'd caused so much trouble. But it was the way he'd been shot that concerned me. I think he was shot at least three times. And I think that's going a little bit far to scare someone off your property. I know that might sound silly because once he died that removed all the problems from Ruatoria, well, *most* of the problems from Ruatoria. But I had nothing to do with that inquiry.

From what I heard he was starting to stir things up again and I suppose Luke did the community a hell of a big favour. But is a person's life worth bloody peace and quiet?

I had a strange reaction actually. A potential trouble-maker had been removed which meant that the cops didn't have to go running to Ruatoria all the bloody time and the people up there were probably going to be a lot happier. But it was the way that he was shot that concerned me.

Email from former Sergeant Nigel Hendrikse: Whether you like Luke or not (he and I certainly had our disagreements and I remember Rana phoning me from Gisborne only a few minutes after I'd left Luke's place, cos he'd phoned Rana and complained about me) we cannot deny that the only thing that took the wind out of their sails was the death of Chris.

I liked Chris, I found him to be articulate and amusing. (I don't think he meant me to find him amusing but all the rambling about Mt Zion and demons and Johnny Too Bad and steedless chariots, but he was only a PAWN IN SOMEONE ELSE'S GAME. I am so pleased that the someone else is mentioned many times, particularly by Bob Kaa, a highly respected and respectable man.)

Poor old Chris knew darn well that the Parole Board were watching him when he came out of prison, but he was torn between living up to the expectations of the Parole Board or his boys, who had for so long said to us cops, "You just wait till Chris gets out, he'll sort all this out." Hmmmm.

(The someone else Hendrikse is referring to is Sue Nikora, an early influence on the Rastas, who got them fired up about land grievances.)

Wednesday, December 5, 1990, The Gisborne Herald, under the headline A high-profile leader...: The man widely regarded as the leader of Ruatoria's Rastafarian group, Christopher Campbell, died in Gisborne last night.

Released from jail just a few weeks ago after serving four years for kidnapping an Armed Offender Squad officer, Campbell was the high-profile character in the group – a spokesman during many court hearings in the mid to late 1980s who was quick to allege sinister plots, cultural repression and religious persecution.

He had a skill as an orator that coloured and lengthened the earlier trials of Rastafarian members. But after a manhunt in the bush behind Ruatoria in 1986, Christopher Campbell faced charges of kidnap, using a firearm to avoid arrest, threatening grievous bodily harm, aggravated robbery, theft of a police radio and theft of a gas grenade.

This incident, in which he held Detective Sergeant Laurie Naden hostage at gunpoint to assist escape into the bush, cost him a seven-year jail sentence.

He was sentenced amid threats that he would not eat again, alleging unfairness during his trial.

The focus of the Rastafarian issue shifted away from Campbell during his four years in jail. But his influence and leadership are said to have continued from within prison. And in October of this year he was released to appear in Gisborne District Court as a "McKenzie friend" on behalf of two Rastafarians on trial for setting fire to a Ngati Porou meeting house and Manutahi Hotel.

Christopher Campbell was 34, the son of a local Ruatoria family.

CHAPTER 6

LAID TO REST

Wednesday, December 5: *A pathologist has been brought to Gisborne today to conduct a post-mortem examination. Donnelly appeared in the Gisborne District Court this morning. A police presence, including Armed Offenders Squad members, was maintained in Ruatoria overnight. Police have moved Donnelly's wife Elizabeth and her seven-year-old daughter, Jess, to Gisborne for safety.*

Thursday, December 6: *Police Minister John Banks asks local police Superintendent Rana Waitai for a report on Luke Donnelly's shooting of Chris Campbell.*

"It is of utmost concern to me that this shooting has taken place," he says. "I am also concerned with and aware of the complete frustration of law-abiding citizens and their apparent inability to live their lives in peace."

Meanwhile Eastern Maori MP Peter Tapsell, Ngati Porou leader Apirana Mahuika and East Cape MP Tony Ryall have asked Ruatoria people to keep cool heads and to leave the issue in the hands of police.

A memorial service is held in Gisborne for Chris Campbell before his body is driven back to Ruatoria. The Rastafarian presence at the service is strong. Filming is clearly not welcomed and the atmosphere at Te Aowera Marae, where Campbell's funeral will be held next Saturday, has turned hostile towards the media.

Police complete their scene examination and the house is released back to Luke Donnelly's family and friends, who begin to secure the property and its contents. The property will continue to be guarded while the situation in Ruatoria remains volatile.

The mood remains quite tense. Many people are depressed and are reacting angrily to the media spotlight. However the town's own media has also been involved. Radio Ngati Porou held a talkback session on the issue. A Rastafarian and a mother of Rastafarians were among those who spoke on air. The talkback was described as "a quite positive session".

Monday, December 10: An appeal has been launched to raise funds for Luke Donnelly.

One of the organisers says it will be known as the Luke Donnelly Appeal. A group of about five or six people decided to set up the appeal. Already Donnelly has been forced to spend eight thousand dollars to shift his stock and furniture from his home at Makarika, where the shooting occurred.

"I've never met the guy, but I feel he deserves to be helped," says the organiser.

Saturday, December 15, 1990: There's a huge turnout for Chris Campbell's funeral at Te Aowera Marae. He is buried at the cemetery there.

Gordon Sutton: The first thing that hit me at Chris's funeral was that I've never seen so many priests at a tangi. Every Maori priest on the Coast was there. And there were so many people there. The whole of Ruatoria was there. It was amazing because the feeling I got from a lot of people was that Chris was hated. And then to get a turn out from so many people, like it's probably one of the biggest tangis ever at Ruatoria. Thousands were there. It was packed. The only thing that was missing was the media. That's one thing the family made clear is they didn't want any media there.

It was like a little Bob Marley funeral, mate. I remember reading a book about Bob Marley's funeral and they reckon everyone was lying in the streets and things like that. I imagine it would have been a bigger version of Chris's funeral.

A lot of people have got a lot of bad things to say about Chris and a lot of people have got a lot of good things to say about him. I've just got my opinion about him from knowing him before he went up there. And like every time I saw him as a Rastafarian, he didn't seem to have changed that much at all.

Former Senior Sergeant Alan Davidson: I know that Chris had said to people that he'd done his jail term and that he'd had enough. "These idiots can play their silly games but I'm not going back." And I know he made that quite clear.

At the same time there were certain things that he wanted in life, and number one was to smoke his hooch. But he was such an enigmatic character that I, deep down, felt that he would not be able to drift into the background. While he was present they had a cause. And when his presence went, the cause fell away.

"BITTERNESS... BEHIND THE SCENES"

New Zealand Herald reporter Ron Taylor makes some insightful observations in an article for the newspaper.

Taylor writes: It has been caused by the depression affecting the whole country, but made worse by the deliberate rundown of the state's East Coast forestry resources.

Created decades ago with the objective of providing jobs, the forests fell into disrepute under the profit-driven criteria of the Labour Government. As a result, the resource has stagnated and the social consequences have compounded. Now the region faces a downturn in horticulture.

For the whole of the Gisborne region the unemployment rate hovers around 10 per cent of the working age population of 53,000. That's bad enough. But in the rural areas centred on little settlements like Ruatoria, more than 80 per cent are out of a job and receiving the dole or some other benefit. Benefit day is peak of the week when there's a spark of life in these rural communities.

Crime is endemic. The only "growth" industry is marijuana...

...Into this environment inject the Rastafarians and other gang elements.

Taylor quotes Gisborne Superintendent Rana Waitai: "The bitterness has always been there but you (Pakeha) don't hear about it. We hear it in the cookhouses, in the dining rooms and behind the scenes.

"What has been misread to be a happy smiling race has in fact been smiling on the surface while all the discontent and sense of failure has curdled away. We have been living in a fool's paradise.

"You can't have people with a feeling of oppression whether it be economic or social. We've bred a large number of our young population like that. They've become acclimatised to the notion of not having to go to work, not being meaningful participants in the community, seeing no future for themselves.

"They are becoming embittered and it's just a matter of time before a most undesirable form of leadership does emerge.

"As a society we're in for a great deal of trouble if we don't do something about a sizable investment into an infrastructure of employment and education. Forestry would appear to be the best bet for that with all its flow on into the community. It's going to cost an awful lot initially, but the alternative is chaos."

In the article, Taylor also quotes Ngati Porou Runanga boss Api Mahuika, who says there's one aspect of the Ruatoria troubles that the wider world hasn't caught on to. He says the trouble is not anti-European, although Pakeha farmers within the community have been embroiled along with Maori landowners. And Mahuika also appears to take a dig at Sue Nikora – an elder relative of many of the Rastas - and her supporters.

Api Mahuika: "If it was anti-Pakeha, why are Maori shooting Maori and kin shooting kin? It's whanau (family). It's got nothing to do with race. It's got everything to do with the misinterpretations, which were fed into them when they were young, of the land tenure system, which was ours traditionally, and the new system. And the perpetrators of that are still there.

"Of course you get these young minds and it gives them an excuse to trample all over other people because, as they say to us, 'we are tangata whenua, it is ours just as it is yours because we were told so because the Treaty of Waitangi says so.' And from there you get the problem.

"Their teachers were telling them that six or seven years ago and that's what it's all about. They used it as an excuse for their behaviour and lifestyle.

"It's no longer on. I just want to make sure that nobody else gets shot."

Ron Taylor's article: There are also moves afoot to get some land back for the Rastafarians and the wider Maori community.

Rana Waitai has been working on that behind the scenes with Api Mahuika, who began discussing the plan with Chris Campbell last year while he was still in prison.

Luke Donnelly: Rana said to me that I had fucked up this deal that he had organised: eighty grand in cash was going to them in Social Welfare funds and a hundred acres at Waipiro Bay. They were gonna get that land to grow their dope. But they could've done that on ten acres.

Ron Taylor's article continues: "I made 47 visits to Chris when nobody else bothered to go near him," says Mahuika.

"At first I was abused but I just sat it out… gradually there was change. But, as I said to the parole board, a lot will depend on the wider community response.

"We are pursuing the issue for land not only with the Maori trustee but others because I believe they (the Rastafarians) need their own patch so they can do the thing they want to do and leave the community alone – and the community can leave them alone.

"Once we reach that stage then we can start building bridges."

He says politicians can't escape much of the blame for what's happened and the events at Ruatoria are a microcosm of what could happen on a wider scale.

When forestry was there, the community didn't have major problems because there was work and a lot of the troublesome had age peers who were able to move among them to keep sanity. They moved away when the work stopped. With them went rationale.

Mahuika's runanga, in partnership with the Gisborne City Council, has started negotiating to buy state forestry assets to give the wider community purpose and bring back a sense of achievement. But it has been frustrated each time. The forests are remote and difficult to serve, and getting the timber out to market from the East Coast will be costly.

On that basis, the argument has been that the state should be realistic in setting a price, just as it was when the trees were planted decades ago to create jobs.

The social gain should be taken into account as much as the dollar in the Government's coffers. So far the argument's been lost, but there's renewed hope with National defeating Labour in the recent election and a new breed in the Beehive.

"I want to resolve the problem in the community because I've got kids growing up, grandchildren growing up, and they're part of that community," says Mahuika. "I want a legacy for them that they have a peaceful and united community."

Friday, December 21, 1990: Luke Donnelly is granted bail by Mr Justice Henry at the Auckland High Court. He will appear in court again (in May) for the taking of depositions.

Friday, December 28, 1990: Police Minister John Banks says cabinet must discuss ways of getting Ruatoria's Rastafarians "off the marijuana and on to the shovel".

Banks said after a visit to the East Coast that the "unprecedented lawlessness" of the Rastafarians needed to be addressed by the cabinet.

"Ruatoria has witnessed an execution, torture, stand-over tactics, arson on a grand scale and is a community held to ransom."

Banks says he'd rather see the Rastafarians working than locked up in jail. "Individually some will work and others are not the slightest bit interested in contributing, but the Maori leadership here believes that collectively they can and would work.

"The cost of getting them working is much less than the social cost of letting them destroy themselves with marijuana and idleness... These people have no direction, no purpose and spend most of their time stoned out of their brains. The Maori community is saying 'enough is enough' and we must do everything we can to give them working opportunities."

PART 11
LUKE ON TRIAL

CHAPTER 1

DEPOSITIONS HEARING

Wednesday, May 8, 1991: It's the first day of depositions for Luke Donnelly in Gisborne.

Chris Campbell's brother-in-law Reece Bolingford tells the court: "I saw Donnelly turn the gun on Chris and shoot him in the lower leg."

Robyn Kapa happened to be driving past the Donnelly address just as everything was getting out of control. She saw two men running on the right hand side of the river. "They were crouching down, looking towards the house and making their way along the river bed."

Kapa says she also saw a man standing behind a vehicle holding a gun up. So she drove to a house and phoned the police. While she was on the phone she heard two gunshots.

Under cross-examination Rasta Bill Kaihe tells lawyer Les Atkins that Campbell had been a peaceful man.

"Did you hear Chris say to Luke, 'I'm going to whip your head off'?" asks Atkins.

"No."

"Did you hear Donnelly say to you, 'You come at me with them, my own fuckin' cousin. Why, Billy? Why?"

Again Kaihe says, "No," and adds that he isn't Donnelly's cousin.

Thursday, May 9, 1991: New Zealand Herald journalist Ron Taylor, who interviewed Luke Donnelly the morning of the shooting, takes the stand during the second day of despositions.

He tells the court that Donnelly feared for the safety of his wife and child because of threats he'd received from the Rastas.

Donnelly and his wife had been escorting their daughter to and from school every day. And he intended to send his wife and child back to Hamilton for a while at the end of the school term.

Chris Campbell's brother Joe, whose property is quite close to Donnelly's, tells the court that he heard several gunshots on the afternoon of December 4. About ten minutes after hearing the gunshots, Campbell says his brother-in-law, Reece Bolingford, came running in, yelling, "Luke, he has just finished shooting at me and them!"

Joe Ward says that when he and the others arrived at Donnelly's address, Donnelly came out from behind a water tank.

"He had a shotgun with him. He came out aiming it at us and said not to fuck him around. Chris was saying things but Donnelly wouldn't listen. Chris said he was sorry."

Under cross-examination by Les Atkins, Ward says they did not yell anything to Donnelly while passing the property.

Atkins suggests that Donnelly didn't wave them up but instead gave the thumbs down sign. Ward disagrees.

Harley Te Hau says that after the vehicle's windscreen was shattered, he was hit by a couple of pellets. He heard Campbell say to Donnelly, 'Come on, come on, Luke, there's no need for this.'"

Later Te Hau saw Campbell get shot in the leg and then he and Bolingford ran down the driveway off the Donnelly property, zig-zagging to dodge bullets.

Friday, May 10, 1991: Iain Kelman, the orthopaedic surgeon who operated on Chris Campbell at Gisborne Hospital, gives evidence.

Kelman operated on Chris Campbell at 8pm on December 4.

He says that when he first examined Campbell, he saw injuries to the right arm and to the legs, but no injuries to the abdomen, chest, head or neck.

The operation was to correct the injury to the arm, a broken leg and other wounds to the legs. Kelman says that by the time Campbell went into surgery his blood pressure had dropped by a marked degree.

Campbell died at 9.10pm that day. The next day Wellington pathologist Kenneth Thompson performed a post-mortem examination on Campbell.

Thompson tells the court Campbell's death was due to shock following blood loss from multiple gun shot wounds.

He says the wound in the left knee had to be a primary entry wound. That means the bullet was unimpeded in its journey from gun barrel to knee. In other words, it didn't ricochet.

It was the same for the right forearm injury: no ricochet. Thompson says the wound was consistent with a whole round entering then exiting.

Cross-examined by Atkins, Thompson says that the multiple small puncture wounds from shotgun pellets were only superficial and not life-threatening. But the injury to Campbell's right forearm was deep and may well have contributed to the death because "it was a major injury".

Atkins says, "If it transpired that in the five hours in the hospital before death the bleeding from that wound was controlled then it would follow that it would not make much of a contribution."

Thompson replies: "That's not necessarily true. The contribution it made in the initial phase in causing blood loss may have had significant bearing on Mr Campbell's progress later on."

Atkins asks him which wounds would have suffered the greatest blood loss.

"It's difficult to speculate when bleeding no longer exists. But the two areas, which I would have expected to cause the most blood loss were the right wrist and inside of the left thigh."

Donnelly's committed to the High Court at Gisborne to face trial for murder.

MURDER TRIAL

Monday, February 17, 1992: Luke Donnelly goes to trial at the High Court in Gisborne for the murder of Chris Campbell. He pleads not guilty.

A lot of the evidence in the trial is a repeat of what was said in the depositions. But occasionally there's something new.

Chris Campbell's brother-in-law, Reece Bolingford, says that when he and the others went up the Donnelly driveway, Campbell told Donnelly's wife to ring the police. When the couple went to the back of the house and Donnelly returned holding a gun and a scabbard, "I heard Chris tell Donnelly to put the gun down. Mr Donnelly was screaming and yelling abuse."

Les Atkins cross-examines Bolingford. Atkins tells the court that in the statement Bolingford made to police he said Campbell had told Luke Donnelly that he was "going to get it one day."

Bolingford agrees that he heard the word utu used but adds he wasn't sure of its meaning.

Atkins puts it to Bolingford that on another occasion he had been with Campbell in a Land Cruiser in Ruatoria and that Campbell told a police constable (Nigel Hendrikse) that "Lukie was going to die". Bolingford says he hadn't heard that and also denies nodding his head in agreement and saying, "Yeah, yeah."

"Did you used to shout out to Mr Donnelly as you drove past his house?"

Again Bolingford denies the allegation.

Atkins asks whether in a statement to police on the day of the killing, he said, "We looked up at Luke's place like we always do, throw him a bit of shit over the fence, sort of like a game. He throws it back at us. We say anything that comes to mind."

"Yes," Bolingford concedes.

"When you said 'we' did you include yourself in that?"

Bolingford says he did.

Had they adopted the same attitude on December 4? Bolingford says they had not; the statement he made on December 4 "was not bang on" because he was still "shaken up".

But he's been caught out by Atkins and his credibility as a witness has been damaged.

*"Would it be that Mr **Donnelly** got his wife to call the police and not Mr Campbell?" asks Atkins.*

Bolingford disagrees.

Did Bolingford hear Campbell say anything on the way up the driveway about burning the house?

"No."

Bolingford tells the court that Campbell didn't say anything to the other men about following him up the driveway. But, really, who would believe him now.

Tuesday, February 18, 1992: *Atkins continues to cross-examine Bolingford.*

He asks if the dog in the car, a staffordshire-bull terrier cross, was urged to attack Donnelly.

Bolingford says it wasn't.

He also tells the court that he heard a further two shots fired as he ran along the riverbed after fleeing from Donnelly's property. Atkins points out that there is no mention of these shots in Bolingford's statement to the police.

Now I reckon this is a good example of how a lawyer whittles away at the credibility of a witness and builds a case. It makes perfect sense that Bolingford heard two shots as he fled the scene. He was there and shots were fired (Campbell had various injuries to prove it and police said there were spent shells lying all over the scene). So he must have heard them. In fact, it would be strange if he didn't hear shots. But hold on. He didn't mention them in his statement to police. Does that mean they didn't happen? Maybe he just wasn't asked about them so they weren't mentioned in his statement. But Atkins is using this innocent omission to help convince the jury that Bolingford is a liar.

Atkins asks if Campbell yelled to Donnelly from the bottom of the driveway about burning his house down and whipping his head off.

"That's a pack of lies," replies Bolingford.

Atkins could just as easily have asked if Campbell had threatened to use Donnelly as fish bait. Whether he did or not is irrelevant, as long as the jury believes there must be a reason why the lawyer is asking. Why would he ask unless there was good evidence Campbell had said that sort of thing.

Anyway, you can almost see where this is going.

Atkins asks Bolingford if he told lies in the statement he made on December 4, 1990. Bolingford concedes he made mistakes but says he didn't lie.

"You have told a pack of lies," says Atkins.

"I'm not lying. I'm not the one here for murder. I know what happened."

And now the clincher.

"Did you discuss this matter with anyone in or near the courthouse?" says Atkins.

"No, I was told not to."

"Did you discuss it with the media or television people?" asks Atkins.

At first Bolingford says no, but Atkins puts it to him that he had said, "When we went to Donnelly's house we had been whacked out."

"Yes, I had been talking to the television cameraman." He says he meant that he'd been tired, not out of it.

Wednesday, February 19, 1992: Les Atkins suggests that Joe Ward and the others had gone on to Donnelly's property as back-up for Campbell.

Ward disagrees but concedes he thought there'd be an argument. "We went up to make sure things did not get out of hand. The Rastaman is a peaceful man. He doesn't go looking for fights. We went up there on a peaceful mission."

Thursday, February 20: Several days of aerial surveillance nets Gisborne police a huge cannabis harvest.

Detective Senior Sergeant Brett Kane, head of Gisborne CIB, says over thirteen thousand plants were found during the operation.

"They were in plantations scattered all over the district and particularly on the East Coast, where one plantation of over one thousand plants was found near Ruatoria."

CHAPTER 2

"CAMPBELL DIED OF SHOCK FOLLOWING BLOOD LOSS"

Monday, February 24: The Wellington pathologist who performed the post-mortem on Chris Campbell gives evidence at the trial of Luke Donnelly. As he did at the despositions hearing, Kenneth Thompson tells the court that Campbell died of shock following blood loss from multiple gun shot wounds. The life-threatening injuries were to the right hand and the left leg.

During cross-examination by Atkins, Thompson rules out the possibility that over-transfusion may have caused Campbell's death. Over-transfusion occurs when too much fluid is given and the lungs become waterlogged, causing heart failure. Campbell received about ten litres of fluid. But Thompson says that was not a large amount for a person who was bleeding.

Answering questions from Mr Justice Henry, Thompson says Campbell would have been unable to use the lower part of his left leg after being shot and there would have been a lot of bleeding.

In the case of the right hand injury there would have been immediate blood loss from the exit wound.

Thompson's evidence completes the Crown case.

Atkins opens the case for the defence.

This includes the written evidence of Constable Nigel Hendrikse, who's overseas on a two-year trip planned long before Chris Campbell was killed. Before he left, Hendrikse gave his evidence in a special sitting in the Gisborne District Court. He was cross-examined and re-examined, then he signed the transcript of his testimony.

As Hendrikse said in an email to the author: "It wasn't normal for me as a cop to be giving evidence for the defence. I was of course always giving evidence for the prosecution in my role as a Police officer. Now I was on the 'dark' side!! The defence."

Email from author to Nigel Hendrikse, August 18, 2009: Hi Nigel, I thought I'd drop you a little line just to get a steer on something. I'm writing up the deps and trial of Luke Donnelly. And I came to the bit where I had to put down some thoughts on your written evidence…

…Anyway, the main gist I was trying to get across was that when Campbell told you that Luke was going to die he may not have meant that he would be the one to kill him. He might have meant that the way Luke was carrying on, someone was going to kill him.

Let me know what you think. Anyway, this is how it reads at the moment:

Constable Nigel Hendrikse's evidence is read to the court. He says Campbell and Bolingford had approached him on November 30 and told him that Luke Donnelly was going to die.

Now this sounds like big evidence. But it needs to be put in perspective. Why would Campbell tell a policeman that? He's not silly and he's just come out of jail. Maybe what he meant was that the police had better sort out Luke because if they didn't someone was likely to kill him. The Rastas believed that four days earlier Luke Donnelly had burned them out of the baches at Whareponga Beach. Everyone else seemed to believe it too. A bit of heat coming back the other way would

have been expected. They were angry. But Luke probably had no more
reason than he normally had to be wary of them.
    When Hendrikse asked who was going to kill Donnelly, Campbell
had replied, "I don't know, but the Lord will see to that." Apparently,
Bolingford, who was also present, agreed.

Email from Nigel Hendrikse to author: …About the comment that
Chris made to me. I liked Chris. We got on well. I think he liked me
because I was absolutely up-front with him. He obviously trusted me
because he used to come into the Police Station to drink hot water with
me. I don't know how many other Police he did that with. Chris was not
a 'common' criminal. He was so unusual in that he was intelligent and I
had such great respect for his brother Barney, who was a fantastic cop.
Chris did bad stuff but he genuinely believed in his cause. A rebel with
a cause. I don't question that. I actually admired the staunchness of the
guy, his toothless grin. Sort of how I admired the staunchness of Luke.
Hard men who you would want to take into battle with you. Yes,
seriously, two guys you'd rather fight with than against. I never felt one
bit of hatred towards Chris. Frustration, despair, futility, yes, but I think
the dope got in the way of clear thinking for Chris. I have hated other
criminals I've dealth with. Wished them dead. Not so with Chris.
    Chris was a guy who was under so much pressure to perform for
many parties. On one hand he had the Parole Board looking over his
shoulder, knowing full well that he'd be recalled to prison if he stepped
out of line. Then the Rastas were on his case. I remember countless
times the Rastas saying, "You wait till Chris gets out, he'll sort this
out," etc, etc. For Chris to actually come to the Police Station to talk
with me showed, I think, that he didn't want to be all bad. He wanted
some sort of resolution, some sort of negotiation, dialogue. It wouldn't
exactly look cool for a hardened criminal to walk into a Police Station
to sit down and have a yarn with a cop. And remember that there were
two very high-powered people hell-bent on getting the Government to
gift land to the Rastas so they could live happily ever after in a smoke-
filled haze at Whareponga Beach, out of harm's way.
    Over the years I have been the recipient of many dope/booze filled
threats from crims. "We know where you live." Blahblah. The comment
that Chris made to me was taken seriously by me. So seriously that I
typed it up and sent it to the Gisborne Police. I think it was a threat that
he hoped somehow that I would pass on to Luke. Make Luke back off.

Luke doesn't back off. I remember being questioned in court as to me introducing the word 'kill' into the conversation. It was true that Chris hadn't used the word. He'd said that Luke was going to die, and I used the word 'kill' cos I knew that a fit healthy youngish guy like Luke was unlikely to die from natural causes any time soon. With the benefit of hindsight, Chris made a very dumb and, as it would turn out, damning comment to me.

I have often thought over the years what a wonderful leader Chris could've been in the community if he had been led down another path earlier in his adult life… a real waste of potential there. And Barney would still be a cop…

(Author's note: I think the "two very high-powered people hell-bent on getting the Government to gift land to the Rastas" were Ngati Porou Runanga chairman Api Mahuika and Gisborne's top cop at the time Rana Waitai. This idea was mentioned in an article by Ron Taylor, which was quoted earlier in the book.)

CHAPTER 3

DEFENDING LUKE

Email from the author to Hendrikse: Hi Nigel,
I'd like to use some of your comments because I feel like I owe it to Luke to have someone lining up on his side because there's no shortage of people who think he got away with murder… … But your email made me pause for thought.

There are three things I'd be interested for you to elaborate a bit on. One is did Chris's comments get back to Luke before the day Luke shot him. So Luke was acting in the knowledge that Chris had made those comments.

Also, can you remember roughly how your conversation with Chris went.

And the third thing is why you decided to be a witness for the defence.

Email from Hendrikse to the author: Hi Angus,

As far as I know Chris's comment to me didn't get back to Luke before the shooting. Bearing in mind that Luke wasn't overly enamoured with Hendrikse the Relieving Sergeant at Ruatoria. We'd had our disputes over points of law… once I even drove out to his place carrying the volumes of Statutes to prove to him that I was right about something… I think it was about his right or lack thereof to shoot someone else's animals on his land… I told him I'd do the shooting to avoid conflict… and he complained to Rana Waitai about me on the phone. Rana didn't worry about it but he did phone me to ask what I'd done to upset Luke. So Luke and me weren't 'mates'. He was pretty fiery… which I guess was a defence mechanism to deal with all the shit that was going on. I guess for me as a cop it wasn't really about me against the Rastas… it was more like the Rastas against the community, and Luke was part of that community, and, of course, the Rastas were also part of the community. I was pretty much 'piggy in the middle', excuse the pun. I didn't really feel like I was part of the community as a relieving cop, I just lived out of a suitcase, and went back to Gissy on my days off. I certainly cared about the destruction in the community but I didn't have that emotional investment in it. My family didn't live there. Even so, I had a pistol under my pillow and a loaded rifle under my bed. I didn't seriously think the Rastas would kill me. But I have to admit it was something that crossed your mind, especially when you'd be lying in bed at 3am and the Rastas would be clip-clopping outside your window on their horses with greatcoats and facemasks 5 metres from your head but there was very little you could do about it… by the time you got up and outside and the bloody security light came on at the back door they were gone in a shower of sparks from the horseshoes on the tarseal.

I can empathise with the way Luke felt. And I've faced 5 guys on my own with rocks and a knife and bottles coming at me, and wishing I had a gun with me as a leveller. The feelings of vulnerability and insecurity. The what-ifs. I guess if I didn't, I wouldn't have slept with loaded weapons. I then have to put myself in Luke's situation of being home with my wife and a carload of the enemy drive up your driveway… what the fuck do you do!!!!

From memory, my conversation with Chris was pretty brief that day. I think he called me over to his car outside the Police Station. It wasn't during one of his visits where he actually entered the Police Station. Maybe that's why it made me write it down cos it wasn't part of a conversation… it was the conversation. I also think from memory that it was that day or the next that I returned to Gisborne at the end of 5 months up there. I think it was a Friday and Chris got killed the following Tuesday. I got called back up there from Gisborne the afternoon he was shot and it was late that night we were all pretty shocked to hear that Chris had died. Through the afternoon we'd been told he'd been shot in the arm. Remember the 'medical misadventure' stuff?? I remember thinking, "Fuck, what's going to happen now."

When the Crown (Police) prepared the file for murder against Luke no one included my report, which really should have been included because it was relevant. So someone told Tony Adeane (now Judge) Luke's lawyer and he called me to his office to tell me that he was intending to call me as a defence witness. I reported as required by Police Regs that this was to be the case, and it went on from there. So I didn't 'decide' to be a defence witness. I was summonsed to be one, but I felt that my evidence was important. I am glad that I actually took the time at that early stage straight after Chris's comment to me to report the matter, cos it gave my evidence more credibility than if I'd reported it verbally after the fact. Of course I wasn't at the trial and actually heard nothing about the trial so don't know if it was a terribly crucial piece of evidence or not, but my guess is that it was.

In my life I'm big on what's fair and what's not, and to my way of thinking it wasn't fair that a carload of Rastas drove into Luke's driveway and created the situation of one man against 4 or 5 in a confrontation. The great leveller in that sort of situation was a gun… I think from memory that the Rastas claimed that Luke had called out to them and told them to come up his drive. If so, what the hell did they think was going to happen, Luke make them a cup of tea!!!

I can hear you think, "But why didn't you ring Luke and tell him." With all the crap that was going on I can't imagine what difference it would've made, probably Luke would have said, "They can get fucked," or such like. The Wild West thing again!

Hope this makes sense.

The other two defence witnesses are surveyor Mark Clapham and firearms expert Dennis Collings.

Clapham visited the Donnelly property and placed an EJ Holden, similar to the Grey Ghost, in the same position on the driveway and took photographs depicting what could be seen.

Clapham uses models to reconstruct the positions of Donnelly and Campbell as described by witnesses, who'd watched events while lying on the ground behind the car.

The court says the Donnelly model can be seen up to thigh level, while the Campbell model can be seen only as far as the mid-calf area. In some cases the models are in places that are entirely obscured from view. The models' hands and arms are not visible.

Tony Adeane tells him that a previous witness said Donnelly's face could be seen. But Clapham says the front wheels of the vehicle would have to have been elevated by six and three-quarter inches to make that possible.

When the Crown cross-examines Clapham, he admits he's never seen the Grey Ghost. He doesn't know the height of the car or the standard of fitness of the tyres. He also agrees that the view a person would have had behind the EJ Holden in December 1990 would have been different to the view from behind it in 1991.

Dennis Collings had been a gunsmith since 1958 and had worked in that capacity part-time for ten years before that. He'd been involved in the use of firearms for hunting and competitive shooting.

His argument is that the bullet, which entered Campbell's left leg, was a rising bullet, which had ricocheted. The hole in the left knee area was consistent with being made by a part of a bullet. And the bullet fragments in the right knee came from the bullet, which had emerged from the left knee.

Collings tells the court that metal removed from the right thigh of Campbell represented about half of the bullet core. Little of the kneecap would be left if a whole bullet had hit the leg.

Collings believes the bullet that hit the left leg had ricocheted so the velocity had diminished. The injury to the left knee was not consistent with a bullet travelling at high velocity.

He says the wounds to the right leg at about knee level were consistent with being hit with parts of a disintegrating bullet.

The entry wound in the right arm was consistent with being formed by part of a .303 bullet, which meant the break-up of the bullet occurred when it hit something hard before entering a limb.

Lawyer Les Atkins asks if it was possible with regards to the left leg, right leg and right arm injuries for them to have been received from one round or two or more.

Collings says one or two similar bullets could have caused the injury to the right knee and forearm.

He's asked if the ricochet from one round could have caused the left knee, right thigh, right knee and right arm injuries.

"Yes, if it disintegrated."

Collings tells the court that the total weight of metal taken from Campbell's body was only about half the weight of a .303 round. A full round had not entered Campbell's right arm because the disintegration of the bullet was too rapid. This was also the case with the left knee wound because only half a bullet core was recovered.

Cross-examined by Crown counsel Bruce Squire, Collings agrees that he has no experience with bullet wounds to human flesh.

"Would it be fair to say that whenever you have expressed opinions concerning impact on tissue and bullet wounds it really is a matter that falls outside your experience?" Squire asks.

"I don't accept that. I don't see a lot of difference between human and other animal flesh."

However he agrees that he has no academic or professional qualifications to give an opinion on the matter.

Basically, Collings believes Campbell wasn't hit directly but by a ricochet off the metal driveway. But Squire points out that the only area of substantial blood loss was in the area found beneath the driveway, where Campbell was found lying. That means that Campbell was shot where he was found lying, not where the ricochets were supposed to have taken place, over by the Grey Ghost. Collings agrees that this would make the ricochet theory impossible.

Tuesday, February 25, 1992: Bruce Squire sums up for the Crown. It goes like this. Christopher Campbell was a human being and the deliberate killing of him was just as much murder as the deliberate killing of any other person. Campbell died from shock due to blood loss from multiple gunshot wounds fired by Donnelly.

On December 4 Donnelly was the only person seen with a weapon. Bolingford heard Campbell tell Donnelly's wife to get the police. "Is that the action of a man hell-bent on having a confrontation with a man with a gun?"

The two shots, hitting the windscreen and the tyre of the EJ Holden, were fired without justification. Then Donnelly shot Campbell and he fell to the ground.

There was no evidence that he intended to inflict violence on Donnelly or that the word gun had fallen from his lips.

Donnelly ordered Kaihe to lie on the ground and "kiss dirt" then told his wife to get the gun belt, rifle and handcuffs.

Firearms expert Dennis Collings had conceded there were no absolutes when it came to the behaviour of bullets when they hit tissue.

Self-defence was not an option open to Donnelly. The two wounds suffered by Campbell were consistent with direct hits from .303 bullets.

Donnelly had wanted to kill Campbell or inflict serious harm. "What is this man doing shooting at a man who is disabled?"

Six empty cartridge rounds had been found, but Bolingford had heard eight shots in all. Ricocheting bullets was just a theory.

Then it's Les Atkins' turn to close for the defence. So this is how he got Donnelly off the murder charge. First he goes through some relevant background issues. "Mr Donnelly was not a person who sympathised with or supported the Rastafarians. He made no secret of it to those who interviewed him." The men who went up that driveway on December 4 would have been in no doubt that Donnelly opposed their actions.

Then there was the dispute that took place at Donnelly's gateway, which involved shouting from both parties. This was the Campbell who told Hemi Hikawai he wanted a quiet life..

Bolingford was lying when he said he heard Campbell tell Donnelly's wife to call the police. The Rastas knew they weren't wanted on the property and they went up there anyway.

The shot, which caused Campbell's death, was fired while he was in the driveway (and posing a serious threat). And neither of the shots aimed were intended to kill or cause bodily injury. Also, Collings said the bullet could have ricocheted off the ground.

Then there was the fact that police had failed to find not just one but two .303 cartridges. Where were they? And there was no metal found where Campbell was lying. So the prosecution's view that the shooting of the left knee occurred when Campbell was lying down an embankment was a strained and unlikely argument.

Because of the background and circumstances on the day, self-defence was open to Donnelly.

CHAPTER 4

DONNELLY GETS OFF ON SELF DEFENCE

Wednesday, February 26, 1992: Mr Justice Henry sums up the case, suggesting to the jury that they come straight to the question of Campbell's injuries to the left knee and right arm. Were they the result of two direct shots? Or is there a reasonable possibility they were the result of a ricochet from one round? Bear in mind, though, that it appeared there'd been two shotgun discharges to Campbell's back and legs, wounds to his buttock from a slug, and that the left knee injury appeared to disable him immediately.

Kenneth Thompson, the pathologist from Wellington, believed the wound in the left knee had to be a primary non-ricochet entry wound.

But firearms expert Dennis Collings believed a ricochet off the driveway caused it.

When it came to the right forearm injury, Dr Thompson believed the wound was consistent with a whole round entering then exiting, while Collings said that part of a ricocheting bullet caused the injury.

"If the bullet which struck Mister Campbell was the first that hit him," Judge Henry says, "then ask yourselves what explanation there can be for the three shotgun wounds suffered at the back of the legs." He reminds the jury that there were two separate pellet shots to the back and legs and the slug which struck the buttocks.

Donnelly had been in possession of two firearms which were capable of killing, and they were more capable of killing when used at short range.

But self-defence applies to both murder and manslaughter. "The crucial question in self-defence is: was it reasonable in the circumstances - that Donnelly believed them to be - to avoid harm to himself and his family - to fire two .303 bullets into Campbell's body."

The jury retires at 11am and is ready to return with its verdict nearly eight hours later at 6.45pm. As the jury prepares to come back, police take up positions around the courtroom and search people before allowing them to enter. Most obviously support Donnelly. The first *verdict of not guilty of murder is greeted with silence. But when the same verdict is returned for manslaughter there are gasps and tears. There is only one dissenting voice: a woman, who leaves the court saying, "So that's justice," and swearing.*

Luke Donnelly is not guilty of the murder or manslaughter of Chris Campbell on the grounds of self-defence.

Judge Henry discharges Donnelly, and Donnelly leaves by a side door and goes straight to a waiting car. His wife Elizabeth leaves the court soon after with friends.

Later that night Donnelly tells the media that police are advising him to get out of town. But he's as staunch as ever. "I have a farm to go back to. I'm not going to run. Otherwise what is the point of the stand I've made and all I've been through in the past fourteen months.

"If they want to keep it up I won't run. I'm not looking for trouble. But I will not back down. I will continue to make a stand. I'm not saying I'm looking for trouble, but if it comes, I won't step out of the way and run."

Donnelly says it's up to the people of Ruatoria to support him. If the Rastafarians want to continue to cause trouble they should say that they, as a town, aren't going to take it.

Donnelly spends the night at a house in Gisborne. There is no party. There is no jubilation, just relief.

Donnelly's cousin Bill says the family had been expecting a verdict of at least manslaughter and were relieved when Luke was acquitted on all charges.

A member of the Campbell family says they don't wish to comment as they feel it won't serve any purpose.

Thursday, February 27, The New Zealand Herald, under the headline, Post-trial clash complaint: Less than an hour after a Ruatoria farmer was found not guilty of murder last night, he told the police of a brush with a Rastafarian who gave evidence against him at his trial in Gisborne.

Mr Luke Donnelly complained to the police that a car he was travelling in, driven by his brother-in-law, was followed by Mr Reece Bolingford, who swerved his own vehicle at them.

"We had to take violent and evasive action. He just missed us when we turned into the driveway of a house I was going to stay in for the night.

"I've told the police and I've been advised for my own good and for that of my friends, relatives and supporters, that I should leave town.

"I'm going to do that, but I'll be back. I'm not going to be forced to leave my home by a bunch of people who should be called ratbags, not Rastafarians."

The police confirmed the complaint. They said they were seeking Mr Bolingford in connection with another incident earlier in the day when it was alleged that he narrowly missed an American tourist crossing the road...

...Mr Donnelly said last night that he had remained confident of his acquittal.

"Really, I can say to you it was all a non-event. I did what I did and I'd do it again if I had to."

Tape of myself after interviewing Luke Donnelly in July 2001 (he didn't want me to tape record our interview: He was saying he was about thirty-eight when he shot Chris. And he lost everything, he said.

He said he sometimes looks at his trigger finger and says, "I wish I'd chopped that finger off. My whole life fell apart after that day."

He said that a couple of days later he was supposed to be going down to the bank to pick up a hundred thousand dollar cheque. I don't know what that hundred thousand dollar cheque was for. But obviously he was getting a hundred thousand dollar cheque for something. And he said he ended up with nothing. *(Luke later told me that the cheque was a loan from the bank to buy some cattle).*

Before the shooting everything was going really well, apart from his ongoing conflict with the Campbells and the Rastas. The farm was coming along well.

Afterwards, he lost all his money and everything he owned paying off legal fees. And when he got acquitted his wife refused to go back to Ruatoria because she thought he was going to go to prison.

He said he couldn't believe it when he got acquitted. He was certain he was going to do time. He thought he'd be lucky and get about six years inside. But he was convinced he'd be put away for killing Chris.

So he was very surprised when he was acquitted. His plan was that he was going to ask for a transfer down to the medium security prison down at Paparua near Christchurch. He was half-way through a law degree so he was hoping to finish his law degree.

But when he got acquitted, life continued.

CHAPTER 5

WHAT HAPPENED AT GISBORNE HOSPITAL?

Even after Donnelly's murder trial there are still plenty of questions about Chris Campbell's death. The main question is: could he have been saved at Gisborne Hospital?

Campbell had been shot several times by Luke Donnelly at just before 2.35pm, which is when the Ruatoria police receptionist received the first call about the incident. According to the coroner's report, he arrived at Gisborne Hospital at 4.15pm and was there what must have seemed an interminable two hours and fifteen minutes until surgeon Iain Kelman arrived to see him at 6.30. And, according to Detective Neilson's notes of his interview with Campbell, he'd been taken into theatre at 7.50pm. That's five hours and fifteen minutes from the first call to police to the beginning of the operation.

And that begs another question: why did it take so long to get Chris Campbell into theatre for surgery?

I sent out a few emails asking medical staff at Gisborne Hospital for their recollections of that afternoon, but didn't get any responses. So I went back to the trial notes. I remembered at least one nurse had given evidence in court. As it turned out, three nurses, Kelman and Doctor Enn Sepp all gave evidence.

Sepp treated Campbell at Luke Donnelly's place. He said, "I felt he was very critical at the time. He had a very rapid heart rate and the external signs of shock. His pulse was very weak. I didn't attempt to take a blood pressure because of the time factor."

Prosecutor Bruce Squire: "If he had not received medical attention at the time, are you able to tell us in your professional judgement how imminent death was if it was imminent at all?"

Sepp: "I think it may have been imminent and it may have taken place in the next hour or two."

So Dr Sepp, with the help of a nurse and the ambulance driver, stopped the bleeding on the two major wounds – the thigh and the wrist - with pressure bandages. Then he inserted an intravenous line and gave Campbell a plasma expander into his circulation to correct some of the blood loss. He also gave him oxygen and then rapidly placed him in the helicopter. Campbell's condition appeared to improve on the way to the hospital.

Luke Donnelly had mentioned a "legend" that Denis Hartley had taken his time flying the chopper.

Dion Hutana told me something similar. After he left the Rastas and finished his jail sentence for arson, Hutana got a suit-and-tie job with the Department of Internal Affairs for a while.

Dion Hutana: One of my bosses at Internal Affairs had access to all the archives about Chris's death. And there was a part in there that when the helicopter came, they grabbed Chris and when they flew him they actually stopped in at Tolaga Bay or Tokomaru Bay and waited for another twenty minutes or so before they carried on taking him to the Gisborne Hospital.

I've heard people say that they took the scenic route around Mt Hikurangi, but I don't believe that.

No I don't believe that either. But that information came from someone who worked in Internal Affairs. I don't know if it's true or not.

There was so much talk about the flight being deliberately delayed on its way to the hospital that I thought I'd ask the chopper pilot about it.

Denis Hartley, May 2010: We didn't stop anywhere. We just went straight in to the hospital. No detours, no nothing. There were three of us in the helicopter. Me, Chris and the doctor (Dr Enn Sepp). And as we were flying along, Chris actually sat up on the stretcher and he started talking to me.

He chatted away quite happily and I thought, "Oh, shit. That's quite unusual for a guy who's been shot," even though it was my understanding he hadn't been shot in any fatal area. He had gunshot pellets over his body but most of the damage was done to his limbs. All right? Even when they loaded him in he was quite coherent.

He was propped up on his elbows for a good quarter of an hour or so. And we were just chatting because I know him and he knows me. And he's like, "Oh, bro, havin' a good flight, eh."

"Are you right there, Chris?"

"Yeah, good, bro."

So he thought he was going to be okay?

Oh yeah, I thought he was, too. I was so bloody dumbfounded when they rang me up that night and told me that he died on the operating table. I was bloody thunderstruck. I just couldn't believe it.

Did you think he was going to be badly injured for the rest of his life though?

No. He was good as gold. He was a bit of a bloody tough nut.

On the helicopter trip was he talking about anything to do with Luke?

No, he was sort of still in a bit of shock. But he knew he was in the helicopter and that he was going to hospital.

So he knew he'd just been shot by Luke but wasn't saying much else about it?

He wasn't talking about it. Na, we didn't even mention that because we didn't want him to jump out the door. He might get agitated.

You were trying to keep him calm?

Actually, they're meant to be strapped in. When they're in the stretcher they're meant to be strapped in, so they can't move. But the straps were round his legs and waist but the strap wasn't around his torso. Why that happened, I don't know.

I was just sitting there flying along. The next thing he was sitting up and leaning towards me in the front of the helicopter going, "Hey bro. This is a good flight this is."

Hahaha. He must have had his own painkillers working, ay.

Hahaha. I just about fell out of the helicopter! I thought he was strapped in properly. But we must have missed it.

Aw well, at least he got a last look at the mountain and everything as he was going in.

In the notes for Luke Donnelly's trial, the nurses say that when Campbell arrived at Gisborne Hospital in the helicopter at 4.15pm he was still in considerable shock.

He was taken to the Accident and Emergency Department's Resuscitation Room. Nurse Patricia Butler says she attended Campbell with Dr David Mathias (a house surgeon), charge nurse Judy Gerber and nurse Pam Morrison.

Butler attempted to take Campbell's blood pressure but it was unrecordable by stethascope. So she called for a Doppler machine to be brought down to pick up his pulse. Campbell had one intravenous line in when he arrived. But, because he was in such shock, another line was inserted in his left arm and a unit of Soluble Plasma Protein Solution was started.

Gradually, the team was able to get Campbell's blood pressure back up.

The bandages on the left leg and right arm were never removed during that time. As the blood seeped through, they were reinforced, bandages put over existing bandages.

Campbell needed lots of fluids. And as these were being introduced there was continued bleeding in the left leg and the blood pooled on the bed between his legs. At some point he was given morphine to ease his pain.

At 5.30pm, nurse Pam Morrison went with Campbell to the X-ray Department, where x-rays were taken of the left leg and the injured arm.

The general duty surgeon had a look at the x-rays and when he saw there was a fracture of the femur in the left leg, he called in Iain Kelman, the specialist surgeon, who arrived at 6.30pm.

A coroner's inquest looked into what happened once Kelman arrived at the hospital. Napier lawyer Russell Fairbrother called for the inquest.

In a letter to Campbell's parents, Willie and Tangiwai (dated March 16, 1992) Fairbrother writes that Donnelly's lawyer Les Atkins has told him "there is serious concern as to the way Chris was treated at Gisborne Hospital". He writes that Atkins has opinions from qualified specialists from outside the Gisborne area who believe Chris's life could have been saved.

*In another letter to the parents (dated September 30, 1992)
Fairbrother writes that he's been contacted by a doctor who has taken a
professional interest in the treatment Chris received in Gisborne
Hospital. "His interest is such that he has published papers in
professional journals and he has a very real concern that two of the
medical staff attending Chris were quite negligent."*

*Fairbrother's notes going into the inquest sum up his argument:
"Young, conscious people with peripheral injuries don't die of blood
loss once they get to hospital." (By peripheral injuries, he means
injuries to the arms and legs as opposed to the head, neck and torso.)
Fairbrother considers it strange that Campbell was able to sign a form
with his left hand and answer questions from Detective David Neilson
just before going into surgery but then died on the operating table.*

*But the surgeon, Iain Kelman, argues at the inquest that Campbell
died of irreversible shock syndrome and that his sudden decline is in
keeping with the phenomenon. Irreversible shock syndrome had been
brought to notice during the Vietnam War and occurred particularly in
young people with severe injury: they recover remarkably well, they can
chat away, but then they deteriorate suddenly and die.*

Kelman explains at the inquest: Shock is a state where the blood
supply to the body is inadequate, meaning that the transport of oxygen
and the removal of waste products from the cells of the body is
impaired. The body itself has a mechanism to compensate for this so
that vital structures such as the heart and brain remain adequately
oxygenated. Because there is diminished blood volume and
compensatory mechanisms come into effect, the body shuts off its own
blood supply to certain non-vital areas, the skin and the intestines as
well as some muscles. This is brought about by the use of the body's
own stores of adrenalin and cortizone-like substances.

In this state the body is compensated and is surviving and, provided
that adequate blood can be replaced soon enough, the body will make a
complete recovery. If, however, this state continues for too long, the
body's compensatory mechanisms fail. The areas, which have
previously been shut off, open up. Blood flows into these areas and
pools in these regions and very slowly returns to the heart, which means
that the heart is not getting back enough blood to pump and therefore
adequate blood supply to the vital organs is then impaired.

Together with this there is the accumulation of byproducts in these areas which didn't have blood supply, particularly in the intestines. Products from bacteria are rapidly absorbed and eventually, when blood flows through them, these toxic products are washed into the system.

These toxic products have a depressing affect on the heart muscle and on the brain generally. They result in the heart being unable to work as a pump and therefore lead to failure.

Once this siutation has been reached it is then termed irreversible, for no amount of extra fluid or drugs can restore the heart's function or restore adequate flow back to the heart...

...They appear to compensate extremely well and this is why a young person in compensated shock is lucid and apparently well. However if the shocked state persists too long, it will eventually fail and blood goes to non-vital areas of the body, toxic products are absorbed and very rapid death ensues.

Fairbrother's notes preparing for the inquest are full of questions over the conduct and decisions of Kelman and anaesthetist Dr James Carstens in theatre. And Fairbrother put his concerns to Kelman during the inquest.

But before addressing those questions, it should be reiterated that the damage to Campbell's body was done before Kelman and Carstens started operating and that more than five hours had passed since Campbell had been shot multiple times.

*During that time, his condition had been fluctuating wildly. On arrival at hospital at 4.15pm his blood pressure was recorded as a very low 60mms of mercury systolic, with a heart rate of 130 per minute. He was resuscitated and by 5.10pm his blood pressure was up to 135. But when Kelman arrived eighty minutes later it was back down to 70. He was resuscitated again. Then, by 7.15, his blood pressure had dropped again. And Kelman suspected that he would have had a low blood pressure for some time **prior** to his **admission** to hospital.*

"The point that I am making," says Kelman, "is that, despite adequate intravenous fluids and blood, his blood pressure continued to drop. He was therefore in a state where the blood pressure was being compensated and then decompensation took place. It was for this reason that I realised that Mr Campbell's condition was serious. He continued to lose blood and my task then was to arrest this blood flow

as soon as possible before the situation deteriorated further. It was for this reason that I took him to theatre for operation."

Campbell's body was severely blood-stained and contaminated with grit and organic material. To save time, the whole theatre team worked to clean it.

Then, shortly after 8pm, with Campbell under general anaesthetic, the operation commenced.

There were three main injuries: to his left leg, right upper thigh and right arm.

The most serious injury was operated on first. It was to the left leg: a large, ragged wound with a considerable amount of muscle injury and a fracture of the femur. The bleeding points were tied off and contained, the fracture was reduced and attempts were being made to internally fix the fracture with a plate and screws. It was noted that the circulation of the leg below the knee was precarious. It required a fasciotomy to allow the return of blood to the muscles so they might survive.

At this point, Dr James Carstens, the anaesthetist, informed the surgeon that Campbell's blood pressure was not sustainable.

Operating was stopped and attempts were made to resuscitate Campbell. External cardiac massage, the giving of intravenous fluids, the use of adrenalin and the use of electrical stimulants to the heart were used and continued for about twenty minutes. But the cardiogram showed no activity from Campbell's heart. His pupils were fixed and dilated. And this situation persisted while resuscitation was being continued. But all of the attempts failed and Chris Campbell was considered to be brain dead by the specialists present at approximately 9.10.

As Kelman says at the inquest, "Only those people who were in theatre at the time could really appreciate the attempts that were made to save his life."

*But Fairbrother wonders whether Kelman was too concerned about trying to save Campbell's **leg** – and got distracted from saving his life.*

Fairbrother cross-examines Kelman: Blood loss could have been controlled to the critical limbs, right arm, left leg, by the application of a tourniquet?

Yes.

The problem with the tourniquet is that after a while it becomes counterproductive and you may lose a limb?

Yes.

But the application of the tourniquet on Campbell to his arm and leg would have stopped the blood loss and retained the compensated state?

Yes.

Was a tourniquet applied?

Yes, to the left leg in theatre in order to gain control of the bleeding sites to identify them and to thereby stop the bleeding.

Was a tourniquet applied to the right arm?

No. We had considered that the left leg was the most seriously injured and therefore needed our attention first. Once that had been completed the plan was to move to his right arm, a tourniquet would have then been applied. However, we considered it counterproductive to apply a tourniquet to the right arm prior to operating on it as it would have remained on perhaps for an extended period, more than an hour, which would have further jeopardised that limb.

A tourniquet can be kept blown up for three hours?

At the very extreme. Surgically, we never leave a tourniquet on for more than two hours in theatre.

Although the literature refers to three hours, can it not in practice be left on for as long as four and a half hours?

This is possible. The resulting injury to that limb could be considerable.

Your aim in surgery was twofold, was it? One was to save a life and as well as that to save both the severely damaged limbs?

Primarily to save his life and stop the bleeding and secondly to save his limbs.

If the information available to you as the operating surgeon had been such that you could not have achieved both aims, save the limbs and the life, is it fair to say you would have moved to saving the life with the risk of losing the limbs?

Without doubt.

Not fair to say, from the information available to you, you were doing a clean up of the left leg as though you had the luxury of elective surgery, the chance of saving the leg as well?

My initial plan and aim in operating on the left leg was to contain the bleeding. As surgeons that was our primary goal and our teaching in order to achieve this is to explore the vessels, stop bleeding and restore normal anatomy.

No point in having a fully limbed corpse.

Quite obviously so.

You could have stemmed the blood loss from the leg and arm at risk to those limbs by packing or the application of a tourniquet?

I could have initially.

It's a fact that when you became aware that control was being lost you stopped the procedures on the leg and packed it so you could turn your attention to resuscitation.

That is the normal procedure when an emergency arises in theatre.

In Fairbrother's notes he writes, "There was no measurement of blood loss."

One way of doing this is to weigh the swabs that have mopped up blood as you go. But, during the inquest, Kelman says that method has been shown to be inaccurate and he hasn't seen it used in about six years.

The second way of measuring blood loss is with a graduated suction bottle. Fairbrother asks if one was used. Kelman says yes.

Another way is by putting a central venous pressure line in through the neck. That tells you what the pressure is like in the veins as the blood returns to the heart. But one wasn't used.

Fairbrother's concerned that there was only one blood pulse reading in the course of an hour when there would normally be six or seven readings. He argues that the fewer readings there are to work with, the harder it is to pick a trend.

He notes that there were also problems with the Datex, the machine used for checking CO2 and doing blood gas analysis. It had to be recalibrated during the operation, which is rare.

Fairbrother: While operating, how long was the machine turned off for?

Kelman: I'm not sure.

It's not recorded?

It is not required of the anaesthetist to report that side.

This machine gives blood pressure and other functions?

Yes.

So on the notes there is no record of oxygen levels?

The pulse oximeter has recorded a 98% suctuation.

At what point was he adequately oxygenated?

I'm unable to say. He's written it at 2030.

The time you noted that you were told the blood pressure dropped?

8.45.

Some 15 minutes later.

Yes.

Did the hospital hold an inquiry into Campbell's death?

The hospital did not hold an open inquiry into his death and the hospital normally holds an inquiry into all deaths. But at the time this death was the subject of criminal proceedings. We were advised by the coroner that such an open meeting would be inadvisable. However, the matter was discussed with the surgeons involved and the anaesthetist.

What annoys Dr James Carstens, the anaesthetist that night, is that everyone runs a magnifying glass over the actions of the surgical team. But, he says, they didn't shoot Chris Campbell. They are merely the people doing their utmost to put him back together again. They can't choose the condition of a victim when he comes to them. They just have to work with what the person pulling the trigger has left them. He says the average layperson has no idea of the stressful conditions under which they work or of the hopeless situations they are handed and expected to make right.

Dr James Carstens, August 5, 2010: I had no warning at all that there was a risk he would die. We had no reason to realise that. After induction of the anaesthetic his blood pressure was stable. His oximeter reading was 98% which meant that his oxygenation was appropriate. His ventilation was controlled so this area didn't need focus. Suddenly, from what I can remember, things just deteriorated. His blood pressure dropped rapidly. It was aggressive, it was fulminant, it was irreversible, it kept on going and I never expected anything like that was going to happen. When this happened all my attention was directed at elevating his blood pressure. Anaesthetic drugs that may lower blood pressure were stopped, blood and fluids given to try and elevate it. All your attention is on the patient and trying to keep the blood pressure up and keep it normal. Time is not spent recording minute by minute changes in blood pressure. The pattern of the blood pressure was downward and aggressively so.

I'd never come across anything like this before. I'd worked at a trauma place, at Baragwanath Hospital in Soweto, where I saw a tremendous amount of violence, gunshot wounds and things like that, but I've never come across anything else like this before or since in my career.

What happened, the events were in train before he even got to theatre. And by the time it was apparent, it was unstoppable and it happened very quickly. I feel that the most likely cause was cardiogenic shock. The patient's heart did not and could not respond to normal resuscitative procedure.

Kelman in the coroner's inquest: In my opinion he died of irreversible decompensating haemorragic shock. The severity of the injury and the time it took to treat him were factors in the ultimate development of irreversible shock. All attempts were made to save his life. However, these failed and I can only say that we attempted to do everything we could and I am sorry that it has happened.

Fairbrother: How long is too long in a case like this?

Kelman: Naturally, these experiments have not been performed in human beings. In animal experimentation it was shown that if the blood pressure had not been returned to normal and maintained at normal after four hours death of these animals ensued no matter what resuscitating procedures were carried out.

Fairbrother: If he had been operated on after 4.15 when he arrived at the hospital it would have avoided irreversible shock syndrome?

Difficult to say, but it could have. The lessons that were learnt in war time were that early resuscitation and early operation saves lives.

Was the possibility of irreversible shock syndrome looked at when he arrived at the hospital?

I was not present at the time. I saw him at 6.30, assessed him and realised the situation was critical.

Excerpts from coroner Alan Hall's conclusion: It is my view and I conclude that Mr Campbell died at Gisborne due to shock following blood loss from multiple gun shot wounds…

… Mr Fairbrother made a submission to me that the time span, that is between the time when Mr Campbell was admitted to Gisborne Hospital and the time that he was seen by a specialist surgeon, in this case Mr Kelman – he was admitted at 4.15pm and saw Mr Kelman about 6.30pm – was perhaps too long and I accept that it is appropriate for me to recommend that the Accident and Emergency Department at hospitals be aware of the possibility of Irreversible Shock Syndrome and take steps to prevent its onset. Obviously it may sometimes be difficult but in this case there is some concern that Mr Campbell was admitted to Gisborne Hospital at 4.15 and not seen by a specialist surgeon until 6.30.

CHAPTER 6

MT HIKURANGI,
THE RASTAS' MT ZION (3)

Saturday, January 5, 1991: Just a month after Chris Campbell's death, it's announced that an application will be made through the Maori Land Court to return Mount Hikurangi – the Rastas' Mount Zion - to Ngati Porou.

For the last one hundred years the mountain has been owned by the Crown and the private owners of Pakihiroa Station, most recently Colin Williams. The station, which was bought by the Department of Maori Affairs, includes two-fifths of the mountain.

To Ngati Porou, Hikurangi is the most sacred of mountains. It is said to be the final resting place of Nukutaimemeha, the canoe which carried the legendary demi-god Maui.

The Minister of Maori Affairs, Winston Peters, and the Minister of Conservation, Denis Marshall, will apply through the Maori Land Court to restore the lease on the mountain to Ngati Porou through the runanga.

The mountain is a part of the Raukumara Range, made up of Taitai, Wharekia, Aorangi, Hikurangi and Whanokao. Hikurangi is the largest with its twin peaks towering 1752 metres above sea level.

Witi Ihimaera, from his novel The Dream Swimmer: As Hikurangi reared out of the waves, the force of the streaming water began to bear Maui's canoe down the slope. Suddenly the waka was caught in an uppermost cleft of the mountain. On days when the air vibrates with psychic energy, the sails and broken bailer of Maui's waka can still be seen. Hikurangi is our Mount Ararat, and Maui's canoe is our Ark of Noah.

The word Hikurangi means "Summit of the Sky", and the mountain has often been regarded as a lodestone for the universe, one of the compass points by which all stars, suns, moons and worlds are charted. It therefore attracts visitants because of its visibility. Tiana saw the comet Tunui a te Ika from Hikurangi when it made its first blazing visitation. The Maori name is, to my mind, a more appropriate one than Halley's Comet and refers to the male organ at tumescence.

In keeping with its cosmological bearing, Hikurangi is the first point on the earth's surface to be touched by the new day's sun. Hikurangi thus enshrines the holiness of the original mountain of Maori folklore, the Hikurangi of myth where there is life eternal. The original Hikurangi is the hearth of the Maori and some say that it lies beyond the dawning sun.

I have always liked to think that there is an invisible plumb line between the mythical Hikurangi and the terrestrial Hikurangi. I have often imagined that if you were lost in space all you would need to do was wait until the sun came up at one end of the universe. You would then look to the other end, waiting for the flash upon the sacred mountain. Once you saw the sword of light, then you could take your bearings.

Hikurangi is where space and time conjoin, a nexus where stars shower and moons collide, and where the past and future visit in the present. It is in all respects a maunga tapu, a sacred mountain, dominating the landscape and destinies of the people who live beneath it. From its peak can be seen the lands of the Ngati Porou.

Friday, March 29, 1991: The three day celebration, during which Colin Williams will return Mt Hikurangi to the people of Ngati Porou, begins today.

Tribal representatives from throughout the country have arrived at Mangahanea Marae in Ruatoria to mark the event.

Williams decided to return the mountain after a lot of soul-searching and, then, negotiations with the Department of Maori Affairs.

Hikurangi is being returned in two parts. The Minister of Maori Affairs transferred title of Pakihiroa Station to Ngati Porou through the

Iwi Transition Agency. However, the transfer included a $300,000 debt incurred by the previous management, Colin Williams. Conditions of the transfer included paying off the debt, which was done just a few days ago.

Today, Ngati Porou are just happy to get Hikurangi back. "It is being returned to Ngati Porou and to Maori and to all the descendants," says kaumatua Petuere Raroa.

"In spiritual terms the taha wairua (or spirit of the ancestors) has been restored."

For Ngati Porou youth, though, the return of the mountain signifies something completely different. Ngahiwi Apanui says, "It makes me feel good because all those waiata that we sing about the mountain finally mean something. And we can sing with absolute certainty that the mountain belongs to us."

Easter Sunday, March 31, 1991: *Around three hundred people and six ministers from various churches are gathered at Colin Williams' Pakihiroa Station, in the shadow of Hikurangi, for the official karakia, church ceremony and hand-back of the mountain.*

After the ceremonies are complete, formal speeches from tribal spokespeople and official guests are held at Uepohatu Marae.

Many of the Maori eders, while happy with the return of the mountain, don't like the terms of the covenant, which say local Maori have to meet the Minister of Conservation's approval before utilising the mountain's resources.

"For the last a hundred and fifty years lands have been cut from under our feet," says Petuere Raroa.

"When you look at Hikurangi and its sacredness to us, we are the true conservators in this land. We have conserved our mountains and the rivers and the coasts but unfortunately we have not been in control of the conservation purse.

"Many of us from this valley shed our blood in the Second World War in the belief that there would be equity between our people. Equity in itself means equal partnership. We've had a say in matters concerning the nation while in matters concerning Ngati Porou we have the greater say.

"When we negotiated the return of the mountain we had always worked under the premise that its return was absolute in control, in authority and autonomy. The permanency of the relationship never

entered our minds. We never thought that such a marriage would take place."

Conservation Minister Denis Marshall says he'll give the greatest consideration to any proposal submitted by Ngati Porou.

CHAPTER 7

DONNELLY'S HOME IS BURNED

Less than a week after Luke's not guilty verdict on February 26, 1992, Inspector Neville Cook of Gisborne police writes to him. The letter is headlined "Firearms prohibition".

"On reviewing the incident, while it is accepted that there had been past threats made against you by members of the group, they were unarmed when they came to your property.

"You resorted to the use of firearms not just to direct them to leave the property but to attack them. You have indicated that you would resort to the use of firearms again under the same circumstances. Your willingness to resort to extreme measures and the use of firearms gives me considerable concern."

Inspector Cook says that he has arranged for Donnelly's firearms licence to be cancelled.

"This prohibition is not intended to remain in force for a lifetime."

Thursday, April 23, 1992, The New Zealand Herald: Ruatoria farmer Luke Donnelly is furious that his home was destroyed in an arson attack, according to relatives.

Two months ago Mr Donnelly was found not guilty of murdering Rastafarian Christopher Campbell outside the house in December 1990.

He was with his wife and daughter in Christchurch when a neighbour saw the three-bedroom Donnelly family home on fire about 12.45am yesterday.

The Ruatoria volunteer fire brigade was called but the house was destroyed.

Police from Gisborne are investigating the blaze, which they have confirmed was deliberately lit...

... Tenants occupying the Donnelly house moved out on Tuesday and it was unoccupied at the time of the fire.

Mr Donnelly could not be contacted last night. His cousin, Bill Donnelly, said he had been in Christchurch to arrange shifting the family's possessions back to the house.

"He is furious," said Bill Donnelly...

...This month a 26-year-old Rastafarian, Raymond (Hata) Thompson, was convicted of threatening to kill Mr Luke Donnelly six months before Mr Campbell was fatally shot.

From the second interview with Luke: There was a second fire at my property at Makarika. I was out there cleaning up and I'd set up a little sleep-out and everything. I was living in the double garage there. A lot of the different places donated different materials for me. It's funny, ay. These people donated things to help me get re-established but they'd say, "Just keep it quiet. Don't say anything to anyone that we're helping you out."

I wanted to acknowledge and thank the people that helped me. But they didn't want it getting out.

In early October, 1992, Gisborne Police Commander Rana Waitai releases a press statement in response to Donnelly's attempts to have his firearms license restored. It reads: "We should feel sad for this human being who is so panicked out of his wits that he used two guns to shoot, a number of times, an unarmed man who lay wounded on the ground before him. Donnelly should stick to his scared-witless-and-panic explanation because he had intended to do it anyway."

Waitai also refers to "the ramblings of Donnelly's imagination."

Not one to take a step back, Donnelly, in the Dominion Sunday Times, criticises Waitai's police work. "Why didn't he bring charges against Reece Bolingford, who tried to run me off the road half an hour after the acquittal? There were witnesses.

"The old people in the Ruatoria district are still terrified of the Rastas. He should get off his fat arse, go up and reassure them that any bullying by the Rastas and he will come down on them like a tonne of bricks.

"At Chris Campbell's funeral, he walked among people all smoking dope and did nothing about it."

Hughie Hughes, Ruatoria electrician: The media reports always described Luke Donnelly as a Ruatoria farmer. I don't believe that Luke ever did any farming while he was here. I don't think he even spent six months in residence here. Well, it didn't seem like he did. He just wanted to have a go at them. He wanted to test himself. He wanted to be a Rambo or something. And I think if I'd been the judge I would've said he was guilty. He wouldn't have got off with an acquittal. I think in his own way he was as bad as the Rastas.

Once he wanted me to make a big show of leaving some appliances outside the back of my shop. Then he was going to set up all his guns around and wait for them to come in and steal them. He wanted me to set up the appliances like bait so he could catch them red-handed. He was ready for a confrontation with these guys. I wasn't interested. He was baiting them all the time. But I don't think they would have done him any harm.

Detective Malcolm Thomas: There's a lot of bad feeling in the community following Chris Campbell's death. I'm driving from Ruatoria back to Gisborne one day and as I'm passing Luke Donnelly's place I hear the sound of chainsaws. By this time the Rastas have already burnt Luke's shed and his house. There's still talk however that Luke's coming back to put a converted railway wagon on the property. So I go up to check out what's happening and find about six Ratafarians armed with chainsaws cutting down all the trees. They're getting rid of all the shelter on the property.

I try to stop them and tell them to put down the chainsaws. But there's only one of me and they're very single-minded about this. They just ignore my request and start to surround me while gunning the chainsaws. It's a very unnerving feeling being alone among all these guys with chainsaws. But that's the sort of situation you have to walk into occasionally in Ruatoria. You're just not sure what's going to happen next. I call up Ruatoria for a vehicle and another cop comes out. Eventually we get hold of the chainsaws and charge the Rastafarians with wilful damage.

The pine trees were planted on the farm in 1953, the year of Donnelly's birth. Donnelly's fences had also been cut, including one fronting onto the main highway, which resulted in stock another farmer was grazing on the property straying. A horse on the property was slaughtered and holes were bashed in the farm's water tank with a sledgehammer. Five Rastas were arrested for the damage to Donnelly's trees and fences. They were Hemi Toi Reuben, Nehe Reuben, Bill Kaihe, John Heeney and Paul William Edwards. All were sentenced to four months' periodic detention and ordered to pay reparation of $300 each.

The goading between Luke and the Rastas continued. Among Ruatoria fireman Tom Heeney's documents is a photo of a chimney with the words Rasta Sux spray-painted down its length. The photo is dated 9/2/93. A note with it reads: "Sign on chimney of burnt-out house at Luke Donnelly's. Possibly done by Luke himself. Photo taken while brigade attended a grass fire on property."

That same month, Luke was considering running for parliament under the tag Independent Labour, even though he was a paid-up member of the National Party. He said he was only going to run if Gisborne Police Superintendent Rana Waitai gained the Labour nomination. Luke's campaign platform was built around law and order, particularly gang and gun problems.

He announced his intentions in the Gisborne Herald on February 26, 1993, a year to the day after he was found not guilty of murdering Chris Campbell: "If what I have in mind were implemented, those who would normally think of joining a gang would find it a totally undesirable lifestyle.

"Existing gangs would be given six to 12 months to wind down their activities and dispose of their regalia and assets. If they chose not to do that they would find that any attempt to maintain their lifestyle would be fruitless."

On gun control: "Common sense says you don't have to have a licence to put your hands on a gun, but you can counter that by laying down stiff sentences for unlicensed people found with a firearm. The problem would virtually fix itself.

"Anyone who might be tempted to bring in a $45 handgun from overseas would be silly to risk a minimum jail term of, say, three years.

"That's another thing I would advocate… minimum instead of maximum jail terms."

Luke never made it to Parliament. But Rana Waitai did as a member of New Zealand First's "Tight Five" Maori MPs in 1996.

PART 12
LIFE AFTER CHRIS (THE NEW TESTAMENT)

CHAPTER 1

BORN AGAIN

Chris Thompson (original Rasta Hata Thompson's brother): Charlie Cheese, Cody, Mike Paiti, Jano Kirikino and a few others all went born-again after Chris died. There were quite a number of them, and their wives. It was true separatism from the Rastas thereafter. When Chris died that's when the divisions started to happen. People began to look at themselves rather than just looking to Chris for guidance. Then you found all these wannabes that kind of leapt up to try and take his place. Cody and Cheese were among them.

Laura: Everyone.

Chris: Well virtually.

See, Cody doesn't strike me as a replacement for Chris. He's too placid a character.

Chris: You haven't seen the other side yet.

Aw, is that right?

Laura: Yeah.

I wouldn't have thought he had an aggressive bone in his body.

Laura: Ouch. Oo-hoo.

Well, that's just how he seems from the couple of times that I've met him.

Chris: Aw, well I've seen it. And this is under the influence of born-again Christianship. We go back to that feeling of being drunk. Like it was very extreme.

What? The born-again side of it?

All of it, the whole situation was extreme. And when division is involved, all those who went their separate ways became extreme in that area that they'd decided upon.

Did they become extremely against each other for a while?

Chris: Yeah, yeah, yeah.

Laura: They were all telling each other, "This is the way to go brother." Ha ha ha. "Come this way brother. This is the path you need to take."

Chris: Some of them were that extreme they just lived through the guidance of the preacher at the time, Arthur Baker. But, for me, they were in a vulnerable state of mind.

So he almost preyed on them.

Chris: Yeah.

Well, maybe that's not the right word.

Well he was doing these numbers like, "You've got to burn your old self, you've got to shed your old skin," meaning turf those colourful clothes, get rid of those hats, cut your hair. Aw wake up! God doesn't judge you on your physical appearance.

Laura: The Rastas were vulnerable and he just took their minds over. And they'd stand blatantly on the street and preach to people. It was extreme. When I look back I think, "My God, how did I get through that." This was all after Chris died. It was bad enough having them there at Mangahanea. But when he passed out and everybody wanted to be the wannabes, well, it was really tough. There were plenty of arguments.

Laura: You know I admire John Heeney and them for where they've come to. That was something that I instilled in those boys at Mangahanea Marae when we were staying there. I told them about the original people to help them empower themselves so that they themselves would know where they're going to in life. So that was something positive that came out of staying there.

And the other thing was – I'm not trying to be like Hori Keeti (the prophet, Pop Gage) but the third eye said to me, "You have to live in there a duration of three months until that faction breaks up into about three or four groups."

And it came out like that. We lived in the house and the first lot went. Then the next lot went. Then the last lot went. My nephew Charlie Turnbull was the one who broke off with the first lot, and he took it to his home. He had the Rastafarian flag on his house and his house was full up with people.

But the others that stayed in town joined Arthur Baker. He's a local born-again Christian man.

They all went different ways. And it ended up being like I was told by my third eye.

But the best part for me was the goodness that came out of it and John Heeney and them got onto the path that they're on now. They're into building houses with those adobe bricks. And that's great.

My nephew Charlie Turnbull, known as Charlie Cheese, eventually became a born-again Christian but he's broken out of that and become his own man. He's a boss in the forestry and he's looking after his wife and his family.

CHAPTER 2

THE STORY OF ED TE RAUNA,
SECOND GENERATION RASTA

I didn't take a note of when I interviewed Ed Te Rauna, but it was at his home in Gisborne, probably in 2001. He was teaching a good friend of mine, Kez Namana, how to speak Maori and she put me on to him.

Ed Te Rauna: I'm twenty-six years old. I suppose I was part of the second generation of Rastas.

I got involved with them when I was just a wee boy. When I was about ten I lost my dad. My dad was the average dad. He worked during the day. He kicked around with his kids on the weekend. He was a forestry worker. To my knowledge he didn't have any affiliation with the Rastafarians. My mum was really unstable at the time so I ended up with my grandmother. So my grandmother brought me up.

And while I was growing up, starting to become a teenager, my father-figures in my life were my uncles, my grandmother's sons, who were Rastafarians. They were the Reubens. Nehe Reuben is known as King Glory. It would be fair to say he was a bit of a father-figure in my life. What a son looks to a dad for - all those qualities he has as a man - I looked to Nehe for. So while I was growing up, starting to become a teenager, starting to become a man, that's how I became to have such strong beliefs in the Rastafarian faith and what was going on in the movement at the time, which was a lot of conflict with the community.

I started off my college years at Te Aute in Hawke's Bay. That was through some family plan to pluck me out of the situation, trying to give me an opportunity. But I think I just needed to be with *my* people, my family, being young and having lost so much as a young fulla. I just longed to be with my family too much. So I blew that opportunity and ended up back in Ruatoria more or less growing up to be a Rastafarian. I didn't even make it through the whole year at Te Aute. I was about thirteen when I arrived back home. I ended up spending another four years at school in Ruatoria. I tried hard to gain some sort of education for my grandparents. But during my education at school, I was also learning about Rastafarianism at home.

It would be fair to say that probably the cannabis had a lot of influence as well. I was always smoking cannabis. It fitted into the lifestyle. It all seemed right for my purpose in life.

Another thing, too, that I was going through at the time was a real spiritual sort of thing. I was really searching for some spiritual strength somehow to help cure my insecurities or my grief or something. I was sort of looking for what they say in religious terms is the truth, those sort of awesome things that life promises. And that was another strong motivator for my believing in the Rastafarian movement. And as I got deeper I learnt that with that particular movement that I had attached myself to there were other issues going on. It became to me like two different cultures entwined. There was the Rastafarianism and then a strong Maori activist thing going on as well in terms of land and stuff like that. But I was just going along with the flow. I was learning this today and learning this tomorrow. And these were the things that started to come out. These were the things I realised that I was a part of, well, a part of fighting for I could say because of some of the things I saw back then.

First of all I thought it was all Bob Marley, and religious stuff and Haile Selassie, all spiritual, all good. And then… I was only fairly young when all the kidnappings and that went on. And I got the fullness of what they went through when they began to come home from jail. The feelings and the beliefs were still in them. They were still in the men who had gone and served time for those things they'd done. And they were even stronger.

I didn't really know Chris that well. I knew what type of man he was. I knew him to be around us. He was like… Well, I don't know what a messiah was like, but I can explain in my own words what he was like when he was around. He was real straight, a real straight-as, straight to the heart dude. He hardly spoke. But when he spoke he expected to be right and expected his word to be done. He was like a real hard man. But I didn't really know him to talk to him.

But the Rastafarians who didn't go and serve time for those things that they did, they almost feared him. They had the utmost respect. They just really bowed their heads to him. He was just awesome like that.

With the activist side of the movement it was like I grew through the levels. By the time I'd received the activist messages, I was strong enough to handle them and strong enough to cope with them. It all made sense. It was unreal, man.

I've got heaps-a different feelings now. And it's hard for me to remember how I was feeling then, when I was accepting all of it.

There were some things that I went through that I don't know if anybody else would understand. This was after Chris Campbell was killed.

To me, in my view, it turned into a cult sort of thing after Chris died. I don't know if I was just growing into my age of discretion and starting to know what was really right and wrong or if it just went out of hand and turned into a cult or something.

The Rastas believed that God was walking with us in the flesh. And they believed that he was one of the bros. And they knew which one. It was old John Heeney.

That's what I mean I'm different today. King Glory, Nehe Reuben, is my family. He's like a father to me. And it hurts me to know that he can believe things as easily as that. I dunno, he might-a seen the guy walking on water or something. But I have real big problems with that.

When Chris got out John Heeney was still inside. Some things went on before they went to jail that I can't explain. Things like the church burnings and that. They had their reasons through what the Rastafarian faith was telling them. You know, "The preacher man is telling lies." Have you heard those Bob Marley quotations from songs? I think that's where they got all their beliefs that the churches were falsely advising and preaching to people.

Then they went to prison and they had a movement in there and John and Chris started recruiting believers in there.

John was Chris's right hand man. But in the early days it had been Beau Tuhura before he drifted off. I think Beau believed he should-a been the leader. And he argued with Chris about it a lot.

When everybody went to jail Beau came back into the picture. A lot of other fullas also came to the front. Beau started trying to throw his weight around and organise everyone again. But it didn't last.

In the long run, out of the three of them, Chris was the strongest character and he was accepted as leader. Beau wasn't really a fighter and you needed to be able to back up your leadership with muscle. John Heeney was fiery as anything, but didn't quite have the physique or the aura to project his power or his strength.

Q: John Heeney, to me, just as an observer, comes across as a bit of a fanatic more than a leader.

Ed: Ha ha ha ha.

I shouldn't, you know… don't tell him that.

Ed: Aw na, this is good for me because I have rarely ever talked about these things. And it's gone and altered my life, you know, altered my life something drastically. Some things I can't get out of my life in terms of trying to move forward in society, things like this here for example is one of the things that he believed in (pulls up his T-shirt sleeve to reveal a big tattoo of the word UTU, revenge) as well as believing in The Bible, you know. (Ed lets the sleeve drop again). That there stays covered up, mate. It's gonna get really covered up if I can get enough money. I'm gonna get it taken off.

That's part of why I say it slowly slipped into being a cult. I believe that they took the gospels and the scriptures and twisted them to suit their own lifestyles. I was just a young fulla. So some of these things if I didn't believe in them, I would be stood over to make me believe. If I questioned anything, it would be, "What?" (Ed flexes his muscles, sets his face aggressively and pretends to be an intimidator looking down on someone). And it was *made* to be righteous. Like the utu was made to be righteous. We were led to believe that we could even *kill* people and be forgiven by God for it, you know.

And I was a strong believer in God and that kind of stuff before I joined the Rastas. And that's part of what motivated me to lean that way in my life. I wanted to believe in God and do all those things, but I wanted to smoke dope at the same time. It suited my lifestyle. I was able to smoke dope and there was still room for me in heaven.

Hata's mum told me that a guy called Charlie Turnbull would have made a good leader.

Ed: He had old leadership qualities, old Charlie Turnbull. But somebody else was already the leader; you know what I mean? Somebody else was already appointed: John Heeney.

Now this fulla Prince of Peace, Eddie Kotuhi, from Wairoa, was one of the guys who was recruited in prison.

I don't know what was happening to the Rastafarian movement in jail, but it was growing. And they were expecting the people at home to be growing as well, to be growing as how they were growing. And they were growing quite criminally minded, I think.

They were still wanting to be righteous. But they were also still wanting to settle some of their vendettas and stuff. And they found a way, I believe, in jail, through enough reading, to make the scriptures fit into their lives. Like I said, they had it that finely down that they could explain to somebody like myself for instance - and this *was* explained to me – how I could go about killing somebody and be forgiven.

The trouble I had with that, mate, is it's in the old Ten Commandments. And like of all the things He said in The Bible, only ten of these things he commanded you, you know. He commanded that you don't do these ten things. He didn't just say it. And I was really sort of terrified to have to make that mistake for me, to make the mistake of believing in a man. I was trying to believe in God and I just about believed in a man, instead of what I should-a been believing in, which was myself. God just comes out of yourself. You've just gotta ask yourself those questions. He'll tell yourself the right answer.

And then there was all this Maori belief from up the Coast that the Messiah was gonna come along. But that's what I mean. They took the Rastafarian faith, and then they took from The Bible and then they took from the Maori beliefs as well. And they applied all the philosophies from those different beliefs and made a religion to suit their lifestyle. Of course, they believe that John Heeney is God. And I don't. I really don't. Aw, he may be. I'll burn in hell for saying I don't because I've known him. I've lived with him. And, shit, He's gotta be greater than that. Like, he's got problems like anyone else: alcohol problems, anger problems. I'm sure if God was walking around down here he'd show us something better than that.

Prince of Peace had a lot to do with how they found their scriptures. They used the laws of the Ringatu Church, started by Te Kooti, for their fellowship. Prince of Peace was made what they used to call… There's a Maori name for it. It's the equivalent of a policeman while the church is going on. He polices the church. And that's what they do in the Ringatu Church. They have these couple of guys going around with long sticks. And because it's so long, incantation after incantation, some people go to sleep. These guys go round and just tap them to wake them up. He was like that, but in jail, that law applied to jail lifestyle was slightly different cos he would go round with a big piece of wood, going rrrr, rrrr (flexes his muscles again). Know what I mean, dude? He'd probably be whacking people. It's just, we're in jail now, and that's what happens in there, stuff like that, stand-overs. That's the whole story right there. Like, when they came out of jail they were just like fire-brands, ay. They were ready to do battle and fired up, mate.

Chris had so many things *on* him. You could write a story about all the things he had on him. He remembered everything that went on before he went to jail and he still wasn't finished with them. I suppose he wanted to make peace. But then again… Their idea of peace was, "You owe us this and that." It wasn't just to go over and say, "Sorry." It was to see things put right.

"THE THIRD COMING OF CHRIST"

Ed Te Rauna: I believe John Heeney thinks he is the person who Pop Gage prophesied. The Rastas consider John to be the third coming of Christ because Haile Selassie was the second coming. And John thinks that he's the one.

Chris thought *he* was the prophesied one and John thought *he* was. And they had a big argue about it when Chris left jail. And this is what the guys all said when they came out of jail. Like, they came out in dribs and drabs at first. These guys are all coming out of jail and coming to the Coast and setting up. But it really started when Prince of Peace and John Heeney came out.

It was Prince of Peace who preached it to everybody. I can't say that John Heeney ever, ever told me that he, you know. But he thrived on it. But I can't say that he ever told me in his own words from his own mouth that he was what Prince of Peace was proclaiming him to be. It was this Prince of Peace, mate, that really, really had the thing.

And apparently they had an argument just before Chris got out. And Chris turned around and said to John, "No, you have to lead them. You have to run the bros."

And John said, "Na, na, na. You're the man." Chris's name was Jah Rastafari, by the way. This was their born-again, get-a-new-name stuff.

Anyway, that's the argument they had. And Chris left John with this: "You have to. You have to take the lead. You're the Joseph," meaning that he was Joseph from the twelve tribes of Israel in the Bible.

And hearing this, Prince of Peace went home, studied up his Bible to find out what the Joseph was and came across the blessings that Isaac, the father, bestowed on his son Joseph. And Prince of Peace believed John Heeney to be all these things. You see, cos if you read it, Joseph gets everything. Even the sun and the moon and the stones bow down to the Joseph. Well, that's where Prince of Peace got his idea that everybody bows down to the Joseph.

That's what Prince of Peace preached to me. That's how I know what that all came from. While he was studying about this Joseph, something sort of dawned on him. "Aw, the Lord is John himself!"

They just come out of jail; they're fit as buggery. Not much people living a laid-back lifestyle are gonna wanna disagree with people like that. And that's how Prince of Peace impressed it upon me anyway. It was cleverly done. The stand-over tactics were very modest. So much so that you couldn't even call it that, I suppose. But it was mild stand-over tactics, just like the body gestures showed us that he was a strong man, and a man that was ready to combat. You know what I mean, bro? You know how you can get the gist of somebody playing up like that.

And he used to preach it to us, knowing that we had a fear of God, in terms of not wanting to wrong the word of God or go against what He says. So we had a fear of God and a love of God and he played on it. He said, "This is what we have to do. It's righteous by God." And how he put it was incredible. It was cleverly put, man.

When John came out, he was even more fired up than I thought Chris was. Chris was going around in a peaceful manner, but everyone in the camp knew how worked up he was feeling toward the people. There was a lot of anger there. They blamed the Ngati Porou people a lot for siding with the police. In their eyes, they thought, "Aw, far out. That's my whanau, that's my grandmother over there. She's housing and feeding the police that are chasing us around the bush." So probably that's how that thing got burnt down or whatever. They were coming across things in their lives, through their own works. It was by no fault of anyone else but themselves. But that's how they were coming across those feelings for people. "Aw, siding with our enemies, ay?" And then there'd be reprisals. But at the end of the day, they put themselves in the situation. The things they were doing were against the law. You had to accept some things they were doing were against the law.

CHAPTER 3

GOTTA "DO SOMETHING FOR THE MOST HIGH"

Ed Te Rauna (interviewed in about 2001): I've separated myself from the Rastas for some time now, about six years. And I've grown a little family, as you can see. My feelings about the moko? Ha ha. It's freaky. I try to have remorse, you know, but there's nothing there. But I do have the regret of putting it on there.

But John freaked out this day. He was asking, "Hey, bro, how did you come up with that name?" He was talking about my Rasta name. I just told him what it meant to me: Lord of the Heavens or Heavenly Lord. So we went down and done that. It became part of my moko.

I do feel like it's *my* moko. And I feel that it's my thing between me and the God that I believe in. But my grandmother will tell me, well, God made me a certain way, so why did I go change it, you know. And I'll say, "Aw, shit, that's right." But I thought, when I did this, that I was doing it for my love of God. I thought, "Far out, that's what God wants us to do. It's richer than this Bible. Far out." That's how Prince of Peace showed it to us, ay, man. He had it *sussed*. He had scriptures spread out through the Bible that he could refer to. He had made a bit of a story about it.

Hata Thompson was strong enough to believe in what he believed in and tell them where to go and shove it. Hata still had a lot of time for those people in a family sort of a sense. But when they tried to make him do things, tried to make him believe things, well he just wouldn't have it. And fortunately for him he was a strong enough character to be able to say those things to people like Chris Campbell. He'd just say, "Aw na, that's not me, man." A lot of people up there had become placid from believing in the gospel things about the faith. And they just didn't have the jolly character to stand up to these guys.

As things got along, there were a lot of things there that I did believe in, a lot of good things, a lot of awesome things. But at the same time I was being introduced to things that I didn't believe in, like this here (pulls up his shirt sleeve and points to his tattoo), utu, me having to go around and deal with somebody because they offended John Heeney. You know what I mean? That was totally wrong. I had to give them a bit of a growling. And if they stood up to a growling, I'd probably have to knock them around a bit. And I just totally disagreed with that. I was very reluctant.

The first time, I got taken out at night. It wasn't too late. But it was night-time. And this is what I was told. Four of the dread guys turned up, sweet as, and they says, "Aw, come to get you. Most High wants us to go and do something, gotta go and do something for the Most High." Most High, being John. That's what he was referred to, as the Most High, not as Lord or God or anything, but he'd acquired that title, Most High. Again, very cleverly put because it could just mean the most high of men or of the Rastas. So very cleverly put, but as we all know Most High is also a title for God.

So they said, "Gotta go and do something for the Most High."

I said, "Aw yeah, sweet" and jumped in the car, because everything we did was for the Most High.

We went to this house and they made me sit in the middle while they were telling me what was going on. They were looking down at me like this, mate (imitates a glare). I was only sixteen or seventeen, still at school, fit as a fiddle. I really felt used in those years before I left them. They took me to this house, man, and they made me beat this fulla up. He was a bit older than me, yeah, quite a *lot* older than me. He was in the Rastas, probably the equivalent of a Mongrel Mob prospect. And at that stage I probably was as well.

They were there to enforce the law that the Most High had sent us around to enforce, to tell this guy to stop mucking around. And the mucking around he meant was, aw, well, this guy was just trying to get a life, you know. He just wanted to have a missus and a bit of a life. He wasn't running away from the Rastas at all. But they thought that he needed to be labouring, hard-core labouring like digging dope holes and stuff like that.

I now see the Rastas as a gang. The movement that I saw progress into what I see today, I believe it's progressed into being a gang. It may have already been like that when I was attracted to them. But I didn't realise it at the time.

It's those sort of incidents that threw me right off. I actually did that. I actually gave the guy some clips. He done nothing to me. But after that I just stood there and bawled my eyes out ay, man. They were all standing right there and growling him. And I couldn't understand why they were growling him. You see? He had his own life. But they were judging him. They needed him to be doing his prospecting or whatever. I was standing by this fulla. I'd just finished jolly slapping him around a bit. And I was just crying. I just stood there crying. And it was a bit of a thing for me, you know. It sort-a shook me up a bit. It give me a look at the people I was believing in. That was a bummer for me ay, man.

From then on I couldn't believe how he (John) could be God.

I don't know what it's like now. But back then they were trying to teach us about that utu stuff. And you can't really justify that sort of stuff, I believe.

There's a lot of things about Maori perspectives that I believe in and there's also a lot of things about *some* Maori perspectives that I don't believe in. In their time they done a lotta good things. In their time they done a lotta awful things as well, Maoris. Yeah, there's quite a dark side to the Maori people. They done some quite rugged things. I mean, some of them, they used to eat each other, man. And along with that they say about how Maori used to have such an awesome spiritual sense. That's right. Well if they had such an awesome spiritual sense, how could they go and do something like that?

It's just because in our modern day we don't have a reference point or something.

Yeah, yeah.

It's just like in those days it would-a just been normal, so that was the accepted. But it's just that Europeans came in and because that wasn't part of their reality it appalled them and they passed their feeling of being appalled on to other Maori people and made the Maori people appalled at themselves, you know.

True. Too much all right.

In a way it's probably no different from eating a cow or a horse or anything really. It's just another form of meat isn't it. But it's just that we have this idea and if you accept that idea then, you know. It's a great way of Europeans, too, to be able to put down another race. But, ah, you have feelings now that some of them don't like you?

Aw, yeah, definitely. I left them in quite an arrogant way. My kids' mum was going with a facially-tattooed Rastafarian. He wasn't at the level of John Heeney and those guys. He was underneath them. This young lady was living up there with them, cooking for their workers, you know. All the work was pertaining to the dope. They'd come down off the hill and she'd have a feed ready for them. Anyway, she went and fell in love with me. And I accepted her wanting to be with me. And that was like an insult to them. It was at the time when they were trying to figure out what was wrong with me. Why don't I come round any more and stuff? I'd already started to move away from the Rastas. And this girl wanted to move in with me even more because I wasn't there. I suppose she wanted to get out too. So she moved in. They wanted to beat me up because she was already with one of the other guys. I don't know. I felt sorry for the girl. Somebody turns up and asks you for help. That's what she was more or less doing, asking for help because she didn't want to be with them. So the bros came around and really put the pressure on. It was like, "You're gonna get it, man!"

I'm like, "Aw well, yeah, I'm here. Here I am. I can't change what I'm gonna do with my life or if I'm gonna get it because of it. Yous all know where I am." But nothing came of it. And we just ended up moving away from there and trying to get on with our lives.

But it goes on until today, mate. I wish I had a letter here so I could show you. Stuff like, "Look, brother, I know you've gone astray. But that's all right. The Lord's forgiving." Stuff like that.

SCRIPTURE-DRIVEN SOLDIERS

(It's worth reminding the reader here that this interview with Ed Te Rauna was done in 2001. The date as I write this note is June 7, 2011. Ed is looking back to the early 1990s when the first wave of Rastas isn't long out of prison, the group has splintered following the death of Chris Campbell and John Heeney is coming to terms with the leadership role that Campbell bestowed upon him in prison. Stand-over tactics may have been used as Heeney asserted his leadership and radical Bible interpretations that would enable Rastas to kill without fear of spiritual reprisal may have been taught (but to my knowledge never utilised). But this was a long time ago. And as I write, in 2011, some of the Rastas, including Heeney, are now involved in crucial, potentially life-saving work in Ruatoria. After years of being at odds with the community, they are now keen to make amends and are playing a positive role. But I'll get to that later.)

Ed Te Rauna, former Rasta: The Rasta beliefs about the twelve tribes of Israel: it would take me a long time to explain something like that. I've kind of like unplugged some of those things from my life. I'm trying to teach myself to not believe in them, you know. I'm trying to re-educate myself.

But there were some awesome things I learnt. Overall, everything I learnt has benefited me today, even the wrong things that I learnt. I now know that I'll never want to do that to somebody again.

These days I just do my own thing. I try not to attach myself to any dogma or religion. I think I've missed out on a lot because of my involvement with the Rastas and it's really hard to re-educate myself. I think I've missed out on my valuable transition in terms of changing from a boy to a man and coping with the things that a man should be able to cope with. I've learnt how to cope with it in other ways and I believe they're not right, like that (points to the tattoo on his upper arm) utu and stuff like that. And it's been really hard for me to re-educate myself.

Although I know I believe in what's right, I have a hard job re-educating myself because of how it was jolly put across to me, man. It was kinda like forced in there.

I might-a been in their eyes some sort of chosen one, chosen child or chosen prospect but I never had any violence come to me.

Was it rare to not have violence used against you?

It was. Apparently it was. It was ordered by old John Heeney that I get a few beatings. I was told by another fulla, he's dead now, Striker Jones, that somebody had been ordered to do something to me. And it was something quite jolly rugged. Shit, you know, I freaked out. I was scared, of course. Striker told me to look out for myself. He said, "Those buggers, they're gettin' silly again." This was when I was moving away from the group.

My missus had made it obvious to everyone that I was the guy that she was interested in. I don't know. She apparently couldn't help herself any time I was around and a glow would come on her. That's what became obvious to everybody. Shucks, man, they just started to turn on me then. And that's when some of these guys were getting ordered to give me a bit of a hiding.

My partner had been with a young fulla. I think he's detached from the Rastas now as well. He was my good friend. But that's a different story.

So I was with them for some time while me and my missus were still gaining a friendship. And they saw this friendship forming and bashings were ordered then. I think somebody up there was definitely looking out for me.

Do you think there was a certain amount of brainwashing by the Rastas?

Aw yeah. That's why I probably called it a cult. It's brainwashing. It's twisted up to suit their own jolly lifestyle.

Do you think they could ever revitalise to the extent it was in the '80s?

That's what I believe he was training us to become.

What? Soldiers?

Yeah. With the scriptures that we used and how they were twisting the Bible around to make it suit a guerilla kind of warfare, it was sweet-as for us to go into someone's house, kill them, and that's what they had in mind, mate. They thought they were gonna cleanse out a jolly nation, I suppose.

The whole nation or just the Coast or Ruatoria?

Well, it seemed like the whole world they wanted to cleanse. So I can't really put a thing on that. But I know they wanted to start at Ruatoria. It was like this, mate. "Well, bro, with those principles in place, those scriptures are there to tell us that it's all right." The scripture goes like this: "To whom thou forgiveth, I shall forgiveth also." That was apparently God's words. And it was used like this: I'll go and take your life but I'll forgive you first. "I forgive you." (Ed pretends to slit someone's throat from behind). Like that. That meant that God forgave that person and that person would go straight to heaven.

That freaky?

It's twisted logic isn't it.

It's *unreal* ay, man. But this is what they believed, ay.

Were there other guys around you believing that or taking it on board, who would've gone out there under that brainwashing?

We lived up in a little bach up at Whakaahu. And it was myself and a couple of older Rastas most of the time. And a couple of occasions we had the addition of (Rangi) Rick Brown - he's Hamana Brown's brother - and this other guy from Nga Puhi. But there was basically just a handful of us learning about these new testimonies that come from the prison wave of Rastafarianism.

So quite often it was just sitting by our fire after dinner, smoking on some weed, having a little church of our own. We'd open with a prayer. They considered me one of their main recruits. I was moulded into exactly what they wanted. I would have been, I believe, a key to their influence over other youths. I was the kind of student that they wanted.

Fortunately for me I was, I don't know, I could say strong enough. I didn't feel strong enough. But from somewhere I just pushed myself away from them. And I'm still coming to terms with it all. I haven't talked about this to anybody. I'm getting the shivers telling you about it because I know some people are gonna be upset. Nobody else is gonna see those guys through my eyes because these older guys are my father-figures and they're teaching me. And they know that I'm full-on, eyes and ears wide open. And they're just pouring it into me, man, cleverly as.

I almost got to that point. I almost believed in the scriptures that they were twisting around. It was just hinted to me that this guy needed to go. He's actually dead now and he actually died from being killed. But I had nothing to do with it and neither did the Rastas.

A lot of those Maori prophecies did have a stronger influence than the Rasta stuff. Those Maori prophecies were where they really defined who they were and why they were.

Were there any prophecies that you particularly remember?

There was one. The guy was a tohunga (holy person) I think. Rikirangi Gage.

Yeah, I know the guy: Pop Gage, Hori Keeti.

Yeah. He prophesised that two leaders would come from the east or something to that effect. And the first one will fall (Chris). And it will be the second one, the one that succeeds him who will be the leader. And that's where John Heeney fits in there as well.

The second one will what? Will be the real leader or be God?

Will be the real leader who will lead these people out of whatever. I dunno.

Slavery or whatever?

Yeah, yeah, stuff like that. Racial oppression and stuff like that. But real rugged stuff like slavery and stuff, which doesn't really go on nowadays, but it was quite a classical prophecy.

But maybe they're not talking about the second leader being John. Maybe they're talking about someone completely different.

Yeah, that's right.

Could be your kids, mate.

Could be. Chris mighta had a kid.

Chris did have a kid. I went and saw his mum and she told me. Where is his son now?

His son was brought up by the mum and her family in Tikitiki and in Gisborne.

Wiki Haua, original Rasta Cody Haua's nephew: Me and Ed Te Rauna went to school together. Ed and me did a lot of fellowship together when we were sixteen and seventeen, often torn between Christianity and the Rastas. He's a top man. One day after sitting with him I went down to the river towards Jeru as I knew they were baptising there that day. I walked off the road and into the water and got blessed in the name of Christ. The interesting thing is I don't call myself a Christian as what that would mean to me is I support the Christians that stole land in the past from our people. I am just a believer in the Lord Jesus.

Ed Te Rauna: I remember one day being with Chris. And there was a guy up there, one of the big time bloody dope growers up there. I'd better not say his name. It would be unfair for the guy. But he was a big guy, a real big guy. And he's real big time. I tell ya, he's real cocky and he's big time. And this is one thing that freaked *me* out. We were just driving along the road. Chris was just fresh out of jail. He knew this guy's always got it and stuff. And we just pull up and Chris hops out. And he just went over to this big time fulla, who was *well* respected, nobody ever messed with him, and asked him for a couple-a ounces. And without a hassle this fulla just reached under the seat of his car and got it out. And while Chris was explaining he'd fix him up later, this fulla was just shrugging off his offers and telling him not to worry about it. Everyone had respect for Chris, even the people who were high up in the community. And I guess that fulla was high up in the community in a sense.

CHAPTER 4

LIVING UP TO THE PROPHECY

Tape recorded note to myself: Cody Haua had been brought up as an Anglican. He pulled out of the Rastas when he became a born-again Christian, after Chris Campbell's death. He doesn't belong to any denomination, but still considers himself a Christian.

He doesn't have a moko on his face, like the modern members of the Ruatoria Rastafarians.

After Chris was killed, John Heeney came up to see Cody at his house in Whakapaurangi Road with two other guys, Prince of Peace and King Glory. Cody thought they wanted to knock him around.

They came up to Cody's old run-down house. And they said that he had to bow down to John and that John was God.

Cody said, "No, I'm not going to bow down to him. He's my friend, not my God."

"You've got to bow down to him because he's God."

"No way." He was waiting for John to jump in and tell these guys, "Wake up."

But he didn't. And that seemed even stranger to Cody.

Dion Hutana, the Rasta who burned down Ngati Porou Marae, interviewed in Mangaroa Prison in Hawke's Bay in the early 2000s: When I pulled away from the dread I broke down and cried for three days and three nights. Robbie Grace from Ruatoria was here then, serving his sentence for murder.

And I thought, "Aw, I'll go over to where that old fulla is," cos I was told he was also a healer, a Maori healer. I thought, "I've got nothing to lose cos I'm right at the bottom of my life now." And he helped me get through it. He helped me back up to a point where I could start again.

Hata Thompson on John Heeney: We're on different paths now. He's got to move along and learn to do things for everyone and not just for himself... He tells me he wants to be a chief. I said, "Aw well, you've got to be fair. Fairness is where it's at, mate."

John and I don't always get on, ay. I think he got a bit jealous of me when he got out of jail. While he was still inside, I ended up running things and I ended up giving a few fullas a clout and changing things and straightening them up a bit because it was getting out of hand. Some of the things that were happening were blatant thuggery, I thought.

I thought, "Aw na, we can't do that." I'm not into stand-over tactics. That's not me: just picking on anybody. If you're going to do something, you do it properly. That's security. But if you've got personal vendettas, *you* deal with it. Don't get us involved. Cos that's what was happening, ay. We started getting involved in personal vendettas. And I wasn't into any of that sort of bullshit. Fuck! I'm getting out of jail and there's another younger generation. And half of them I didn't even know.

Farck! I had to pull a lot of their heads in and try to get them on the right track, which was pretty hard, especially when they were most likely getting commands or something. And my actions didn't go down well with Chris and the other one (John Heeney). But I said to them, "Man, it just had to happen. And if you were out here, you'd see it, too."

Chris and John were still in jail and they had this leadership carry-on happening between them. But I was out, and I could see what the young guys were doing.

And I just didn't want to see the bros back home going to jail for fuckin' bullshit. You're no good in jail. I learnt that when I went there. You're no good to no one.

Interview with Hata Thompson's mum Laura (Aunty Ga-ga) and younger brother Chris:

Laura: According to the prophecy, there is leadership that has to come through from here. There is a person who will come out of here to make sure the people are looked after.

Did Chris Campbell think he was that person?

Laura: Oh yeah, I suppose he thought he was.

Chris: Well I'd be blatant. I'd say yeah. To be honest I'd say yeah, and likewise for today for John (Heeney). Well, *he* believes he is. He believes he's the new advent, the third advent.

When you say advent you mean like he's the latest reincarnation of Haile Selassie or something?

Laura: Yeah.

Chris: When I look at the core group and the names they've allowed themselves to take and claim as their own, well those were all given by John. In a way it's like how Jesus acquired John the Baptist, acquired Judas Priest, all of these fullas and his apostles, well likewise for John. I think the same effect took place for Chris. But he had a by-far larger gathering.

Do you think John might be flogging a dead horse sort-a thing?

Laura: Yeah.

Chris: Well I believe so.

Laura: It's assumption on his part.

207

Chris: I wouldn't say assumption. Like I'd say good on him because at the end of the day he still has people following him and that's all part of his drug for himself. Flogging the wrong horse for me would be seen like this: the way he's going about achieving his goals is a bit lopsided. There's no equality in it. You don't demand because people are entitled to their free agency as individuals at the end of the day and it says in The Pipera (The Bible) about free agency.

Even though I have a dislike for taking pieces here and there to suit your daily need or your on-the-spot requirements I do, however, believe that a lot of revelations are coming to pass these days. For instance with the uprising of our people, because that's what they were calling it back in Chris's day: an uprising. Now in John's case I'd call it a retry because he's trying to stimulate something that happened then or re-stimulate it according to then. And it's obvious; "Open your eyes, brother. You saw it never happened then. Why are you following that same formula?" I know it sounds like I've got a personal dislike for John, but not really. We have our differences in perspective and perception and beliefs. Like, back then I really believed.

How old were you then?

About seventeen or eighteen. And I really believed that what they were preaching at the time or what they were delivering to my ears, my inner soul I should say, my mind, I believed in it to be true. But where I went wrong for myself when I reflect is I over-ate. You know how it is when you over-eat, you're gonna spew?

Yeah, yeah, yeah. I used to love rice risotto. But now I just can't be bothered with it. You know what I mean? You just go too far on it.

Yeah but for me it was like, where I went wrong was I was just drinking so much from out of the book and actually soaking in so much that I'd lost contact with the real world. I'd allowed myself to go to that extent where it was just falling out of my mouth. "You're blasphemous," and you're this and you're that. You know, I became the preacher there drunk at the end of the day on what I thought I'd empowered myself with. I used to sit there and I've been through many a different faith to get a perspective from different angles. And the one thing I note with a lot of the faiths is that they believe theirs is the only way and that there are no other alternatives. And yet I believe - the way I see things now - there is an alternative. It's called allowing them to come freely, and seek freely like, say, how you're seeking to fulfill what you must (in writing this series of books) and I think, 'Good on you.'

But for me with John and them, John was not a part of a lot of what happened back then because he was in jail.

What is it across John's forehead?

Chris: Te ahi o te atua.

The fire of god?

Chris: Well you could say the fire of god. But the way I look at it is the wrath of god.

The wrath of god.

Cos it's a fiery thing, ay, wrath. To me that's where it's all stemming from.

Mmm. Can I use your loo?

It's a longy.

Hata Thompson: These days the Williams are more inclined to meet the local Maori people half-way. I think with all the things that have happened they want to heal the wounds. And it's the same with us, too. Like when Diesel Dick (Maxwell) was alive, he tried to stir it up. And the same happened when John (Heeney) got out of prison. I had to go and tell Dick to pull his head in. And he didn't like me telling him because he's way older than me. And I said, "Well, you know, what's gonna happen is eventually these young fullas are gonna give you a hiding, mate. And it won't be one. You know. You might take one of them on and give him a hiding. But they're just gonna stretch you out in a lump, mate. And you won't win. Eventually, they're gonna get you. It's only a matter of time. So you better use a bit of this (taps the side of his head) some time."

He had a black cloud following him around, that fulla.

I tried to tell him that. "You've got a black cloud hanging over your head, mate. It won't be long. You're gonna get the chop." But he wouldn't listen.

There are two types of respect in this world. There's respect for who you are. And there's respect because you'll give them a hiding if they don't respect you. And that second one's not the respect you want. It's the other one.

Diesel was not meant to lead. He had no brains on *him* I'm sorry to say. Our bro was the brains out of all of us; Chris was the brain.

John Heeney's got a good mouth, got a good mouth, you know, sometimes. He does get carried away a bit and gets too deep into the

Most High and it becomes very hard to pick up what he's up to or what he's on about. Personally, I wouldn't say I've turned a new leaf; I've just grown up.

CHAPTER 5

ARSON AND BURGLARY

December 17, 1992: Gisborne Police confirm they're investigating a complaint that water on Luke Donnelly's property has been poisoned.

Police Commander Rana Waitai says Donnelly made a complaint about it in September and the Ruatoria police had sent a sample to the DSIR for testing. The sample was found to have a cyanide concentration of 22 micrograms a millilitre. At that level someone would become ill if they drank five litres of water.

Waitai says the cyanide would have dissipated over time and the original concentration would have been much stronger.

Of course the Rastas are the main suspects and comments made by one of them to the author suggest they were responsible.

But it wasn't just being Luke Donnelly that was considered a crime by the Rastafarians. Supporting him was also an unpopular move.

On Monday, January 11, 1993, Tom Fox's house is extensively damaged by fire. Tom and his son-in-law Boxy are supporters of Luke Donnelly and were involved in his vigilante group, the Ruatoria District Rangers.

The CIB and Fire Safety officers find that the fire started in the kitchen. At first they think it isn't suspicious. But they change their minds when it's noticed that several items, including two TVs, a stereo, a sheepskin rug and a shotgun, are missing.

Rastafarians Hamiora Sam Keelan and Rangi Rick Brown are later charged with arson and burglary.

A police summary of the case, obtained by the author, says: "When questioned about the complainant's house fire and burglary, the defendant Brown at first denied responsibility, but later said that he had gone to the complainant's property with an associate, and after stealing electric items, lit two candles that he had found inside the house, with the intentions of burning the house down. He said that he placed these candles against a kitchen and bedroom wall as a means of delaying the fire.

"The defendant Brown said that the complainant, a kaumatua, had recently shown support for a man who had been charged with the murder of their Rastafarian leader and for this reason he set fire to his house. He said that he had no regrets for his actions."

Keelan and Brown are drinking at the Manutahi Hotel in Ruatoria before the fire and are seen at various places on the East Coast that day in an orange Ford Escort car.

During Keelan's trial, his lawyer Phil Dreifuss says that while driving past Hiruharama Marae, where a tangi was in progress, Brown spotted Tom Fox's car. He told Keelan about problems he had with Fox and it was decided they would rob his house.

After they had taken items from the house, Keelan waited in the car for a minute before Brown came. Brown did not tell Keelan about the fire.

Keelan tells the court he didn't know Fox's house had been burned until he saw an article in the Gisborne Herald about it.

"I'm sorry for the fact that Mr Fox's house was burned down and for the fact that I was involved in taking items from the house."

Later they swapped a vacuum cleaner for half a bottle of whisky and sold some of the other items.

Two days after the fire, Detective Malcolm Thomas stopped the orange Escort in Gisborne. Keelan was driving and Brown was a passenger. The missing shotgun was found in the car.

Brown was also apologetic. "The act I did was stupid and I apologise to Tom Fox," he said at his sentencing. He was jailed for three years for arson, burglary and unlawful possession of a firearm while Keelan was jailed for his part in the burglary.

Otago Daily Times, Friday, May 7, 2010: Four New Plymouth Black Power members have been found guilty for their parts in the violent death of a man who only worked for a member of rival gang the Mongrel Mob.

Peri Niwa, 31, was stabbed to death at the back of a New Plymouth house in 2008 while fleeing from armed Black Power members who had turned up at a party.

During the trial it emerged how the gang jealously defended its turf. Mr Niwa was not a gang member, but worked for a team of scaffolders run by an out-of-town Mongrel Mob member.

The High Court jury in New Plymouth last night found Matiu Pahau, 22, guilty of Mr Niwa's murder.

Mahana Edmonds, 39, **Rangi Rick Brown, 40,** and Adrian Tony Fenton, 27, were found guilty of manslaughter. All four were found guilty of the commission of a crime with a firearm and have been remanded for sentence.

CHAPTER 6

THE DEATH OF DICK MAXWELL

Tuesday night, March 9, 1999: *Dick Maxwell is stabbed, bashed repeatedly about the head with a boat oar and drowned.*

Police find his body lying face down in the water of the beach at Horoera, a tiny settlement, four kilometres east of Te Araroa, on the road to the East Cape lighthouse. There are multiple stab wounds to the body and head. A weapon and other items useful to the murder investigation are located at the scene.

Watene Wanoa, a twenty-seven year old man from Te Araroa, is arrested and charged with Maxwell's murder.

Thursday, March 11, 1999, The Gisborne Herald: The name of the man killed near Te Araroa on Tuesday night was released this morning. He was James Dick Maxwell, 39, who lived in the Te Araroa area.

I don't like to point out mistakes by The Gisborne Herald. They gave me my start in journalism and the diligent, thorough and extensive coverage of the Ruatoria Rastafarians by their journalists – accessed by me through the newspaper's archives as well as through various people's personal scrapbooks – has been one of three main sources of information for this series of books (along with trial notes and my own interviews).

But I can't overlook this one small mistake.

The man who was killed wasn't James Dick Maxwell. His name was Dick James Maxwell.

A full obituary under the headline "Dead man was widely linked to Coast arsons" was run on page 24. He was also called James Dick Maxwell in the obituary.

I can't help but feel the printing of the wrong name was somehow a fitting finale to the career of Diesel Dick. The 1987 trial of five police officers accused of kidnapping and assaulting him captured national headlines and ensured he was notorious enough to warrant an obituary. But maybe he was not as legendary an outlaw as he himself believed and he obviously wasn't big enough to have his name printed correctly.

People say that in his latter years he developed a chronic alcohol problem and that his behaviour when he drank made him a lot of enemies.

Monday, August 23, 1999: *Watene Wanoa's trial for the murder of Dick Maxwell begins in the High Court in Gisborne. Through the testimonies and written evidence of Linden Miles, Mark Cottle, John Reedy, George Mathieson, John Woolf and Hemi Hikawai, the first glimpses of what transpired on March 9 are gained.*

Linden Miles is the proprietor of the Kawakawa Hotel, at Te Araroa. Maxwell visits his hotel at 4.30 in the afternoon. Miles lends him twenty dollars and gives him a box of beer. It's the last time he sees Maxwell alive. Later that night James Warnock comes to the hotel and tells him that Maxwell's been stabbed. Miles calls the police, who later return to the hotel with Wanoa.

"Wanoa was pretty hyper. I'd never seen him like that before," says Miles. "He told me, 'I killed a man today, Linden.'"

Mark Cottle is a volunteer officer for the St John Ambulance Service. He arrives at Te Araroa at midnight. He sees Wanoa, dressed only in underpants, talking to constables George Mathieson and John Woolf.

Cottle goes down to the beach and finds Maxwell face down in a channel of water. "I checked his vitals. There was nothing. There were *multiple stab wounds to the chest and head and various cuts elsewhere."*

There's a blood-stained shirt not far from the body and an oar lying nearby. There are clots of thick blood on the rocks and on the water. At the campsite he sees empty beer bottles and an empty whiskey bottle. There's also a truck that's covered with blood on the inside. "I couldn't help but notice it." The blood's splattered all over the cab, on the steering wheel, the seats, the floor, on clothing, on gumboots and on the dashboard.

St John ambulance driver John Reedy hears Wanoa tell a police constable, "No one makes a threat on my life and gets away with it." He hears Wanoa say he wasted Maxwell with a boat oar.

Wanoa tells Constable Mathieson, "I've done him in. He's in the sea." Mathieson goes down to the beach where he sees a shoulder sticking out from a crevice. The person is face down with his nose and mouth in the water. It's 12.08am. Mathieson places the body on rocks. He recognises the body as being that of Maxwell. The dead man is wearing only shorts.

Constable Woolf takes Wanoa to Te Araroa Police Station. At about 2am, he begins to write up his notes from the interview with Wanoa.

This is how Wanoa describes the day's events to Constable Woolf.

Wanoa and Maxwell are drinking together outside Wanoa's caravan near the beach. Maxwell starts to get aggro after drinking whiskey and grabs the knife. There are two "rumboes", both on the beach.

"He grabbed the knife off me. I had to go hard out to get it back. I stabbed him. If I didn't do him over he would come back and do me. I stabbed him heaps of times. Then I rolled him over onto his face to drown. If I didn't he would come and get me. I could hear him crying. I threw him into the channel."

Counsel Paul Mabey, of Tauranga, needs to build up a case of self-defence for Wanoa. He has to make Maxwell seem so scary that for him to walk in the room is grounds to kill him in self-defence.

Detective Hemi Hikawai of Gisborne CIB conducted the scene operation at 8.40am the day after Maxwell was killed.

Mabey asks Hikawai if he's aware of recent events (three years ago) in which Maxwell's brother received serious injuries, allegations that Maxwell cut someone's hand off and his reputation for being intimidating and acting as a law unto himself.

"Yes," says Hikawai.

Mabey asks if Maxwell showed disregard for the rights and property of others.

"Yes, he could be like that," replies Hikawai.

Tuesday, August 24: Pathologist Dr Wayne Elmsley tells the court that Dick Maxwell died by drowning after receiving other severe injuries.

Maxwell's skull and underlying tissue suffered considerable bruising consistent with blunt trauma. The injuries were extensive and visible above the left ear, at the top of the head and at the front of the head. Dr Elmsley believes about seven blows caused the injuries, as there were seven lacerations. There were extensive fractures of the base of the skull and the brain was also slightly swollen caused by someone hitting the skull.

Crown prosecutor Denys Barry asks if an oar could have caused these injuries.

"An oar is a blunt instrument but any blunt instrument could have caused these injuries," says Dr Elmsley.

He says there were also stab wounds and bruises to other parts of the body likely to have been caused by both sharp and blunt instruments.

Maxwell's lungs were hyper-expanded or very blown up. When he cut across Maxwell's lungs watery fluid escaped, which was characteristic of drowning.

"In my opinion this man died of asphyxiation by drowning in sea water after receiving other severe injuries."

Defence lawyer Paul Mabey asks if Maxwell's brain injuries were capable of being fatal.

"Yes, I think so, if not treated immediately." Brain swelling could often be fatal but it took a while to reach its maximum extent. "The swelling I saw was not the feature of coning you see in death by swelling."

Mabey asks if coning's a reference to the swelling of the brain, which forces the brain stem down towards the spinal column.

"Yes."

Does the brain stem control such things as involuntary responses like breathing and heartbeat? Could a force down onto the spinal column lead to these responses being cut off?

"Yes, but I don't think this happened here. But the process had commenced." The process occurs at a different rate in different people and took hours to maximise.

Mabey asks Dr Elmsley if he's certain death was by drowning.

"This man was making respiratory efforts," says Dr Elmsley. If Maxwell was dead when he went into the water there would have been some fluid in his air ways but not to the extent of hyper-expansion. One lung was very heavy and weighed one kilogram.

Detective Kevin Ford (a childhood friend and classmate of the author) interviewed Wanoa on March 10 (the day after the killing). Afterwards, Wanoa signed the detective's notes of the interview.

This is what Wanoa told Ford. "We were on the piss by the caravan at Horoera Beach. He grabbed me by the throat. I grabbed the knife and stabbed him. No (expletive) tries to strangle me, and gets away with it. We rolled on the ground. I punched him. I think I was kicking him too. I've got sore feet. I don't know how many times I punched him. I was buzzing."

Wanoa got a bread knife from the table. Maxwell went to Wanoa's truck and Wanoa followed him. "I dragged him out and told him to go." Wanoa went to lie down but could hear Maxwell walking around. "I went outside to rumble again." Wanoa said he took a five centimetre long butcher knife. "I just didn't want to be killed."

Maxwell ran down the beach. "I ran after him. He grabbed the knife off me and said he was going to bleed me. I grabbed an oar. I know what he's like. If he didn't kill me tonight, he'd kill me tomorrow. I hammered him. We were in the sea. I just bashed him, bashed him, bashed him."

Ford asked Wanoa why he chased Maxwell down to the beach. "I wanted to waste him. I rolled him over face down after I finished bashing him. I wanted to make sure he was dead."

Ford asked Wanoa why he rolled Maxwell into the sea. "He was already gone. I had to do it. Otherwise I would've been dead."

***Wednesday, August 25, 1999:** Watene Wanoa takes the witness stand today.*

This is his recollection of events on March 9.

Maxwell and James Warnock unexpectedly turn up at his campsite. They're drunk and have a box of beer with them.

*Wanoa brings out a bottle of whiskey and starts talking to Warnock.
"Maxwell was just chanting away to himself."*

*Within ten minutes Maxwell has "skulled" a quarter of the whiskey.
He says he's going to kill Wanoa and grabs him by the jersey. "I
whacked him and told him to fuck off – don't touch me."*

*About ten minutes later Maxwell starts saying his name and pulling
him. A little later, Wanoa goes to walk past Maxwell. "He jumped up
off the ground and grabbed me around the throat. I just grabbed him. I
pushed him away."*

Maxwell gets up and starts to walk towards Wanoa.

"I grabbed a knife off the table."

*He stabs Maxwell "to get him away from me". Maxwell "rolled
over".*

*Wanoa isn't sure how injured Maxwell is. He goes back inside his
caravan. He can hear Maxwell rummaging around "in my truck".*

*Wanoa remembers he has a knife in the truck. He goes out to the
truck to get it.*

"He might have grabbed it.

*"I went to the truck and pulled him out by his hair. I told him to fuck
off."*

*Wanoa returns to his caravan and lies on his bed. "I could hear
Maxwell outside. He said he wanted to cut my throat and bleed me."*

*Wanoa goes outside to chase Maxwell away. He takes the knife with
him.*

*He chases Maxwell down to the beach, but Diesel Dick manages to
get hold of the knife.*

"We flipped up. We were rolling around. He grabbed the knife."

*They end up on the rocks to the left of the channel, which is full of
water. He grabs Maxwell's hands from behind so "he wouldn't try to
stab me."*

"It happened fast. We ended up fully on that channel."

Wanoa pushes Maxwell, gets out of the channel "and just took off".

*"Maxwell was coming behind me. My oar was lying on the beach. I
just picked that up.*

"I spun around. He was right behind me. I whacked him with it."

He doesn't want Maxwell "to get me, because he would stab me".

*He hits Maxwell with the oar "a few times" and Maxwell falls to
the ground.*

"I thought he was dead. I just freaked out. I just rolled him over into the water. I walked up to the caravan. I was freaked out because I thought he was dead."

Paul Mabey tells his client that Linden Miles thought he looked upset later that night.

"No one wants to kill someone."

Mabey asks Wanoa what he meant when he said to Detective Ford, "I know what he's like."

Wanoa says Maxwell was a violent man who had put his brother in hospital after hitting him with a mere.

"Maxwell thinks he owns everything. He gets what he wants. I didn't want to end up like his brother."

Wanoa's cross-examined by Crown prosecutor Denys Barry.

Wanoa says there was a period of about sixty to ninety minutes from Maxwell's arrival to the first stabbing incident. It was another thirty minutes before he pulled Maxwell out of the truck.

He says he didn't see James Warnock leave the campsite.

He lay on his bed for about five minutes before chasing Maxwell down to the beach.

He estimates it was a fifteen to twenty minute period from when he chased Maxwell down the beach until he struck him with the oar.

Barry tells Wanoa he had plenty of opportunities to escape.

"It's my place," says Wanoa.

Surely, Maxwell wasn't much of a threat after he was stabbed?

"He was coming towards me. He was fit as."

He can't have been a threat when he was struck by the oar.

"I had to kill him or he would have killed me. One of us was going to die that night – either him or me."

Wanoa told police he rolled Maxwell into the surf so Maxwell "wouldn't come back".

"That was after I thought he was dead."

"You told Detective Ford, 'I just pushed him into the water with my feet to make sure he didn't come back.'"

"I was still freaking out."

"You were making sure he was dead."

"I thought he was already dead."

This is an important point because if Maxwell was barely alive, barely breathing, he's of no immediate threat. Therefore deliberately pushing his nose and mouth underwater is tantamount to murder, *especially as the pathologist has already testified that Maxwell drowned.*

Thursday, August 26, 1999: *DSIR forensic scientist Noreen McGavin says, in written evidence, that Maxwell had 289 milligrams of alcohol per 100 millilitres of blood in his system. (The legal limit for driving is eighty milligrams.) The scientist says there was no alcohol in Wanoa's body when the specimen was taken ten hours after the fight. It's possible however that he could have had 0 to 215 milligrams of alcohol ten hours before.*

Maxwell had enough cannabis in his blood to suggest he had smoked a single cannabis cigarette thirty minutes to four hours before his death.

Wanoa may have smoked a single cannabis cigarette ninety minutes to twenty-four hours before the sample was taken.

Dr Patrick McHugh (whose sister Stephanie was a school friend of the author) says he examined Wanoa on the morning of March 10. Wanoa told him he'd been involved in an assault and had an injured right hand.

McHugh says Wanoa had been held around the neck by two hands. There was tenderness over Wanoa's right hand and scratches over the chest. There was no significant bruising, swelling or tenderness over the neck. But it was possible bruises could still have developed within another twenty-four hours.

Paul Moana says he visited a man at Punarukou on the afternoon of March 9. Maxwell, James Warnock and William Crawford lived at Punarukou, close to Pikitanga Marae.

Moana says he could hear Maxwell, Warnock and Crawford chanting like a haka eighty metres away on the other side of a creek. Maxwell had the loudest voice and the chant was: "Horoera, kill the fuckin' cunt, Horoera, kill the fuckin' cunt."

Now it's time for the final addresses, where the defence and the prosecution take a square peg of real life – wild and crazy and unpredictable as it usually is when someone gets killed – and cram it into the round hole of the law.

Crown prosecutor Denys Barry explains to the jury that under self-defence everybody's justified in using reasonable force in the circumstances as they believe them to be.

Barry asks if there was an imminent or serious threat in this case and whether Wanoa had an opportunity to seek protection without using force.

He points out that there was a thirty-minute period where Wanoa went to the truck and pulled Maxwell out. Wanoa could have left the campsite. Instead, he effectively became the aggressor. Maybe Wanoa used reasonable force at the beginning. But he told Constable Woolf that he'd stabbed Maxwell "heaps of times" and rolled him onto his face to drown. He told Detective Ford, "I just pushed him into the water with my feet to make sure he didn't come back." He chased Maxwell on to the beach. "You might think Wanoa was attacking him again," says Barry.

"When Maxwell got hold of the knife on the beach, he was fighting for his life you might think."

Wanoa had said that if Maxwell did not kill him that night, Maxwell would kill him the next day. But, says Barry, protecting against a future threat is not self-defence.

Now it's defence counsel Paul Mabey's turn.

He says Wanoa said many things to many people on that night and in court. It was a good insight that he told Detective Ford that he was "freaked out", and that he told Linden Miles, "No one likes to kill a man."

Wanoa could have run away but, as he told the court, it was his place and his truck.

In the first fight, Maxwell made a threat and tried to strangle Wanoa. Before chasing Maxwell to the beach, he heard him say he was going to cut Wanoa's throat and bleed him.

Mabey reminds the jury that pathologist Wayne Elmsley said Maxwell's head injuries were potentially fatal if he were left alone on the beach. Mabey told the jury not to focus on the single act at the end when Maxwell was rolled into the sea. Maxwell was a violent man who had previously attacked his brother with a mere.

Wanoa described Maxwell as being "fit as" after the first fight while the pathologist said many of Maxwell's wounds were superficial.

Wanoa believed one of them was going to die that night. If Wanoa believed that he was justified in killing Maxwell.

The jury goes out at 11.50am and comes back at 7.50pm. A group of about twenty-five of Wanoa's relatives and supporters are waiting in the court for the verdict.

Watene Harold Wanoa is found not guilty of the murder or manslaughter of Dick James Maxwell. The supporters burst into cheers. After being discharged by the judge, Wanoa is surrounded by his friends and family. He joins them in a prayer. Then Wanoa walks out of the court. His punishment for stabbing the body and head repeatedly, bashing the head with an oar seven times and then drowning Diesel Dick Maxwell? Nothing.

Afterwards, Paul Mabey says he's naturally pleased for his client.

"It shows the jury system is the best system," he says. "They thought long and hard about their decision. I think it's the right decision."

When writing about a man like Dick Maxwell, there is no shortage of people who want to bag him. But everyone has a positive side. And I got a glimpse of Dick Maxwell's while talking to a lawyer in Gisborne. When I asked the lawyer if I could quote him about Dick, he never got back to me so, out of respect to the lawyer, I won't name him and, out of respect to Dick Maxwell, here are the comments.

"I always found Dick really good, really personable. There was another lawyer here back then, Grant Vosseler, who used to get on with Dick really well. Dick was going for bail one time and Grant gave his own address and said, 'He'll stay with me.' He'd put Dick up at his house.

"It used to annoy me, and it still does, people bagging Dick when they don't know him. He was always a friendly guy. He'd come in here, bring me some food out of his garden or something like that. Whenever we were at court in Ruatoria, because his mother lived directly across from the St John Ambulance Hall, he'd come and get us at the court smoko, take us over there, food on the table. They'd really look after us. And Dick would put that on.

"But, you know, full of gin I wouldn't want to see him. Alcohol was definitely his downfall.

"I think if Chris Campbell hadn't been killed, he could have kept a guiding hand on Dick. Because it was only after Chris died that Dick really went to the pack. Before that he was a fine specimen to look at. After Chris died he started drinking heavily, he got a pot tummy on him and started to slouch and just didn't look after himself. Because Chris really did instil good values, I thought, on those guys. And someone like Dick needed that kind of leadership.

"I remember one time Dick was playing some music and I actually had a Miles Davis tape in my car. Tutu, I think it was. And I said to Dick, 'Aw, you'll probably like this.' So we were sitting in his house listening to it and I forgot to take it with me. I remember I got to Tokomaru Bay and I thought, 'Shit, I left that bloody tape behind.' And it was quite a significant tape to me because we actually had it playing in the maternity ward when my wife gave birth to our eldest daughter. And I thought, 'I'd like to get that tape back.' Of course, I didn't think I'd ever see it again. Six months later Dick's in town for something and he turns up here with my tape, says, 'You left this at my home.' Just little things like that really impressed me about Dick."

Wiki Haua, Cody Haua's nephew: Diesel's death didn't surprise me. The bro was notorious as. I had a real soft spot for Dick though. He had all that bravado and reputation but when it came to my grandmother, he had respect and that I admired. I remember him coming to our house one day full of swagger and talking himself up and Nanny Punky came out of the room and told him off big time for talking crap. If it had been anyone younger Dick would've taken them on. He turned to her and said, "Sorry Aunty," gave her a kiss on the cheek and asked her if she wanted a cup of tea.

When Dick got beaten up by the cops that's how I knew it was true. When he got to our place to get a ride into town, he told Nan what happened. I know he wouldn't have lied to his Aunty Punky. He respected her too much.

The police were disappointed and frustrated by the not guilty verdict in the trial of Watene Wanoa for the murder of Dick Maxwell. As one officer who worked on it said, "It was as cut and dried as a murder case gets, but still he got off on self-defence."

But things can't have been easy for Wanoa following the trial. On July 31, 2005, he was found dead in a house at Waihau Bay. He had committed suicide. Police said there were no suspicious circumstances.

EPILOGUE

Original Ruatoria Rastafarian Hata Thompson: What we were doing was really a fight, a spiritual fight in a sense. And it's still going on today.

Even though it seemed wrong at the time, we get a different reaction now. People say, "We looked at you fullas and we watched you fullas. And we didn't have the guts to do what you fullas were doing back then. We just stood there silently and watched. Not that what you fullas were doing was right. But at least you were doing *something* that got the attention of everyone." They say, "Some of the things were wrong."

And I agree with that also.

I was young then. And I was blinded by rage and anger more than anything. But as I've grown up I've cottoned on to it more. I am still an angry person deep down. It just takes a while for it to come out. When it does come out, "Woah," I'm bad, ay. I get bad. I just can't help myself. But I try to keep that under wraps.

I try to look at things from different angles. I try to see the logic in situations. I try to think, "What are the benefits gonna be? What are the long-term benefits?"

You eventually grow up.

I look at my time in jail. It taught me really, jail. It taught me a lot actually. It taught me to *watch* people. I came out of there and I could pick people straight away by just looking at them or talking to them. I could tell who was fake and who wasn't. You could just pick it up. It's just something like a sixth sense. I guess it comes from all different types of people in jail. You've got crooks, you've got liars, you've got thieves. You're living with all the criminal elements. Eventually your mind will become sharp to them, you know. They'll take you for a ride, a lot of them. "Aw yeah, fresh meat. We'll make a monkey out of him." And that's what they do. There's no rules in there, mate. It's survival. You can make it easy on yourself. Or you can make it hard. The easy way is to walk away.

I'd say now, today, in this day and age Chris Campbell would probably be a good man now. He would've kept the brothers together. That's what I reckon. But I was striving for other things when I was with him. I said to him that I had other things that I had on *my* mind that

I had to take care of. But we come out of jail and our views had changed. My perception of God had changed. One thing I still agreed with Chris about was that Haile Selassie was the second advent of Jesus Christ. And I still believe that. I'm not gonna doubt myself because that's to do with the Bible, see.

I see us slowly getting pushed off the land. The forestry's killing us. The pollen from the trees gets into everything. I'm sure it's not good for us.

I'm not into forestry, mate. I'm going into possum trapping. I just bought me a hundred traps this morning. By trapping possums I'm doing a service to my generations that follow after me. And when we wipe out the possums it helps us bring back all our native bird-life.

Former Rasta Ed Te Rauna: After Chris died everyone just split up. A lot of people went to the church. It was a born-again church. Those that stayed with the Rastas also split up. It was like the hard ones got harder and the ones who were just there to be holy and righteous, they went that way. But even they've broken up now. It's really just John's group that's still going. And I think it's a shame really what's happened with the Rastas. I think he's more or less flogging a dead horse. And he's more or less been the one that's flogged it to death.

It's a real shame that such good things had to be ruined. Some people will never believe in the things they once believed in because of what they went through with those guys. People like me. One day you believe in good things and holy things and righteous things. Now the poor things don't know what to believe in.

I'm doing all right but I still feel shaken by what I've been through here (points to his head) and what's been through here (points to his heart). I'm shaken that I came so close to believing in some of the things that they believe or that John Heeney believes anyway.

Hata Thompson: Chris was fighting for equal rights and justice. He just wanted a fair deal for Maoridom. Just give us a fair deal and I'm sure we'll give everyone in this land a fair deal.

You'd find that there's a bit of bad amongst everyone. We're always portrayed as being evil. But I don't believe that.

I've been with rugged people all my life. They're just rugged and swearing and all that. That's how they were brought up. It came up from when they were kids, hearing it from their parents. It goes from generation to generation. And it's in this little kid inside them. They just pick it up around them. They don't know no different. It could be beautiful to them; you know what I mean. Not to other people, but to them it's just what they're used to. It's not their fault. It's how you bring them up, I suppose.

See, I don't drink any more. About ten years ago I started drinking. I went for about five or six years and I'm just giving it up again. I've been off for two years now. I've given up the cigarettes. And now I'm just about ready to give up the herb. I've slowed down now that I'm getting older. I'm looking for business angles now. I go out with my mates now and they let me drive because I'm the sober one. I drive them to the pubs. I go with them and I stay there all night.

I had to give up the cigarettes because what was happening I was smoking that much cigarettes I was starting to get pains in my throat and I couldn't breathe, especially waking up in the mornings and going to sleep at nights. I was going, "Phoo, I can just barely breathe." And I'd have to prop myself up and sleep like that. I thought, "Na, there's gotta be a better way than this. It's not worth it." So I had to make that decision there and then to give up the cigarettes. And I knew that every time I had a puff it brought it on and I realised, "Aw, this is the problem."

It was real hard giving up smoking. But it just got to the stage where I couldn't breathe one time. It was like I had asthma. I gave up for a couple of days and I could feel myself clearing.

And I don't mind not drinking. It doesn't make you any more better than the next man just because you don't drink. You can still go out and have a good time.

Beau Tuhura, interviewed in the early 2000s: I'm nearly fifty now. I've given up the alcohol. And I've never regretted it either.

When I spoke to Cody Haua in the early 2000s, he hadn't given up alcohol. But he'd given up marijuana. We were offered it when he took me around for my second meeting with John Heeney. But we both declined.

(I don't know if Hata, Beau and Cody have continued their abstinence in the years that have passed but I know that at the time I

interviewed them they were all taking steps to improve their health and their lifestyles.)

Wiki Haua, Cody's nephew, a second generation Rasta, and one of twenty-two kids brought up by Nanny Punky: The last few years I was in high school I looked after my Nan. I owed my whole life to her and it annoyed me that as she was nearing the end of *her* life she had to put up with all the dramas that happened with the Rastas. She wanted more for me, so she sent me away to family in Palmerston North at the end of 1991 and died a few months later. I didn't like it that she died alone after doing so much for so many other people. I've often wished I could have been there. But she'd had enough. Uncle Cody found her at home.

A lot of Kiwis over here in Oz have spoken to me about what happened in Ruatoria. My manager, wife and a couple of friends have now read the books and I think they look at me in amazement with how I am. A few people have even told me to write a book about my life. I'm now a lending manager with a bank over here in Oz and I often wonder how I managed not to go the other way and how on earth I ended up the way I am now. I call myself Ngati Corporate to the other Kiwis.

Jeremy Williams, farmer and member of the famous settler family who had his house and his woolshed burned down in separate arson attacks (interviewed in the early 2000s): Gary McCormick, when he did a Heartland programme on the East Coast, he asked me what I thought about our kids going to Kohanga Reo. And I said, "I'm pleased. We want them to learn and it's a bit like Latin. I mean some people say you don't actually speak Latin, but it exercises your mind." And I use the example that my great grandfather was a fluent Maori speaker. My grandfather could also speak it a bit. And my grandmother was the first person to record Maori action songs. She even toured Australia doing concerts in 1948 and playing these little records. My father learnt Maori at school and knew a few phrases. I learnt almost none and now my children are now learning it and I think it's great.

I'm sure that us joining the Kohanga Reo has helped normalise things. It's quite nice to see kids, whose fathers were Rastas and definitely anti-social in their behaviour ten or twenty years ago, growing up normally and playing JAB rugby. Our kids go into town and play JAB rugby and they're all giving it a go together. There were some awful wounds a few years ago and time does seem to be healing a lot of them.

The family that run Kohanga Reo, the Bartletts, just at the beginning of our road, have been involved with our family for years. Lionel Bartlett shore in the shearing gang. He worked for Geoff Cotterill for years. All their children are all about my age. A couple of Lionel and Kiriana's daughters run the kohanga reo and they're good people. They ran the kohanga reo in Maori, but they'd mix it up a little bit so the Pakeha kids understood as well.

But as far as farming goes, times have changed. There are six or seven couriers go up the Coast. I break something on my tractor I can get a part up there that day or the next one. My dog's got a bung eye, the vet puts a tube of ointment on the courier, it goes straight to Hikurangi Food Market and the RD brings it out. Then you've got the internet. And we've now got mobile phone coverage.

Whereas my parents went to Ruatoria a lot: grocery-shopping, haircuts, Dalgeties, Williams and Kettles, that sort of thing, now we tend to go to Gisborne for most of that.

We get groceries at the Hikurangi Food Market and I bank in Ruatoria but my agri-business bank manager is a guy in town. And I communicate with him by fax or I take my disk to him and we do the budget in his office.

My father would have had a meeting with his Ruatoria bank manager once a year. I have communication with my banker most months and about three major sessions with him up here at the farm a year.

I need some advisers. I've got a farm consultant. My father never had one. I need a lawyer. And I want a lawyer who's not just going to tell me how to write a will. I want a lawyer who can say, "Hey, you can save money by doing this and doing that." I want an accountant, and he's not some sort of desk-bound boffin in town here. He's someone who understands my business. And I want a banker.

All those guys are based in Gisborne, except for my farm consultant who's in Napier now. But I'm the fulla in the middle. They work for me.

My father's generation and earlier, a lot of them trembled in fear of the bank manager, or the crusty old lawyer. I don't want that. I don't want to feel frightened of any adviser. So it's all changed.

Napier lawyer and former Labour MP Russell Fairbrother: As I talk to you I've got this quite strong mental image of Chris Campbell. His eyes were quite bright and he had this, not really a smile but he had a very pleasant face. And he was totally animated. But he wasn't irrational and he could always bring you back to where he started from if he started off on one of his tangents. And so he was never unhooked or never incoherent and I don't know what his basic grievance was but he certainly felt that Maoridom and the Ruatoria area had let he and his generation down. And the picture I got was that he gave the Maoris in their teens and early twenties some self-pride and self-respect. And being anti-establishment and smoking the dope and doing petty crime was part of a bonding exercise where they were seen to be marshalling their forces.

I think Chris certainly had a vision for that coast which was much bigger than the Coast. I think if he hadn't died he would have been a legitimate leader in his time - I've no doubt about that - probably of the Alan Duff mould.

His mother and father were absolutely lovely people. His dad was non-aggressive and his mother was simply lovely. Chris also had a brother Pani, who was a policeman, and Chris was always conscious of that and whilst he rejected everything Pani stood for he never rejected Pani. And Pani also never rejected Chris.

The source of his charisma? He had an absolute belief in what he was talking about and I don't think there was any bullshit in it. So when he spoke it was with a real fervour, which was contagious.

He knew The Bible very well because his parents were quite religious. And I don't think he misused The Bible but he knew how to quote it and he knew how to adapt it to his beliefs. Well I didn't think he was mad, let's put it that way.

Yeah, I think he had something special. I couldn't tell you what it was but he's not someone who you remember and then put to one side. And the more you talk about him the more you remember about him.

Rasta leader John Heeney, early 2000: I end up getting a two-year trespass notice from Bella's Dairy, which is Luke Donnelly's shop in

Childers Road, in Gisborne. I get it because I'm walking past there one day when I'm drunk. I've been drinking down the road with the brothers. I'm not pissed but I've had a couple. And I know where he stays. And I just write a note and leave it at the shop for him. It just says, "The End."

And that would have been the end of the Ngati Dread series of books if I hadn't called the former Ruatoria policeman Nigel Hendrikse in May 2011.

I was producing 3 News and we were doing a story on whether more police should carry firearms in locked boxes in their cars. Hendrikse had been in the news recently because John Gillies, the Mongrel mob member who had stabbed him in the back with a screwdriver, paralysing him, was about to be released from prison. I knew that the incident with Gillies was just one of several during Nigel's police career where he had found himself unarmed against an assailant with weapons. So I figured a comment from him would be timely and relevant to the debate. Normally, I would have got a reporter to ring him. But, because I'd dealt with Nigel while writing this book, I rang him.

It didn't make any difference. He politely declined. He didn't want to say anything in the media that could hinder or stop Gillies from getting a job after he was released from jail. So I didn't get the quote I wanted for the story. But I was really impressed. John Gillies had stabbed him, yet Nigel was still willing to give him a shot at redemption.

Nigel asked me how volume three was getting on. I said, as I'd said to many people, that it was at the printers ready to go; I was just waiting for my wife Tui to do the cover art.

"Too scared to push the go button, ay?"

"Well, there might be a bit of that, too," I conceded. "I know I've pissed off Rastas, cops, farmers and vigilantes with the other two books. This one will piss them off all over again... plus everyone else in the community, too."

"You know," said Nigel, "I heard a lovely story from there the other day."

"Ooh, what was that?"

"Apparently, John Heeney's driving the fire truck there now."
"What!?"

"Yeah. John Heeney's in the Ruatoria voluntary fire service."

"Oh my God! You don't mind if I make a few inquiries about that do you?"

"No, not at all."

"They reckon Tom Heeney and Maurice Mataira used to say, 'They light 'em, we fight 'em,' when talking about their sons."

"Yeah."

"Now it's gone full circle, ay. They light 'em, we fight 'em, they fight 'em."

That night, when I got home, I told Tui.

"It's a good thing I didn't do that cover, ay," she said.

"I'll say."

"If I'd drawn the cover when you wanted me to, you wouldn't have been able to get this story in."

"I know."

"And you'd have felt it was unfinished.'

"True... and I thought you were just being lazy."

"I knew there was something stopping me from doing that cover."

I made some inquiries. The Gisborne Fire Service didn't want to talk to my tape recorder and said that John Heeney didn't either. So I made some more inquiries elsewhere.

It turns out that John Heeney became a member of the Ruatoria volunteer fire service in the mid-2000s. He joined up with fellow Rasta Whare Taukamo and they have become not just good but "excellent" fire-fighters, "the backbone of the service".

They've fought many major fires in Ruatoria and around the East Coast and are available at a moment's notice to get the fire truck out.

Unfortunately, the Ruatoria voluntary fire service has struggled to attract staff. But at the time of writing, May 2011, it had just had its first influx of new recruits in years. One of those is David Mataira. In 1989 he and Johbn Heeney were convicted of the 1985 arson of the Ruatoria courthouse-cum-police station.

So there is a trend in the community of mature men trying to put right the wrongs they committed when they were young and reckless.

And who's the officer in charge of this team? His name is Royce Mathieson and the fact that he can now work with the Rastas is another example of how far the people of this troubled township have come. Royce is the brother of former "vigilante" Graeme Mathieson, who was charged with but later got off the 1986 arson of John Heeney's house.

So while I liked the idea of finishing this series of books with the words The End, it seems obvious to me now that that idea had more to do with style than substance. And it had a sinister undertone that is probably not as accurate now as when it was said back in 2000. Luke Donnelly's left the region and things have obviously moved on from then.

I know in movies they always used to finish with the words The End. But in TV news – a medium with which I am much more familiar – we often use two other words as a headline to describe a situation: Developing Story.

So while this series of books and this version of events will stop at the end of this sentence, the resilience and the ability of the people of Ruatoria to bounce back, despite the hardships they meet along the way, will continue to be A Developing Story.

www.ingramcontent.com/pod-product-compliance
Lightning Source LLC
LaVergne TN
LVHW051046080426
835508LV00019B/1738